Anonymous

The Official Handbook for the National Training School for Cookery

Containing the lessons on cookery which constitute the course of instruction in the

school

Anonymous

The Official Handbook for the National Training School for Cookery
Containing the lessons on cookery which constitute the course of instruction in the school

ISBN/EAN: 9783744797641

Printed in Europe, USA, Canada, Australia, Japan

Cover: Foto ©Paul-Georg Meister /pixelio.de

More available books at **www.hansebooks.com**

THE OFFICIAL HANDBOOK FOR THE

NATIONAL TRAINING SCHOOL FOR COOKERY

CONTAINING

THE LESSONS ON COOKERY

WHICH CONSTITUTE

The Course of Instruction in the School

WITH

LISTS OF UTENSILS NECESSARY, AND LESSONS ON CLEANING UTENSILS.

COMPILED BY R. O. C.

AND TESTED IN THE NATIONAL TRAINING SCHOOL.

"The number of inhabitants who may be supported in any country, upon its internal produce, depends about as much upon the state of the *Art of Cookery*, as upon that of *Agriculture*, but if Cookery be of so much importance, it certainly deserves to be studied with the greatest care. Cookery and Agriculture are arts of civilized nations: Savages understand neither of them."—*Count Rumford's Works, Vol. 1*

LONDON:
CHAPMAN AND HALL, 193, PICCADILLY.
1877.
[*All rights reserved.*]

LONDON:
BRADBURY, AGNEW, & CO., PRINTERS, WHITEFRIARS.

PREFACE.

I. THIS work has been written to explain in an easy way the first principles of good Cookery, and in the form of lessons is especially addressed to those who wish to carry them into practice. It has been the aim of the writer to leave no detail, however small, vaguely stated. It is taken for granted that the learner has no knowledge on the subject. The loose expressions, such as "a pinch," "a little," found in all cookery books, are therefore avoided, and precise quantities are given.

II. The work is not to be regarded as an exhaustive cookery book with numerous recipes. It aims to be rather a grammar than a dictionary.

III. The lessons give a sufficient number of examples of cookery illustrating many degrees of cost: thus the rich may have a dish of curried rabbit for 3s. 8d., and the poor may have a dish of curried tripe for $10\frac{3}{4}d$.

IV. The work has been used and tested in the National Training School for Cookery since 1875, and the instructors now employed in local schools throughout the country have been taught and practised by means of these lessons.

V. It has been found that it is most convenient to practise the lesson with the instructions in sight close at hand. An edition of each lesson has been printed on separate sheets of thick paper, for the use of students and teachers, which may be obtained at the National Training School for Cookery, or at any of the local schools.

VI. The writer requests that the notice of any errors and omissions which are inevitable in a work of this kind may be communicated to R. O. C., at the National Training School for Cookery, Exhibition Road, London, S.W.

R. O. C.

July, 1877.

CONTENTS.

PREFACE

LISTS OF UTENSILS

LIST OF CLEANING MATERIALS

LESSONS ON CLEANING

LESSONS ON COOKERY

INDEX

LIST OF UTENSILS REQUIRED IN A FIRST CLASS SCHOOL KITCHEN,

AND THEIR AVERAGE COST.

LIST NO. I.

	£	s.	d.
3 copper stewpans, varying in size from 3 pints to 3 quarts	1	18	6
3 enamelled stewpans, sizes from 1 pint to 2 quarts	0	9	6
1 copper sautépan, 12s.; 12 iron saucepans, sizes from 1 pint to 2 gallons, £1 2s. 9d.	1	14	9
Iron pot for boiling	0	9	6
Stock pot, to hold 8 quarts	0	15	0
Frying pan	0	2	0
Iron omelet pan	0	1	0
Fish kettle	0	8	6
Frying basket and pan	0	8	0
Copper preserving pan	1	5	0
2 gridirons	0	9	0
Best brass bottle jack	0	15	0
Block tin screen and dripping pan	1	3	6
Steamer and saucepan	0	8	6
Weights and scales, to weigh from ¼ oz. to 14 lbs.	1	9	0
Coffee mill, £1 2s.; 1 marble mortar and hardwood pestle, £1 5s.	2	7	0
6 kitchen knives, 7s. 9d.; 3 kitchen forks, 5s.	0	12	9
12 iron spoons, 4s.; 6 wooden spoons, various sizes, 1s. 6d.	0	5	6
1 fish slice, 1s.; 1 egg slice, 9d.	0	1	9
3 larding needles, 2s. 3d.; 1 trussing needle, 9d.	0	3	0
1 set of skewers, 2s.; 1 corkscrew, 1s.	0	3	0
1 flour dredger, 1s. 6d.; 1 sugar dredger, 2s.	0	3	6
1 paste board, 3s. 6d.; 1 chopping board, 3s. 6d.	0	7	0
1 rolling pin, 1s. 6d.; 1 cutlet bat, 3s. 6d.	0	5	0
1 chopper, 3s. 6d.; 1 saw, 4s. 6d.	0	8	0
1 box of fluted cutters, 4s. 6d.; 1 box of round cutters, 3s. 6d.	0	8	0
1 box of vegetable cutters	0	5	6
1 egg whisk, 1s. 6d.; 1 grater, 1s.	0	2	6
2 flour tubs, or 1 double bin	0	9	0
2 cake tins, 2s.; 1 coffee pot (French), to hold 3 pints, 4s. 6d.	0	6	6
Carry forward	£18	4	9

	£	s.	d.
Brought forward	18	4	9
2 block tin jelly moulds, sizes 1 pint and 1 quart . . .	0	6	0
2 white china moulds, sizes 1 pint and 1 quart . . .	0	1	6
1 iron kettle, to hold 3 quarts, 7s. 6d.; 3 baking sheets, 7s. 6d.	0	15	0
2 Yorkshire pudding tins, sizes 1 pint and 1 quart . .	0	2	6
2 tartlette pans, and 12 patty pans	0	3	0
2 soufflée tins, sizes 1 pint and 1 quart	0	3	0
2 strainers, for gravy, &c. 5s.; 1 silk sieve, 2s. . . .	0	7	0
2 wire sieves, 6s.; 4 hair sieves, various sizes, 10s. . .	0	16	0
1 seasoning box, 5s.; 1 spice box, 2s. 3d. . . .	0	7	3
1 tin cullender, 1s. 6d.; toasting fork, 1s. . . .	0	2	6
1 paste brush, 1s.; 1 steel, 2s.	0	3	0
1 string box and scissors, 4s. 6d.; 1 basting ladle, 2s. .	0	6	6
1 jelly bag and stand, 9s. 6d.; 1 tammy cloth, 2s. 3d. .	0	11	9
6 pudding basins, sizes from ½ pint to 3 pints . .	0	3	6
12 basins (8 common, sizes from 1 quart to 4 quarts, and 4 lip basins, from 1 quart to 1 gallon) . . .	0	14	0
6 dishes, 5s.; 6 pie dishes, sizes from 1 pint to 2 quarts, 5s.	0	10	0
24 plates, 8s.; 1 salting pan, to hold 3 or 4 gallons, 4s. 6d.	0	12	6
1 bread pan and cover, 3s.; 1 cheese pan and cover, 3s. .	0	6	0
3 wooden trivets, various sizes	0	2	6
1 black board for lectures (size about 5 feet by 4 feet) .	2	5	0
Kitchen range . . . . . . from £9 to	10	0	0
Gas stove . . . . from £12 to	14	0	0
Frymometer (for testing the heat of fat for frying) .	0	10	6
Frymometer [Cetti's, 11, Brooke Street, Holborn], for testing the heat of the oven for baking	0	10	6
Fitting frymometer in the oven door	0	5	0
	£52	9	3

LIST OF UTENSILS REQUIRED IN A SECOND CLASS SCHOOL KITCHEN,

AND THEIR AVERAGE COST.

LIST NO. 2.

	£	s.	d.
5 iron saucepans and covers, sizes 1 pint, 1½ pint, 1 quart, 1½ quart, and 4 quarts	0	9	1
1 iron saucepan and steamer	0	6	0
1 gridiron	0	1	8
1 frying pan	0	1	6
1 iron kettle	0	5	6
1 tin cullender	0	1	0
1 Yorkshire pudding tin	0	0	10
1 baking tin	0	1	0
1 paste board	0	4	0
1 rolling pin	0	1	6
1 brass bottle jack	0	10	0
1 tin roasting screen and ladle	0	19	6
1 coal scuttle	0	3	6
1 coal shovel	0	0	9
1 cinder sieve	0	2	3
1 set fire irons	0	3	6
6 iron spoons	0	2	0
6 knives and forks	0	12	0
3 wooden spoons	0	0	6
6 tea spoons	0	1	6
6 basins, various sizes	0	2	6
3 pudding basins	0	1	0
3 pie dishes	0	1	0
6 dishes, various sizes	0	5	0
12 meat plates	0	4	6
Seasoning box	0	4	6
1 toasting fork	0	1	0
1 dust pan	0	0	10
1 salt cellar, 1s.; 1 pepper box, 6d	0	1	6
1 mustard pot and spoon	0	2	6
1 hand bowl	0	2	0
Carry forward	£5	13	11

	£	s.	d.
Brought forward	5	13	11
1 steel	0	2	0
1 dish tub	0	4	0
2 brown pans	0	2	0
3 jugs	0	2	0
1 meat saw	0	2	0
1 chopper	0	2	3
Scales and weights	0	4	6
1 corkscrew	0	1	6
1 grater	0	1	0
1 coffee pot, 2s. 3d.; 1 tea pot, 3s.	0	5	3
1 cake tin	0	1	0
1 flour tub	0	2	6
Black board for lectures (size about 5 feet by 4 feet)	2	5	0
Small range . . . . about	2	12	6
	£12	1	5

LIST OF CLEANING MATERIALS AND UTENSILS REQUIRED,

AND THEIR AVERAGE COST.

	£	s.	d.
1 pail, wooden	0	3	6
Scrubbing brush	0	2	0
Set of blacklead brushes	0	4	6
Sweep's brush	0	1	0
Flue brush	0	1	6
Sink brush	0	0	9
Sieve brush	0	0	9
Dust pan and brush	0	4	6
Broom (hair)	0	3	6
Bass broom	0	2	0
2 tubs, 4s. 6d. each	0	9	0
1 hearthstone	0	0	6
1 box of blacklead	0	0	6
Whitening	0	0	1
Rottenstone	0	0	1
Bath brickdust	0	0	1
½ quire emery cloth	0	0	9
6 lbs. of soda	0	0	7
1 bar of scrubbing soap	0	0	11
Sand	0	0	6
Salt	0	0	6
White chalk	0	0	2
1 yard of house flannel	0	0	6
1 leather	0	1	0
1 pair of gloves	0	0	9
1 coal shovel	0	3	0
1 cinder sifter	0	2	6
1 dust pan and coal hammer	0	6	3
1 coal scuttle	0	4	6
1 set of fire irons	0	10	6
	£3	6	8

LESSONS ON CLEANING STOVES, GRATES, AND KITCHEN UTENSILS.

TO CLEAN AN OPEN KITCHEN RANGE.

1. We should rake out all the cinders and sift them into a scuttle for use.

N.B.—All the dust should be thrown away.

2. We take a sweep's brush and sweep down all the soot from the flues and oven.

3. We mix some pounded black lead in a gallipot with enough water to make it into a smooth thick liquid.

4. We dip the black lead brush in the mixture, and black-lead the whole of the range, beginning from the top of the stove, by the dampers, and then downwards.

5. When the black lead is dry we brush it all over with a dry brush.

6. We then take another brush and polish the range all over, so as to make it quite bright.

N.B.—The bars of the stove should be done in the same way.

7. We take the sweep's brush and sweep the remaining soot and dust from the stove and the hearth.

8. We polish the steel handles and bolts of the oven by rubbing them with emery paper.

9. The brass handles and bolts we should polish with bath brickdust and a leather.

10. We get a flannel and a pail of hot water, put in it some soda, and wash the hearth all over.

N.B.—We must not wet it too much.

11. We take a hearthstone and rub it all over the hearth.

12. We then wring the flannel out in the hot water, and smooth the hearth over, rubbing it lightly all in one direction.

13. We must black-lead and polish the inside of the fender in the same way as we did the range, and brighten the rim of it by rubbing it with emery paper.

Now it is finished.

TO LAY A FIRE.

1. We should place a few sifted cinders at the bottom of the grate.

2. We then put in a piece of crumpled paper, and arrange the sticks over it, laying them across each other.

3. We now put a few pieces of coal on the top, rather to the front, so as to leave a good draught at the back to draw the fire.

4. When the fire is lighted and has burned up a little we can add more sifted cinders mixed with the coal.

5. We should only put small quantities of coal and cinders on the fire at a time.

Now it is finished.

TO CLEAN A CLOSE KITCHEN RANGE.

1. We proceed in the same way as for an open range (see notes 1 and 2),

2. We must now take down the doors of the flues at the back of the range, and take off all the lids of the flues over the oven and boiler.

3. We take the turk's head or flue brush, push it carefully up each flue at the back, so as to sweep them as clean as possible.

4. We must then put it in the flues above the oven and boiler, and sweep all round.

5. We should pull out the drawer just below the oven, in which we shall find the soot has fallen.

6. We empty all the soot away and sweep out the drawer clean.

7. We now take the sweep's brush and sweep down the range.

8. We black-lead, polish the range, and clean the hearth and fender as described for an open range (from note 3 to end).

9. We take down the iron plate-rack across the top of the range, and rub the bars with emery cloth.

10. We should dust the fire-irons, and if they are rusty, they should be rubbed with emery cloth or oil and leather.

Now it is finished.

TO CLEAN A GAS STOVE.

1. We require the same materials as for a kitchen range.

2. We lift out the bars at the top, and rub them with emery cloth until they are quite clean and bright.

3. We wash the top of the stove with a flannel dipped in hot water and soda, so as to remove all grease and dirt; we then wring out the flannel, and partially dry the top of the stove.

4. We now black-lead and polish it in the same way as for the kitchen range.

N.B.—We must be careful not to stop up the gas holes with black lead.

5. We place the bars back over the stove.

6. We polish the brass handles of the gas burners with bath brickdust and a leather.

7. We wash the tiles round the stove with the flannel, hot water, and soda.

8. We dry them with a cloth.

Now it is finished.

TO CLEAN AN IRON SAUCEPAN.

1. We should wash the saucepan well in hot water and soda.

> N.B.—All the black should be removed from the outside and bottom.

2. We must soap the palm of one hand, and rub the inside of the saucepan.

> N.B.—In washing any greasy utensil it is best if possible to use the hand instead of a flannel, as the latter retains the grease and so keeps putting the grease on again instead of rubbing it off.

3. We mix some sand and powdered soda together, and then dip the soap into it and rub the inside of the saucepan until it is quite clean and bright.

4. We now rinse it in water and dry it with a cloth.

5. We should clean the lid in the same way.

> N.B.—A white enamelled stewpan is cleansed in the same way, great care should be taken to remove all the stains off the white enamel inside.
>
> N.B.—Salt might be mixed with the sand and used to remove the stains from the enamel.

Now it is finished.

TO CLEAN A COPPER STEWPAN.

1. We mix some sand and salt together on a plate, half the quantity of salt to that of sand.

2. We wash the stewpan well in hot water and soda.

3. We soap the hand, dip it in the salt and sand, and rub the inside of the pan until all stains are removed and it has become clean and bright.

4. We rinse it out well in the water, dry the inside quickly, and then turn over the pan and clean the copper outside.

5. We should rub it in the same way with a soaped hand dipped in sand and salt.

> N.B.—If there are many stains on it, an old half lemon or vinegar might be used to remove them.
>
> N.B.—Only the copper part should be cleaned with lemon or vinegar.

6. We now rinse it again thoroughly, and dry it quickly with a cloth.

Now it is finished.

LESSONS ON COOKERY.

ROASTING.

Now we will show you how to roast meat at an open range, but first we must see that the fire is clear and bright.

1. We must take the shovel and put it in at the back of the fire and push all the red hot coals to the front.

2. We put fresh coal at the back, packing it together rather closely, but taking care that we leave a draught at the back, to draw the fire and make it burn clear and bright.

3. We must fill in all the spaces in the front of the fire with small lumps of coal or coke.

> N.B.—If it be a close range with which we are dealing, we should pull out the *centre damper only*, which will create a draught at the back, and help to draw the fire up quickly.

4. We now take our joint, say *a leg of mutton.*

5. We must see that it is quite clean, and, if necessary, we must scrape it with a knife and wipe it over with a clean cloth.

> N.B.—Meat should not, as a rule, be washed in water, as it takes some of the goodness out. If meat has been kept some time and is not quite fresh, then you might wash it with a little vinegar and water, but it must be well wiped afterwards.

6. We take the *leg of mutton* and with a sharp knife cut off the *knuckle bone.*

> N.B.—The *knuckle bone* we put aside ; it can be used with *beef* for *beef tea*, or be put in the *stockpot*, or the trimmings and one pint of water will make gravy for the joint when done, allowing it to simmer while the joint is roasting.

B

7. We trim off the *piece of flank* and remove the thick *piece of skin* from the part where the leg joins the *loin*. (These trimmings must be put aside, as they can be used for other purposes.)

8. We must now *weigh* the *leg of mutton*, so as to find out how long it will take to roast it, as a *quarter of an hour* is allowed for *each pound* of weight, and *one quarter of an hour* besides.

> N.B.—When we have a joint *without bone*, such as *rolled ribs of beef* or *topside of beef*, we must allow twenty minutes to *each pound* of weight, as it is all solid meat.

9. We take the *leg of mutton*, which weighs say *seven pounds*, it will therefore take *two hours* to roast.

10. We put the *roasting screen* in front of the fire to keep off the draught and keep in all the heat.

11. We put the *dripping pan* down on a stand within the screen, close to the fire, with the dripping ladle.

12. We hang the *roasting jack* up from the mantelpiece over the dripping pan.

> N.B.—Some roasting screens contain the dripping pan and the jack, which are of course more convenient.

13. We take the *hook* of the *roasting jack* and pass it through the *knuckle-end* of the leg.

14. We must *wind* up the *jack* with the *key*, before we put the joint on, so as to make it twist the meat round.

15. We must put the joint close to the fire for the *first five minutes.*

16. After that time we can draw the joint a little further back, or it will cook too quickly and become burnt and dried.

> N.B.—Meat that is frozen must be placed some way from the fire at first, and then drawn gradually towards it, as it must thaw slowly or it may become tough.

17. We must baste the joint every *five* minutes with the drippings that run from it into the pan, using the dripping ladle.

18. We let the joint roast for *two hours*, as its weight is *seven pounds.*

19. After that time, and just before we dish up the

Lessons on Cooking Meat.—Roasting.

joint, we must sprinkle about a *saltspoonful of salt* over it, and then *baste it well*.

20. We must take a large dish and warm it well.

21. Now we can take the hook of the jack, and place the joint on to the hot dish, and draw out the hook.

22. We take about a *gill of hot stock* and pour it into the dish. [This makes the gravy, and when the joint is cut, the juices from the meat will add to it.]

23. We must take a piece of demy paper and cut it like a fringe. This we put round the end of the knuckle bone.

N.B.—The dripping in the pan should be poured into a basin, and when it is cold there will be under the crust of dripping a good gravy. When the *dripping* is required for use it must be carefully removed from the top of the *gravy*, and clarified. (See Lesson on "Frying.") Nearly all joints can be roasted in this way. Attention should be paid to the rules explained above concerning joints of meat without bone.

Now it is finished.

BOILING.

Now we will show you how to boil *meat*.

1. We must give attention to the *fire*, and build it up gradually with small pieces of *coal*, so as to make it burn clear and bright.

2. We must not have a smoky *fire* for boiling, or the *meat* will get smoked, we should start with a good *fire*, and keep it up by adding occasionally small *coal*, and so prevent smoke as much as possible.

> N.B.—We do not require such a clear bright fire as for roasting.

3. We now take a saucepan sufficiently large to hold the *joint* to be cooked.

4. We fill the saucepan almost full of *cold water*, and put it on the fire to warm.

> N.B.—*Salt* should always be added to the *water* in the saucepan to make the *water* taste, unless the *meat* to be cooked is already *salted*, in which case it should be omitted.

5. We now take the *joint*, say, for example, a piece of the *silverside of beef salted*.

6. We must see that it is quite clean, and if necessary we must scrape it with a knife, and wipe it over with a clean cloth.

> N.B.—*Meat* should not as a rule be washed in *water*, as it takes some of the goodness out. *Meat* that has been kept some time, and is not quite fresh, might be washed with *vinegar and water*, but it must be well wiped afterwards.
>
> N.B.—*Salt meat* must not be washed with *vinegar and water*, but only with *salt and water*.

7. We must now weigh the piece of *salt beef*, so as to find out how long it will take to boil, as *ten minutes* are allowed for each *lb. of meat*.

> N.B.—This rule refers to the boiling of all meat except *pork*, which requires *fifteen minutes* to each *lb. of meat*.
>
> A.—In boiling *meat* to be eaten the *joint* should be first plunged into *boiling water*, in order that the albumen on the outside of the joint may become hardened, and so prevent the escape of the *juices of the meat*.
>
> B.—The temperature of the water should then be lowered gradually (by adding a small quantity of cold water and drawing the saucepan to the side of the fire), and the *meat* allowed to simmer gently, or it will become tough.

C.—In boiling *meat* for the purpose of making *soup*, the *meat* should be put into *cold water*, in order to extract all the goodness from the *meat*.

D. The water should be brought gradually to boiling point, then moved to the side of the fire, and left to simmer gently for some length of time.

N.B.—*Salt meat* must be put into *warm water*, so as to extract a little of the *salt* before the pores of the skin are closed up; if the *meat* were put into *boiling water* the pores of the skin would be closed, and the meat would be hardened by the *salt* not being allowed to escape.

8. When the water in the saucepan is warm, we take the *beef*, which weighs, say, *eight pounds* (it will therefore take about *one hour and twenty minutes*), and put it in the saucepan; there should be only just enough water to cover the joint.

9. We let the water just boil up, and then we should move the saucepan to the side of the fire, and let it simmer gently for the remainder of the time.

10. As soon as the water comes to the boil we must take a large spoon and *skim* the water carefully.

N.B.—The *scum* should be skimmed off directly it rises, or it will boil down again in the *meat* and spoil it. *Scum* is the *impurity* which rises from the *meat*.

N.B.—We must be very careful not to let the *meat boil*, or it will be *hardened* and *tough*.

11. When the *meat* is sufficiently cooked, we take it carefully out of the saucepan and put it on a hot dish for serving. We pour about *a gill* of the *liquor* (in which it was boiled) round the *joint* (this makes the *gravy*, and when the *joint* is cut the *juices* from the *meat* will add to it).

N.B.—The *liquor* from *boiled meat* can always be used for different purposes, and should therefore never be thrown away, but poured into a clean basin and put aside to cool, the *fat* should be carefully removed from the top of the *liquor*, while it is cold, before being used. *Salt liquor* is often used for making *pea soup*.

Now it is finished.

BAKING.

Meat, Bread, Pastry, &c.

Now we will show you how to *bake meat*.

1. We must have a *good fire*, and keep it up, adding by degrees small pieces of *coal*, as the *oven* is required to be very *hot*.

> N.B.— If it is a close range with which we are dealing, we should pull out the *damper* placed over the *oven* in order to draw all the *heat* of the *fire* towards the *oven*. The *ventilator* of the *oven* should be *closed*.
>
> N.B.—In kitchen stoves there is usually either a *handle* at the top of the oven, to be pulled out for opening the *ventilator*, or a *slide ventilator* at the bottom.

2. We should test the *heat* of the *oven* by the *thermometer* which is fixed in the door of the oven, the heat should rise to 240° Fahrenheit.

3. We take the *joint*, see that it is clean, as directed in "Lesson on Roasting," Note 5, and weigh it, so as to find out how long it will take to *bake*, as ten *minutes* are allowed for each *pound of weight*.

> N.B.—When we have a *joint without bone* we must allow about *fifteen minutes* to each *pound of weight*, as it is *solid meat*.

4. We take the *hot water tin*, on which the *stand* for the *meat* is placed, lift up the *upper tin* or *tray* and fill the *under tin* half full of *warm water*, we then fit on the *upper tin*.

> N.B.— In one corner of the upper tin is a small hole or escape for the steam. The *water* below must only *just reach* this *hole*, and *not* come into it.
>
> N.B.—The *water* is placed in the *tin* to prevent the *tin* and the *meat* from getting burnt, and so causing a disagreeable smell.

5. We place the *stand* on the *hot water tin* to raise the *joint* and prevent it from standing in its own *dripping*, which would sodden and spoil the *meat*.

6. We now take the *joint*, which weighs say *seven pounds* (it will therefore take *one hour and ten minutes* to *bake*), and put it on the *stand*. We should dredge *flour* over it.

7. We put the *tin* with the *meat* in the *oven*. The *oven* should be kept *very hot* for the first *five minutes*, in order to form a *brown crust* on the outside of the *joint*, to keep in the *juices* of the *meat*. After that time the *ventilator* of the *oven* should be *opened*, so as to allow the *steam* to escape, or the *meat* would get soddened.

> N.B.—*Meat* that is *frozen* must be gradually warmed, to thaw it before shutting it up in the hot *oven*, or it would be tough.

8. We must *baste* the *joint* every *fifteen minutes* with the *drippings* that run from the *meat* into the pan, using the *dripping ladle*.

> N.B.—*Joints* that are not very *fat* must be even more frequently *basted*, or they would burn: if there is not sufficient *dripping* from the *meat*, a little extra *dripping* should be put into the pan.
>
> N.B.—*Joints* that have *no fat* should be covered with a piece of *whitey brown paper* which has been spread with *butter* or *dripping*—it will prevent the *meat* catching too quickly.

9. We should turn the *joint* over occasionally, as the upper side will get browned quicker than the lower.

> N.B.—*Potatoes*, washed and peeled, or a small *suet* or *dripping and flour pudding* (see " Puddings," Lesson No. 28), or a *Yorkshire pudding* (see " Puddings," Lesson No. 29), might be baked under the *meat*, but they should only be put in *half an hour* before the *meat* is finished.

10. Just before we dish up the *joint*, we should sprinkle about a *saltspoonful of salt* over it, and then *baste* it well.

11. We serve the *joint* on a hot dish (as described in " Lesson on Roasting," Note 22, and act with regard to the *dripping* according to the " N.B." after Note 23.)

> N.B.—*Pastry* or *bread*, &c., should not be *baked* in the oven at the same time as the *meat*, as the *steam* would prevent their *baking* properly. For baking small *patties* and *tartlets* made of *Puff Paste*, the heat of the oven should rise to 300° Fahrenheit. For *meat pies*, *tarts*, &c., the heat should rise to 280°. For *bread* the heat should rise to 280°, and must be reduced after a *quarter of an hour* to 220°.

Now it is finished.

FRYING.

And Lessons on Clarifying Butter, Fat, and Dripping.

The principles of frying.

1. We must have a clear bright fire.

N.B. We must be very careful it is not smoky.

2. We should be careful that the utensil used is very clean, for if there is anything sticking at the bottom of the pan, it will quickly catch or burn, and so spoil the contents.

3. We should clarify all *fat* (*not lard*), *dripping,* and *butter*, before using them, to remove the impurities from the former, and the butter-milk, and other watery substance, from the latter.

N.B.—*Fat* need not be clarified more than once. After using it we should always pour it off carefully in a basin, and when it is cold we should remove the sediment from the bottom of the cake of *fat*. *Butter* must be clarified each time it is used, to remove all watery substances.

4. We must have the *fat* very hot; good frying depends on the *fat* being properly heated.

5. We should test the heat of the *fat* by a frimometer, if possible; the heat should rise to 345 *degrees* Fahrenheit for ordinary frying, and 400 *degrees* for *whitebait*.

N.B.—If there is no frimometer, the heat of the *fat* may be tested by the look—as *fat* gets quite still and begins to smoke when it is very hot—or by throwing in a small piece of *crumb of bread*, and if it fries directly a light brown, the *fat* is ready for use.

6. We should use a deep pan with plenty of *fat*, so that anything put in may be entirely covered.

7. We can fry *bacon* in its own *fat*, it only requires watching and turning till it is done (see Lesson on "Liver and Bacon," from Note 1 to Note 5).

8. We can fry *chops* or *steaks*, or *slices of meat*, in either an oz. of *clarified dripping or butter.*

9. We should melt the *fat* first, but it does not require to be heated.

10. We must be watchful, when the *meat* is frying, not to allow it to burn; we should turn it over occasionally.

N.B.—If there is a gridiron it is much better to grill *chops* and *steaks*, as it prevents their being greasy (see Lesson on a "Grilled Steak"). For frying *Fish*, see "Fish," Lessons Nos. 3, 6, 7, and 13. For frying *Meat, Rissoles, Potatoes,* &c., see "Cooked Meat," Lessons Nos. 2 and 6; "Australian Meat," Lesson No. 8; "Entrées," Lessons Nos. 4 and 11; and "Vegetables," Lessons Nos. 3 and 4.

Lessons on Frying and Clarifying Fat.

To render down or clarify *fat*.

1. We take any scraps of *cooked* or *uncooked fat*, and cut them up in small pieces.

2. We put the pieces in an old but clean saucepan, and pour in just enough *cold water* to cover them.

3. We put the saucepan on the fire and keep it boiling; it will take about *an hour*, the lid should be off the saucepan.

4. We must stir the *fat* occasionally, to prevent it from burning or sticking to the bottom of the saucepan.

5. When the *water* has evaporated, and the pieces of *fat* are cooked, we should pour the melted *fat* through an old sieve into a basin, and when cold it can be used for all frying purposes instead of *lard*.

To clarify *dripping*.

1. We should put the *dripping* in a saucepan, and put it on the fire to boil.

2. When it boils we pour it into a basin in which there should be *half a pint of cold water*.

3. When the *dripping* is cold, we take a knife and cut round the edge, so as to take out the *cake of dripping*.

4. We should scrape off all the sediment that will be found on the bottom of the *cake*, and wipe it dry with a cloth.

To clarify *butter*.

1. We put the quantity of *butter* required for present use in a small saucepan, and put it on the fire and let it boil.

2. When the *butter* has boiled, we must take a spoon and remove the *white scum* from the top.

3. We should then pour the clear *butter* carefully into the pan for use, as below the *butter* will be a little more *watery substance*.

Now it is finished.

COOKED MEAT.

Lesson No. 1.

HASHED MEAT.

Average cost of "*Hashed Meat.*"

INGREDIENTS.

	d.
1 lb. of scraps of cold meat and bone	6
2 small onions	1
1 carrot	¼
½ a turnip	¼
1 bunch of herbs (consisting of 1 bay leaf, a sprig of marjoram, thyme, parsley,)	½
About a tablespoonful of flour	
1 dessertspoonful of mushroom ketchup	1
Sippets of bread	
Salt and pepper	¾
½ an oz. of butter	
	9¾

Time required, about two hours ; or, if the stock for the gravy is already made, then only half an hour.

Now we will show you how to *Hash Cold Meat.*

1. We take any remains of *cold meat*, cut off all the meat from the bone, and cut it into thin slices.

2. We chop the *bone* in pieces and put them into a saucepan.

3. We take *one onion*, peel it and cut it in quarters.

4. We take *one carrot*, wash it, scrape it, and cut it in quarters.

5. We take *half a turnip*, peel it, and cut it in half.

6. We take a *sprig of parsley*, wash it, and dry it in a cloth.

7. We take *one bay leaf, one sprig of marjoram* and *thyme*, and the *parsley*, and tie them tightly together with a piece of string.

8. We put the *herbs* and the *vegetables* into the saucepan with the *bones*, and pour in enough *cold water* to cover them.

Lessons on Re-Cooking Meat.—Hashed Meat. 27

9. We put the saucepan on the fire and when it boils we should add *pepper* and *salt*, according to taste.

10. We now put the lid on and move the saucepan to the side of the fire to stew gently for *one hour, or one hour and a half;* we should watch it and skim it occasionally.

11. We take a *small onion*, peel it, and cut it in slices.

12. We put *half an ounce of butter* into a frying pan.

13. We put the pan on the fire, and when the *butter* is melted we add the *sliced onion*, and let it fry a nice brown.

14. We must shake the pan occasionally to prevent the slices of *onion* from sticking to the bottom of the pan and burning.

15. When the *onion* is sufficiently browned, we strain off the *butter* and put the *onion* on to a plate.

16. When the *bones* have stewed long enough, we should strain off the liquor into a basin.

17. We wash out the saucepan and pour back the liquor.

18. We put a *tablespoonful of flour* into a small basin.

19. We add *a tablespoonful* of the *liquor* to the *flour* and stir it into a smooth *paste*.

20. We stir this *paste* gradually into the *liquor* in the saucepan.

21. We also add the *browned onion* and a *dessertspoonful of mushroom ketchup*.

22. We put the saucepan on the fire and stir the *sauce* until it boils and thickens.

23. We let it boil for *two or three minutes*, until the *flour* is cooked.

> N.B.—We should be careful to stir the sauce smoothly while it boils, or it will be lumpy.

24. We then move the saucepan to the side of the fire, and when it is off the boil we lay in the pieces of *meat* to warm through.

> N.B.—We must not let the sauce boil while the meat is in it, or the meat will get hard and tough.

25. We cut a *thin slice of bread*, and cut it into square pieces.

26. We cut these square pieces in half, cornerwise, making the pieces into triangles.

27. We put *one ounce of clarified dripping* (see Lesson on "Frying") in a frying pan to melt.

28. When the *dripping* is quite hot we put in the *sippets of bread*, and let them fry a light brown.

29. We should turn them, so that they get browned on each side.

30. We put a piece of *kitchen paper* on a plate, and when the *sippets* are fried we turn them on to the paper to drain off the grease.

<small>N.B.—If liked, the bread could be toasted before the fire instead of fried; in which case the bread should be cut into sippets after it is toasted.</small>

31. For serving, we put the *slices of meat* on a hot dish, in the centre, strain the *sauce* over them and put the *sippets of bread* round the edge of the dish.

Now it is finished.

COOKED MEAT.

Lesson No. 2.

MEAT FRITTERS.

Average cost of "*Meat Fritters.*"

INGREDIENTS.

	d.
Slices of cold meat	6
6 oz. of flour	1
1 tablespoonful of salad oil }	
Salt }	1
2 eggs }	
Dripping for frying }	2
	10

Time required, about half an hour (and one hour for the batter to rise).

Now we will show you how to make *Meat Fritters, i.e.* frying meat in batter.

1. We put *six ounces of flour* and *half a saltspoonful of salt* into a basin.

2. We add a *tablespoonful of salad oil* and mix the *flour* into a smooth paste.

N.B.—We must be careful that the oil is quite sweet. If oil is objected to, one ounce of melted butter can be used instead.

3. We now stir in smoothly by degrees, *half a pint* of *tepid water;* we must be careful that there are no lumps.

4. We break *two eggs*, put the *whites* on a plate (the *yolks* we should put in a cup, as they will not be required for present use).

5. We sprinkle a *quarter of a saltspoonful of salt* over the *whites of the eggs*, and whip them to a stiff froth with a knife.

6. We stir the whipped *whites of the eggs* lightly into the *batter.*

N.B.—In winter, clean snow might be used in the batter instead of the whites of eggs.

N.B.—This batter might be made without the whites of eggs, in which case it should be mixed with half a pint of beer, instead of the water, but the batter made with beer will not rise as much as when eggs are used.

N.B.—The beer will not taste after the batter is fried.

7. We stand the *batter* aside *for one hour* to rise, or until required for *frying*, but it should not stand longer than *two hours*.

8. We put *half a pound of clarified dripping* (see Lesson on "Frying") into a saucepan, and put it on the fire to heat.

9. We take some *cold meat*, and cut it up into thin slices.

> N.B.—Cold boiled, or roast pork, or boiled bacon is very nice fried in batter.

10. When the *batter* has risen and the *fritters* are required for use, we stir the *batter* lightly with a spoon, so as to be sure that there are no lumps settled at the bottom.

11. When the *dripping* is quite hot and smoking, we take the *slices of meat*, dip them in the *batter* so that they are quite covered, and then drop them into the *hot fat*.

> N.B.—We must not put in too many slices at a time, as they should not touch each other.

12. We must turn them over so that they are fried a nice brown on both sides.

13. We put a piece of *kitchen paper* on a plate.

14. As the *fritters* are fried, we take them carefully out of the fat with a *perforated spoon*, and put them on the paper to drain off the grease.

> N.B.—We must be careful to skim the fat from time to time, or the little loose pieces of batter will burn and spoil the fat.
>
> N.B.—Slices of apple or orange can be fried in this batter in the same way, only that the batter should be sweetened, and sugar sprinkled over the fritters when they are fried.
>
> N.B.—Fish can be fried in batter the same way, only that the batter is usually made with beer instead of white of egg.

15. For serving, we turn the *fritters* on to a hot dish.

Now it is finished.

COOKED MEAT.

Lesson No. 3.

GOBLET PIE.

Average cost of a "*Goblet Pie.*"

INGREDIENTS.

		d.
Any scraps of cold meat		
2 tablespoonsful of chopped suet		1½
2 do. of moist sugar		¾
2 do. of currants		¾
2 do. of plums		½
2 do. of chopped apples		½
¼ lb. of flour	}	¾
¼ of a teaspoonful of baking-powder		
1 oz. of dripping............................		½
		4¾

Time required, about three-quarters of an hour.

Now we will show you how to make a "*Goblet Pie.*"

N.B.—This pie is made with equal quantities of ingredients.

1. We take any scraps of *cold meat* (the smallest scraps would do that would not do for anything else), put them on a board, and chop them up as finely as possible (there should be about *two tablespoonsful of chopped meat*).

2. We take about *two ounces of suet*, put it on a board, cut away the *skin*, and chop it up very finely (there should be about *two tablespoonsful*).

3. We take *two small apples*, peel them, cut out the core, and chop them up finely (there should be about *two tablespoonsful*).

4. We take *two tablespoonsful of plums*, stone them, and chop them up in small pieces.

5. We take *two tablespoonsful of currants*, wash them, dry them in a cloth, and pick them over.

6. We put all these *ingredients* into a basin with *two tablespoonsful of moist sugar*, and mix them all well together with a spoon.

7. We then turn the mixture into a small pie dish.

8. We put a *quarter of a pound of flour* into a basin, and mix into it a few grains of *salt*, and a *quarter of a teaspoonful of baking powder*.

9. We take *one ounce of clarified dripping* and rub it well and lightly into the *flour* with our hands, until it resembles *sifted bread crumbs*.

10. We now add to it sufficient water to mix it into a stiff *paste*.

11. We flour a board and turn the *paste* out on it.

12. We take a rolling-pin, flour it, and roll out the *paste* to the shape of the pie dish, only a little larger, and to about a *quarter of an inch* in thickness.

13. We wet the edge of the pie dish with *water*.

14. We take a knife, dip it in *flour*, and cut a strip of the *paste*, the width of the edge of the pie dish, and place it round the edge of the dish.

15. We should cut this strip of *paste* from round the edge of the *paste*, leaving the *centre* piece rather larger than the top of the pie dish.

16. We wet the edge of the *paste* with *water*.

17. We take the remaining piece of *paste*, and place it over the pie dish, pressing the edges together with our thumb.

N.B.—We must be very careful not to break the *paste*.

18. We take a knife, dip it in *flour*, and trim off all the rough edges of the *paste*, round the edge of the dish.

19. We take a knife, and with the back of the blade we make little notches in the edge of the *paste*, pressing the *paste* firmly with our thumb, to keep it in its proper place.

20. We make a little hole with the knife, in the *centre* of the *pie* to let the *steam* out while the *pie* is baking.

21. We put the *pie* into the oven (the heat should rise to 220°), to bake for *half an hour*.

Now it is finished.

COOKED MEAT.

Lesson No. 4.

CURRY.

Average cost of a "*Curry*" (made with cold meat).

INGREDIENTS.

	d.
Scraps of cold meat	6
2 oz. of clarified dripping	1
(or butter 2*d.*)	
1 apple	½
1 onion	½
1 dessertspoonful of curry powder	} 1
Salt	
	9

Time required, about three quarters of an hour.

Now we will show you how to make a *Curry*.

1. We put *two ounces of clarified dripping* or *butter* into a saucepan, and put it on the fire to heat.

2. We take *one onion*, peel it, put it on a board, and chop it up as finely as possible.

3. When the *dripping* is quite hot we put in the *chopped onion* to brown; we must be careful it does not burn.

4. We should shake the saucepan occasionally to prevent the *onion* from sticking to the bottom.

5. We take the *cold meat* and cut it up into small pieces.

6. We take *one small apple*, peel it, take out the core, and chop it up very finely on a board.

7. When the *onion* is sufficiently brown we should strain it off, and pour the *dripping* back into the saucepan.

N.B.—We should put the browned onion on a plate.

8. We now put the pieces of *cold meat* into the saucepan, and let them brown on both sides.

9. We add *one dessertspoonful of curry powder*, the *chopped apple*, and a little *salt*, according to taste.

10. We now pour in *half a pint of cold water*, and put back the *browned onion*.

> N.B. If the onion had been left in while the meat was browning, it would have got burnt.

11. We should stir smoothly and carefully until it boils, and then move it to the side of the fire to simmer for *half an hour*.

12. The lid should be off the saucepan as the *sauce* is to reduce.

13. For serving we take the *meat* out of the saucepan and put it on a hot dish and pour the *sauce* over it.

> N.B. *Boiled rice* should be served with the *curry* (see Lesson on "Rice").

Now it is finished.

Lessons on Re-Cooking Meat.—Shepherd's Pie.

COOKED MEAT.

Lesson No. 5.

SHEPHERD'S PIE.

Average cost of a "*Shepherd's Pie.*"

INGREDIENTS.

	d.
Scraps of cold meat	6
1 small onion }	
Pepper and salt }	½
1½ lb. of potatoes	1½
1 oz. of butter	1
½ a gill of milk	½
	9½

Time required, about an hour and a half.

Now we will show you how to make a *Shepherd's Pie.*

1. We take *one and a half pound of potatoes,* wash them, and boil them as described (see "Vegetables," Lesson No. 1.).

N.B.—This quantity of potato will cover a quart pie dish.

N.B.—Any remains of cold potatoes should be used instead of boiling fresh ones.

2. We put *one ounce of butter* and *half a gill* (one gill is a quarter of a pint) of *milk* into a saucepan, and put it on the fire to boil.

3. We put the *boiled potatoes* into another saucepan, and mash them up with a fork or spoon.

4. When the *milk* boils we pour it into the *mashed potatoes,* and stir them into a smooth paste.

5. We put the saucepan on the fire and let the *potatoes* just boil; we must be careful they do not burn.

6. We take any *scraps of cold meat,* cut them in small pieces, and put them in a pie dish in layers.

7. If there is not much *fat* with the *meat,* we should mix a few slices of *pork fat* with the *meat.*

8. We take *one small onion,* peel it, and chop it up as finely as possible on a board.

9. We sprinkle each layer of *meat* with plenty of *pepper and salt*, and a little of the *chopped onion*.

10. We fill the dish half full of *cold water*.

> N.B.—If there is any cold gravy it would, of course, be better than the water.
>
> N.B.—The pie dish should be quite full of meat, and rather heaped in the centre, so as to raise the crust of potato.

11. We take the *mashed potato* and put it over the top of the *meat*, smoothing it over neatly with a knife.

12. We take a fork, and mark all over the top of the *potato*.

> N.B.—If liked, the mashed *potato* might be mixed with half its weight of flour into a dough, to make a more substantial crust; it must be then rolled out with a rolling-pin like pastry.

13. We put the pie dish into the oven, or into a Dutch oven in front of the fire, for *half an hour*, to brown the crust of *potato* and warm the *meat* through.

Now it is finished.

COOKED MEAT.

Lesson No. 6.

FRIED RISSOLES.

Average cost of "*Fried Rissoles*" made of cold meat.
(This quantity makes about 8.)

INGREDIENTS.

	d.
Scraps of cold meat, 2 oz.	1
2 tablespoonsful of chopped suet	1
2 do. of bread crumbs	½
2 do. of chopped parsley	
1 tablespoonful of chopped herbs, marjoram and thyme	½
2 eggs	2
Crumb of bread	
Salt and pepper	1
Use of dripping for frying	
	6½

Time required, about half an hour.

Now we will show you how to make *Rissoles* with cold meat.

1. We put about *half a pound of clarified dripping* into a saucepan and put it on the fire to heat.

2. We take some *scraps of cold meat*, and chop it up as finely as possible on a board, when chopped there should be about *two tablespoonsful.*

3. We take *two ounces of suet*, put it on a board, cut away the *skin* and chop it up as finely as possible. There should be *two tablespoonsful.*

4. We take a grater and grate some *crumbs of bread* on to a piece of paper.

    N.B.—More than *two tablespoonsful of bread crumbs* will be required, as the *rissoles* should be dipped in *bread crumbs* before they are fried.

5. We take *two or three sprigs of parsley*, wash it and dry it in a cloth.

6. We put the *parsley* on a board and chop it up finely; there should be *two tablespoonsful.*

7. We take a *sprig of marjoram* and a *sprig of thyme*, take away the stalks and rub the leaves through a strainer, or chop them up finely on a board.

> N.B.—The *stalks* of the *herbs* are bitter to taste, and can therefore only be used for flavouring and not for eating.

8. We put the *meat, suet,* and *two tablespoonsful of bread crumbs* into a basin and mix them together.

9. We now add the *herbs* and a *teaspoonful* of *salt*.

> N.B.—If liked, a little chopped *onion* or chopped *lemon peel* might be added.

10. We break *one egg* into the basin and mix all together lightly.

11. We take a board, flour it, and turn the *mixture* on to it.

12. We also flour our hands, to prevent the *mixture* from sticking.

13. We form the *mixture* into little balls, and we should sprinkle a little *flour* over them.

14. We break an *egg* on to a plate, and beat it very slightly with a knife.

15. We put the *balls* into the *egg* and egg them well all over.

16. We now put them into the *bread crumbs* and cover them well, but not too thickly.

> N.B.—We must be careful to finger them as little as possible.

17. We put the *rissoles* into a frying basket, a few at a time, as they must not touch each other.

18. When the *fat* in the saucepan is quite hot and smoking, we put in the frying basket and let the *rissoles* fry a pale brown.

19. If there is not sufficient *fat* to cover the *rissoles*, we must shake the basket occasionally, that they may get fried on all sides alike.

> N.B.—If there is no frying-basket, we should carefully put the *rissoles* into the *fat* with a spoon, and then we must turn them over, so as to get them equally browned.

20. We put a piece of kitchen paper on a plate.

21. When the *rissoles* are fried, we turn them carefully on to the paper to drain off the *grease*.

22. For serving, we put them on a hot dish.

Now it is finished.

COOKED MEAT.

LESSON No. 7.

MINCED MEAT.

Average cost of "*Minced Meat*" with rice or potatoes.

INGREDIENTS.

	d.
Scraps of cold meat	3
1 tablespoonful of mushroom ketchup }	1
Pepper and salt }	
½ lb. of Patna rice or 1 lb. of potatoes	1½
	5½

Time required to cook the potatoes, half an hour; to cook the mince, five minutes.

Now we will show you how to make a *Mince* of cold meat.

1. If the *mince* is served with *rice* (see Lesson on "Rice"), or if with *mashed potatoes* (see "Vegetables," Lesson No. 2).

2. We put any *scraps of cold meat* on a board, and mince it up with a sharp knife.

3. We put the *minced meat* into a saucepan with about a *tablespoonful* (or enough to moisten the mince) of *mushroom ketchup*, or some *gravy*, and season it with *pepper and salt* to taste.

4. We put the saucepan on the fire to let the *mince* just warm through.

5. We should stir it occasionally, to prevent the *meat* from sticking to the bottom of the saucepan.

6. For serving we turn the *mince* on to a hot dish, with a border of *boiled rice* or *mashed potato*.

Now it is finished.

AUSTRALIAN MEAT.

LESSON No. 1.

MULLIGATAWNY.

Average cost of "*Mulligatawny Soup*" (3 quarts) made from "*Australian Meat.*"

INGREDIENTS.

	s.	d.
2 lb. tin of Australian calf's head............	1	0
2 lbs. of Australian mutton	1	2
2 apples	0	1
2 leeks.....................................	0	1
2 carrots, 1 turnip..........................	0	1½
2 good-sized onions	0	1
2 tablespoonsful of flour ....⎫ 1 tablespoonful of curry powder ....⎬ Salt and sugar ....⎭	0	1
A bouquet garni (of parsley, thyme, marjor, m and 2 bay leaves)	0	1
	2	8½

Time required three hours.

Now we will show you how to make *Mulligatawny Soup*.

1. We take a tin of *Australian mutton* and open it carefully.

2. We take a spoon and carefully remove all the *fat* from the top of the *meat*.

> N.B. – The *fat* should only be removed from that part of the meat which is required for immediate use.
>
> N.B.—The *fat* should be clarified, by putting it into boiling water, and when cold can then be used as dripping.

3. We take *two pounds of the mutton* out of the tin, put it in a basin with *two quarts of warm water*.

4. We take *two apples*, peel them, and put them on a plate.

5. We cut the *apples* in *quarters*, cut out the *core*, and then cut the quarters into slices, and put them into a saucepan with *two ounces of the clarified fat*.

6. We take *one turnip* and *two good-sized onions*, peel them, cut them in pieces, and put them in the saucepan.

7. We put the saucepan on the fire, and give one stir to the *vegetables* with a wooden spoon.

Lessons on Australian Meat.—Mulligatawny.

8. We take *two leeks*, wash them well in cold water, and cut off the green tops of the leaves.

9. We cut the *leeks* up and put them in the saucepan.

10. We take *two carrots*, wash them, scrape them with a knife, cut them in pieces, and put them in the saucepan.

11. We give one stir with a wooden spoon to mix the *vegetables* together, and let them fry for *ten minutes*.

12. We also add a *sprig of parsley*, a *sprig of thyme*, a *sprig of marjoram* and *two bay-leaves*, tied tightly together with a piece of string.

13. When the *vegetables* have fried for *ten minutes* we take *half a pint of the liquor* (in which the meat is soaking), pour it into the saucepan, and let it boil and reduce to a quarter of a pint.

14. We should stir the *vegetables* occasionally.

15. We put *two tablespoonsful of flour* and *one tablespoonful of curry powder* into a basin, and mix them into a smooth *paste* with *one gill* (quarter of a pint) of the *liquor*.

16. We stir this mixture into the saucepan with the *vegetables*.

17. We now put the *meat* and the remaining *liquor* into the saucepan, put the lid on and let it come to the boil.

18. When it boils we should put one *saltspoonful of salt* and *half a saltspoonful of moist sugar* into the saucepan.

19. We now move the saucepan to the side of the fire and let it simmer for *two hours and a half*.

20. We should watch it, and skim it occasionally with a spoon.

21. After that time we strain off the *soup* through a strainer into a basin.

22. We pour the soup back into the saucepan.

23. We open the *two pound tin of calf's head*, remove all the *fat* from the top, and stir the contents of the tin into the soup in the saucepan.

24. For serving we pour the soup into a hot soup-tureen.

Now it is finished.

AUSTRALIAN MEAT.

Lesson No. 2.

BROWN PURÉE.

Average cost of "*Brown Purée*" (1 pint and a half) made from "*Australian Mince Meat*."

INGREDIENTS.

	s.	d.
1 lb. of Australian mince meat	0	7
2 carrots and 1 small turnip	0	1½
2 leeks	0	1
2 sticks of celery	0	1
1 onion, stuck with 4 cloves		
A bouquet garni (of 2 bay leaves, thyme, and marjoram)	0	1
A sprig of parsley		
1 teaspoonful of Liebig's extract	0	1
	1	0½

Time required, about two hours.

Now we will show you how to make a *Brown Purée*.

1. We take a tin of *Australian mince meat* and open it carefully.

2. We take a spoon and carefully remove the *fat* from the top of the meat.

> N.B.—The *fat* should only be removed from that part of the *meat* which is required for immediate use.
>
> N.B.—The *fat* should be clarified by putting it into boiling water, and when cold can then be used as dripping.

3. We take out *one pound of meat*, scrape off the *jelly* (which we put aside), and put the *meat* in a mortar.

4. We pound the meat well with a pestle.

5. We put *two quarts of water* into a saucepan, and put it on the fire to boil.

6. We take *two carrots*, wash them, and scrape them with a knife.

7. We take *two leeks*, cut off the outside green leaves, wash them thoroughly in cold water, and cut them in quarters.

8. We take *two sticks of celery*, wash them, and scrape them clean with a knife.

9. We tie these *vegetables* into a small bundle with string.

10. We take *one small turnip* and peel it.

11. We take an *onion*, peel it, and stick *four cloves* in it.

12. When the *water* in the saucepan is quite boiling, we put in all these *vegetables*.

13. We also add a *bouquet garni*, consisting of *two bay leaves*, a *sprig of thyme* and *marjoram*, tied tightly together.

14. We take a *sprig of parsley*, wash it in cold water, wring it in a cloth, and put it in the saucepan.

15. We take the *jelly* which came from the *meat*, and a little more out of the tin, and put it in the saucepan.

16. We also stir in *one teaspoonful* of *Liebig's Extract*, or ten or twelve drops of caramel (see note below) for colouring.

17. We let the *vegetables* boil gently for one hour and a half.

N.B.—The lid should be on the saucepan.

18. After that time we stir in the *pounded meat*, and season according to taste.

19. We take a cullender and strain the *purée* through on to a hot dish.

N.B.—For making caramel (browned sugar) for colouring gravies, &c. We put a quarter of a pound of moist or loaf sugar into an old saucepan, and put it on the fire and let it burn until it has become quite a dark brown liquid ; we add to it half a pint of boiling water and let it boil for five minutes, stirring it occasionally ; we then strain it, and pour it in a bottle, and it is ready for use at any time.

Now it is finished.

AUSTRALIAN MEAT.

LESSON NO. 3.

IRISH STEW.

Average cost of "*Irish Stew*," made from *Australian Meat*.

INGREDIENTS.

		d.
1½ lbs. of Australian meat	....	10½
1½ lb. of potatoes	....	1½
½ lb. of onions	....	1
		1 1

Time required, about one hour.

Now we will show you how to make an *Irish Stew*.

1. We wash *one and a half pound of potatoes* well in cold water, and scrub them clean with a scrubbing brush.

> N.B. If the *potatoes* are not very good, or are in any way diseased, we should take a sharp knife, peel them, and carefully cut out the *eyes* or any *black specks* about the *potatoes*, but it is much better to steam or boil them in their skins.

2. We take a potato steamer, fill the saucepan with hot water, and put it on the fire to boil.

3. We take *half a pound of onions* and peel them.

4. When the water is quite boiling we put the *potatoes* in the steamer, and sprinkle them over with *salt*.

> N.B.—As the onions are to be eaten with the potatoes, we put them in the saucepan of boiling water, and they can be boiled while the potatoes are being steamed.

5. We place the steamer on the saucepan of boiling water, and cover it down tight to keep the steam in.

6. We let the *potatoes steam*, and the *onions boil*, for *half an hour*.

7. We take a tin of *Australian meat* and open it carefully.

8. We take a spoon and carefully remove the *fat* from the top of the *meat*.

> N.B.—The fat should be clarified, by putting into boiling water, and when cold can then be used as dripping.

9. We take *one and a half pounds of meat* out of the tin and cut it in slices.

10. We should take a fork and put it in the *potatoes* and the *onions* to feel if they are quite tender.

11. When they are sufficiently cooked, we take the *potatoes* out of the steamer, put them on a board, peel them carefully, and cut them in slices.

12. We take the *onions* out of the saucepan, put them on a board, and cut them in slices.

13. We take a large saucepan, put in a layer of *potatoes*, then a layer of *onions*, and then a layer of *meat*.

14. We should sprinkle a little *pepper* and *salt* over each layer of *meat* for seasoning.

15. We pour *half a pint of warm water* into the saucepan, put it on the fire, and let the *meat* and *vegetables* simmer until they are thoroughly warmed through.

16. For serving we turn the *Irish Stew* out on to a hot dish.

Now it is finished.

AUSTRALIAN MEAT.

Lesson No. 4.

SAUSAGE ROLLS.

Average cost of "*Sausage Rolls*" (about two dozen) made from "*Australian Mince Meat.*"

INGREDIENTS.

	d.
½ lb. of mince meat	3½
1 lb. of flour	2¼
½ lb. of dripping	4
1 teaspoonful of baking powder	} ½
Seasoning	
4 sage leaves	
1 egg	1
	11

Time required, half an hour.

Now we will show you how to make *Sausage Rolls*.

1. We take a tin of *Australian mince meat* and open it carefully.

2. We take a spoon and carefully remove the *fat* from the top of the *meat*.

N.B.—The *fat* should be *clarified* by putting it into a basin of boiling water, and when cold can then be used as dripping.

3. We take *half a pound* of the *mince meat* out of the tin, put it in a basin, and season it well with *pepper and salt*.

4. We take *four sage leaves,* put them on a board, and chop them up as finely as possible with a knife.

5. We mix the *chopped sage* well into the *mince meat* with a spoon.

6. We put *one pound of flour* into another basin.

7. We add to it *one teaspoonful of baking powder, salt* (as much as would cover a *threepenny piece*), and *half a pound of clarified dripping*.

8. We rub the *dripping* well into the *flour* with our hands.

N.B.—We must mix it thoroughly, and be careful not to leave any *lumps*.

9. We add enough *water* to the *flour* to make it into a stiff *paste*.

10. We flour the paste board.

11. We turn the *paste* out on the board.

<small>N.B.—We should divide the *paste* in two, so as not to handle it too much.</small>

12. We take a rolling pin, flour it, and roll out *each portion* into a thin sheet, about *one-eighth of an inch* in thickness.

13. We cut the *paste* into pieces about *six inches* square.

14. We should collect all the scraps of *paste* (so that none is wasted), fold them together, and roll them out and cut them into squares.

<small>N.B.—There should be about *two dozen squares* of paste.</small>

15. We should put about a *tablespoonful* of the *mince meat* into the centre of each square of *paste*.

16. We fold the *paste* round the *meat*, joining it smoothly down the centre, and pressing the *ends* of the *paste* together with our finger and thumb.

17. We take a baking tin, grease it well, and place the *sausage rolls* on it.

18. We break *one egg* on to a plate, and beat it slightly with a knife.

19. We take a paste brush, dip it in the *egg*, and paint over the tops of the *rolls*.

20. We place the tin in a hot oven to bake for 15 *minutes*.

<small>N.B.—We should look at them once or twice, and turn them if necessary, so that they shall be equally baked.</small>

21. For serving we take the *rolls* off the tin and place them on a hot dish.

Now it is finished.

AUSTRALIAN MEAT.

Lesson No. 5.

CURRIED RABBIT.

Average cost of "*Curried Australian Rabbit.*"

INGREDIENTS.

	s.	d.
2 lb. tin of Australian rabbit	1	0
2 oz. of butter or dripping	0	1
2 moderate sized onions	0	1
1 good sized apple	0	0½
1 dessertspoonful of curry powder	0	1
Salt and flour		
Patna rice served with the curry	0	1½
	1	5

Time required, half an hour.

Now we will show you how to make a *Curry of Australian Rabbit.*

1. We take a *two pound tin of rabbit* and open it carefully.
   N.B. Any other *meat* could be used for the *curry* instead of the *rabbit*.

2. We take a spoon and carefully remove all the *fat* from the top of the meat.
   N.B.—The *fat* should be *clarified* by putting it into a basin of boiling water; and when cold can be used as dripping.

3. We put *two ounces of butter* or *clarified dripping* into a stewpan.
   N.B.—If the *fat* from the *rabbit* has been clarified in time, it can be used instead of the butter or dripping.

4. We put the stewpan on the fire to heat the *fat*.

5. We take *two moderate sized onions*, peel them, and cut them in slices.

6. When the *fat* is quite hot, we put in the *onions* to fry brown.
   N.B.—We must watch it, and stir the onions occasionally, and not let them burn or stick to the bottom of the pan.

7. We turn the *rabbit* out of the tin on to a plate.

8. We take a *good sized apple*, peel it, take out the core, and chop it up as finely as possible.

Lessons on Australian Meat.—Curried Rabbit.

9. When the *onions* are sufficiently browned we take all the pieces carefully out of the stewpan with a perforated spoon, and put them on a plate.

10. We take the pieces of *rabbit*, dry them in a cloth, and sprinkle them over well with *flour*.

11. We now put the pieces of *rabbit* into the stewpan to fry a nice brown.

12. We must turn the pieces occasionally so as to let them brown on both sides alike.

13. We put a *dessertspoonful of curry powder* into a cup, and mix it into a smooth paste with a little *cold water*.

14. When the *rabbit* is browned, we put the *chopped apple* and the fried onion into the stewpan.

15. We stir in smoothly the curry paste, and then add *half a pint of cold water* or *stock*, and *salt* according to taste.

16. We give one stir with a spoon and mix it all together.

17. We now put the lid on the stewpan, draw it rather to the side of the fire, and let it stew very gently for about *a quarter of an hour*, until the apple is quite tender.

18. We must boil the *rice* as directed. (See Lesson on "Rice.")

19. For serving, we turn the *curry* on to a hot dish, the *rice* can be put as a border on the same dish as the *curry*, or served on a separate dish.

Now it is finished.

AUSTRALIAN MEAT.

LESSON NO. 6.
MEAT PIE.

Average cost of a "*Meat Pie*" (a quart dish) made from *Australian mutton* or *beef* and *kidneys*.

INGREDIENTS.

	s.	d.
1½ lb. of Australian mutton or beef	0	10½
½ lb. Do. kidneys	0	3¾
¾ lb. of flour	0	1½
¼ lb. of dripping	0	2
1 teaspoonful of baking powder pepper and salt	0	0½
	1	6

Time required, about three-quarters of an hour.

Now we will show you how to make a *Meat Pie*.

1. We take a tin of Australian *mutton or beef* and open it carefully.

2. We take a spoon and carefully remove the *fat* from the part of the meat which is required for use.

> N.B.—All the *fat* should not be removed, as the *meat* not required for immediate use will keep better with the *fat* on the top; but a tin of *Australian meat* will not keep more than two or three days after it has once been opened.

3. We take a tin of *kidneys*, open it carefully and remove the *fat* from the part of the meat which is required for use.

> N.B.—The *fat* should be *clarified*, by putting it into boiling water, and when cold can then be used as dripping.

4. We take *one and a half pound* of the *meat* (*mutton or beef*) out of the tin and cut it neatly into nice sized pieces, and season the pieces with *pepper and salt*.

5. We take *half a pound of the kidneys* and cut them up in pieces.

6. We put *three quarters of a pound of flour* into a basin with a small *teaspoonful of baking powder* and *salt* (to cover thinly a *threepenny piece*).

7. We take a *quarter of a pound of clarified dripping* and rub it well into the *flour* with our hands.

> N.B.—We should be careful not to leave any lumps.

8. We add sufficient *water* to make it into a stiff *paste;* it will take rather less than *one gill* (quarter of a pint).

9. We take a board, flour it, and put the *paste* on it.

10. We take a *quart* pie-dish and fill it with the pieces of *meat* and *kidney*.

11. We take a little of the *jelly* out of the tin and put it in the dish with the *meat*, to make the *gravy*.

12. We take a rolling pin, flour it, and roll out the *paste* to the shape of the top of the pie-dish, only rather larger.

>   N.B.—We should keep our hands floured, to prevent the paste sticking.

13. We take a knife, dip it in the *flour*, and cut off a strip of the paste about *one inch* wide.

>   N.B.—This strip should be cut off from round the edge of the *paste*, leaving the centre piece the size of the top of the pie-dish.

14. We wet the edge of the pie-dish with *water*, and place the strip of *paste* round the edge.

15. We now wet the strip of *paste* on the pie-dish.

16. We take the piece of *paste*, lay it over the top of the pie-dish, pressing the edges together with our thumb.

17. We take a knife, flour it, and trim off the rough edges of the *paste*.

18. We take the knife, and with the back of the blade, we make little notches in the edge of the paste, pressing it with our thumb, to keep it in its proper place.

19. We should make a small hole in the *centre* of the *paste*, to let out the steam, whilst it is baking.

20. We can ornament the top of the pie with the remains of the *paste*, according to taste.

21. We put the *pie* into a quick oven to bake for *half an hour*.

22. We must look at it occasionally, to see that it does not burn.

Now it is finished.

AUSTRALIAN MEAT.

Lesson No. 7.

FRICASSÉE OF MUTTON.

Average cost of "*Fricassée of Mutton,*" made from Australian meat.

INGREDIENTS.

	s.	d.
2 lbs. of Australian mutton	1	2
2 oz. of butter	0	2
1½ oz. of flour } Pepper and salt }	0	0½
1 doz. mushrooms	0	4
Bread	0	0½
About 1 pint of milk	0	2
	1	11

Time required, about half an hour.

Now we will show you how to make *Fricassée of Mutton.*

1. We put *two ounces of butter* into a saucepan and put it on the fire.

2. When the *butter* is melted, we stir in *one and a half ounce of flour*, and a little *pepper and salt* according to taste.

3. We now pour in *three quarters of a pint of cold milk*, and stir smoothly with a wooden spoon, until it boils and thickens.

4. We take *one dozen of mushrooms*, peel them, and cut off the end of the *stalks*.

5. We add these *mushrooms* to the *sauce* and let them stew gently, until they are quite tender.

6. We take the *peel* and *stalks* of the *mushrooms*, wash them in cold water and put them in a small saucepan, with about *a gill of milk.*

7. We put the saucepan on the fire and let it stew gently, to extract the *flavour* of the *mushrooms.*

8. We take a *two pound* tin of *mutton*, open it carefully, and remove all the *fat* from the top of the *meat* with a spoon.

N.B.—The *fat* should be clarified by putting it into boiling water, and when cold can then be used as dripping.

9. We turn the *meat* out of the tin and cut it in small pieces.

10. We cut a thin slice of *crumb of bread*, put it on a board, and cut it up in small square pieces.

11. We cut these square pieces in half, cornerwise, making them into triangles.

12. We put *three ounces of clarified dripping* into a frying pan and put it on the fire to heat the *fat*.

13. We take a piece of kitchen paper and put it on a plate.

14. When the *fat* is quite hot and smoking, we throw in the *sippets of bread* and let them fry a pale brown.

15. We then take them out of the frying pan, and put them on the piece of paper to drain off the grease.

16. We sprinkle a little *salt* over the *sippets*, and keep them warm till required for use.

17. When the *mushrooms* are sufficiently cooked, we should strain the *milk* (in which the mushroom peelings were stewed) and stir it smoothly into the sauce.

18. We draw the saucepan to the side of the fire, and when the *sauce* is a little cooled, we put in the *slices of mutton* and let them just warm through.

N.B.—We must be careful that the *meat* does not boil, or it will be hardened.

19. We now take out the pieces of *meat* and put them on a hot dish.

20. We pour the *sauce* over the *meat*, and arrange the *mushrooms* in the centre.

21. We place the fried *sippets of bread* round the edge of the dish.

Now it is finished.

AUSTRALIAN MEAT.

LESSON NO. 8.

RISSOLES.

Average cost of "Rissoles," made from Australian meat.

INGREDIENTS.

	d.
½ lb. of Australian meat	3½
½ lb. of flour	1¼
4 oz. of dripping	2
Salt and pepper } A few sprigs of dried herbs }	½
1 egg	1
2 oz. of vermicelli or some bread crumbs } Clarified dripping (for frying) }	½
	8¾

Time required, one hour.

Now we will show you how to make *Rissoles* of *Australian meat.*

1. We put *one pound of clarified dripping* into a saucepan and put it on the fire to heat.

N.B.—We must watch it and be careful it does not burn.

2. We put *half a pound of flour* into a basin with *salt* (to cover thinly a *threepenny piece*), and *four ounces of clarified dripping.*

3. We rub the *dripping* well into the *flour* with our hands, until it is quite a *powder.*

4. We then add a little cold water and mix it into a stiff paste.

5. We *flour* a board and turn the *paste* out on to it.

6. We take a tin of *Australian meat*, open it carefully, and with a spoon remove all the *fat* off the part of the meat required for immediate use.

N.B.—The *fat* should be *clarified* by putting it into boiling water; and when cold can then be used for dripping.

7. We take *half a pound of meat* out of the tin and scrape off as much of the *jelly* as possible.

8. We put the *meat* on a board and chop it up as finely as possible.

> N.B.—*Minced meat* might be used, which would not of course require chopping up.

9. We take a small bunch of *dried herbs* and rub the *leaves* into a powder.

> N.B.—The *stalks* of the *herbs* need not be thrown away, as they can be used in soups for flavouring.

10. We sprinkle the *herbs* over the *meat*, also a little *pepper* and *salt*, and a little *flour*.

11. We take a rolling pin and roll out the *paste* as thin as possible.

12. We cut the paste into *rounds* with a *cutter* (which should be dipped in *flour*); the *rounds* should be rather larger than the top of a tea-cup.

13. We put some *meat* into the *centre* of each *round* of *paste*.

14. We break an *egg* on to a plate and beat it up slightly with a knife.

15. We take a *paste-brush*, dip it in the *egg*, and just wet the edges of the paste with the *egg*.

16. We fold the paste carefully over the *meat*, pressing the edges together with our thumbs.

17. We take *two ounces of vermicelli* and rub it between our hands, crushing it up as finely as possible.

18. We put this crushed *vermicelli* on to a piece of paper.

19. We put the *rissoles* into the plate of *egg*, and *egg* them well all over with the brush.

20. We then turn them into the crushed *vermicelli*, and cover them well with it but not too thickly.

> N.B.—We must be careful to finger them as little as possible, so as not to rub off any of the *egg* or *vermicelli*, or the *rissoles* will burst while frying.
>
> N.B.—Bread crumbs might be used instead of vermicelli.

21. We take a frying basket and put in the *rissoles*; we must be careful that they do not touch each other.

22. When the *fat* in the saucepan is quite hot and

smoking, we put in the frying-basket and let the *rissoles* fry for a *minute or two* until they have become a pale brown.

23. We take a piece of kitchen paper and put it on a plate.

24. As the *rissoles* are fried we turn them from the frying-basket on to the piece of paper to drain off the grease.

25. We then put them on a hot dish and they are ready for serving.

Now it is finished.

AUSTRALIAN MEAT.

Lesson No. 9.

SAVOURY HASH.

Average cost of a "*Savoury Hash*" made from *Australian Mutton*.

INGREDIENTS.

	s.	d.
1½ lb. of Australian mutton	0	10½
1 oz. of butter	0	1
½ oz. of flour		
½ an onion		
½d. of mixed pickles, or 1 teaspoonful of vinegar	0	1
1 dessertspoonful of chopped herbs		
Pepper and salt	0	0½
1 dessertspoonful of mushroom ketchup	0	0½
	1	1½

Time required, about ten minutes.

Now we will show you how to make a *Savoury Hash*.

1. We put *one ounce of butter* into a saucepan and put it on the fire to melt.

2. We take *half an onion*, peel it, and cut it in slices.

3. We put the *onion* into the *butter*.

4. We also stir in *half an ounce of flour*, and let all fry for a *minute or two* to brown.

5. We take a tin of *Australian mutton*, open it carefully, and remove the *fat* from the part of the *meat* required for immediate use.

N.B.—We should clarify the fat by putting it into boiling water, and when it is cold it can be used as dripping.

6. We take *one and a half pound of the mutton* out of the tin.

7. If all the *meat* is required for present use, we should turn it all out of the tin, and we should then rinse out the tin with *half a pint of warm water* to make the *gravy* for the *hash*.

N.B.—If all the meat has not been taken out of the tin, we should take some of the jelly out of the tin, and melt it in half a pint of warm water to make the gravy.

8. We pour this *gravy* into the saucepan with the *flour* and *butter*, and stir well until it boils and thickens.

9. We now move the saucepan to the side of the fire to keep warm.

10. We take a *halfpenny worth of mixed pickles*, and chop them up finely.

11. We stir the *chopped pickles* or a *teaspoonful of vinegar* into the *sauce*.

> N.B.—If the flavour of the pickles or the vinegar is disliked, they might be omitted.

12. We take *a sprig or two of parsley* (wash it and dry it in a cloth), and *a sprig of marjoram* and *thyme*, take away the stalks, and chop up the leaves finely on a board. (There should be about a dessertspoonful.)

13. We cut the *meat* up into neat pieces, and sprinkle over each piece some of the *chopped herbs* and a little *pepper and salt*.

14. We put the *meat* into the saucepan of *sauce* and let it just warm through for about *five minutes*.

15. We now pour into the *sauce* a *dessertspoonful of mushroom ketchup*.

16. For serving we put the *meat* on a hot dish and strain the *sauce* over it.

Now it is finished.

AUSTRALIAN MEAT.

Lesson No. 10.

MINCE.

Average cost of "*Mince*" served with "*Mashed Potatoes.*"

INGREDIENTS.

	d.
1 lb. of Australian mince meat	6
1½ lb. of potatoes	1½
1 oz. of butter	1
1 gill of milk	½
1 tablespoonful of mushroom ketchup } Salt and pepper }	1
	10

Time required, about forty minutes.

Now we will show you how to make a *Mince* served with *Mashed Potatoes.*

1. We take *one and a half pound of potatoes*, wash them well in cold water, and scrub them clean with a scrubbing brush.

2. We take a sharp knife, peel them, and carefully cut out the *eyes* and any *black specks* about the *potato*.

3. We put them into a saucepan with cold water, enough to cover them, and sprinkle over them *one teaspoonful of salt*.

4. We put the saucepan on the fire to boil the *potatoes* for from *twenty minutes to half an hour*.

5. We should take a fork and put it into the *potatoes* to feel if the centre is quite tender.

6. When they are sufficiently boiled, we drain off all the water, and stand the saucepan by the side of the fire, with the lid half on, to steam the *potatoes*.

7. We put *one ounce of butter* and *one gill* (quarter of a pint) *of milk* into a small saucepan, and put it on the fire to boil.

8. When the *potatoes* have become quite dry, we should take the saucepan off the fire and stand it on a piece of paper on the table.

9. We should mash them up smoothly with a spoon or fork.

> N.B.—The best way to mash potatoes is to rub them through a wire sieve; we can then be sure there are no lumps left.

10. When the *milk* boils we should pour it into the *mashed potatoes*, and stir it till it is quite smooth.

11. We add *pepper and salt* according to taste.

12. We stand the saucepan of *mashed potatoes* by the side of the fire to keep warm until required for use.

13. We take a tin of *Australian mince meat*, open it carefully, and remove all the *fat* from the part of the *meat* required for immediate use.

> N.B.—This fat should be clarified by putting it into boiling water, and when cold it can be used as dripping.

14. We take *one pound of the mince* out of the tin, put it in a saucepan with *one tablespoonful of mushroom ketchup,* and stir it into a paste.

15. We put the saucepan on the fire and let the *mince* just warm through.

> N.B.—We should be very careful that it does not boil, or the meat will get hardened.

16. For serving we make a wall of the *mashed potatoes* round the edge of a hot dish, and we pour the *mince* in the centre; we should stand the dish in front of the fire to colour the *potato* a pale brown.

Now it is finished.

ENTRÉES.

Lesson No. 1.

CURRY.

Average cost of a "*Curry (Indian) of Rabbit,*" &c.

INGREDIENTS.

	s.	d.
1 rabbit or chicken, etc.	2	6
Half an ounce of coriander seed		
2 cloves of garlic		
1 dessertspoonful of turmerick		
8 berries of red pepper	0	6
2 inches of the stick of cinnamon		
6 cardamomums		
A small piece of green ginger, about the size of a nut		
5 small onions	0	2
Salt		
3 ounces of fresh butter	0	3¾
Half a pint of cream or good milk	1	0
The juice of half a lemon	0	1
	4	6¾

Time required, about two hours.

Now we will show you how to make a *Curry*.

1. We take a *rabbit* [which has been skinned and properly prepared for cooking] and put it on a board.

2. We cut it up in the same way as for carving, thus :— taking care that the pieces are nearly all of one size.

> N.B.—*Chicken, veal,* and *other meats* would serve the purpose for curry as well as rabbit.

3. We take *a quarter of an ounce of coriander seed*, put it into the mortar and pound it very finely with a pestle.

4. We take the pounded seed out of the mortar and put it on a piece of paper; we must scrape out the mortar cleanly so that none be lost.

5. We take *two cloves of garlic*, peel them with a sharp knife and place them in the mortar.

6. We also put into the mortar *a dessertspoonful of turmerick*.

7. We add *eight berries of red pepper* and *one inch* of the *stick of cinnamon*.

8. We put in *four cardamomums*.

9. We take a piece of *green ginger* about the size of a nut and slice it very thinly.

10. We take *three small onions* and peel off the two outer skins.

11. We divide the onions into quarters and place them and the sliced ginger in the mortar.

12. We must now pound up all these spices and the onions as finely as possible with the pestle.

13. We now add to them the pounded *coriander seed* and mix them all up together.

14. We turn all this pounded mixture out of the mortar into a half-pint basin.

15. We take a *teacupful of cold water* and rinse out the mortar, and then pour the water on to the pounded mixture in the basin.

16. We take the pieces of *rabbit* and wash them in cold water.

17. We take the pieces of *rabbit* out of the cold water and place them on a sieve to drain.

18. We take a stew-pan and put in it *three ounces of fresh butter*.

19. We put the stew-pan on the fire to melt the butter.

N.B.—We must be careful that it does not burn.

20. We take *two small onions* and peel off the two outer skins.

21. We divide the *onions* in half down the centre, and cut them up so that the slices are in half circles.

22. We put these sliced onions into the melted butter, we add also *two cardamomums* and let them fry a pale brown.

23. We then take the onions carefully out of the stew-pan with a slice, and place them on a piece of whitey-brown paper to drain off the grease.

Cooking Meat.—(Entrées).—Indian Curry. 63

24. We now take the basin of spices, and add as much cold water as will make the basin three parts full.

25. We add to the basin of spices a small *dessertspoonful of salt*.

26. We now pour all the contents of the basin into the melted butter in the stew-pan, to cook for about *twenty minutes*, stirring well all the time with a wooden spoon.

> N.B.—To test when the spices are sufficiently cooked, you should smell them, and if they are quite done, no particular spice should predominate.

27. We now place the pieces of *rabbit* in the stew-pan to brown.

28. We must turn the pieces of *rabbit* occasionally so that they get brown on all sides.

29. We now pour into the stew-pan a *teacupful of cold water* to make the meat tender.

30. We put the lid on the stew-pan, and let it all cook steadily for about an hour.

31. We must watch it carefully, and stir it perpetually.

> N.B.—A good deal of stirring is required.

32. We must add by degrees a teacupful of cold water, to wash down the bits of spice which will stick to the sides of the stew-pan.

33. We must also add by degrees, *half a pint of cream*, or good *milk* [*water* might even be used instead] and mix it well together with a wooden spoon.

> N.B.—We must be careful that no pieces of meat or spices stick to the bottom of the pan.

34. We now take half the *fried onions*, chop them up finely, and add them to the *curry*.

35. We then put into the mortar *five coriander seeds*, and *one inch of the stick of cinnamon*, and pound them well together with a pestle.

36. When the *rabbit* is quite done, we take the pieces out with a fork, arrange them nicely on a hot dish, and pour the gravy round.

37. We then sprinkle over the *rabbit* the remainder of

the *fried onions*, and the pounded *cinnamon* and *coriander seed*.

38. We take a *fresh lemon*, cut it in half, and squeeze all the juice of it through a strainer over the *rabbit*.

N.B.—*Boiled Patna rice* should be served with the above *curry*.

Now it is finished.

ENTRÉES.

Lesson No. 2.

QUENELLES OF VEAL.

Average cost of "*Quenelles of Veal (about* 12) *and the Sauce.*"

INGREDIENTS.

	s.	d.
1 lb. of the fillet of veal	1	3
2 oz. of butter	0	2
2¾ oz. of flour	0	0¾
¾ pint of 2nd white stock	0	3
2 eggs	0	2
1 dozen button mushrooms	0	6
1 gill of cream	0	6
1 teaspoonful of lemon juice	0	0½
Salt		
	2	11¼

Time required, about three-quarters of an hour.

Now we will show you how to make *Quenelles of Veal.*

1. We put *one ounce of butter* and *two ounces of flour* into a stew-pan and mix them well together with a wooden spoon.

2. We add *one gill* (quarter of a pint) *of second white stock.*

3. We put the stewpan on the fire and stir well until it boils and thickens, and leaves the sides of the stewpan.

4. We now pour this mixture or *panada* (as it is called) on to a plate.

5. We stand the plate aside to cool.

6. We take one pound of the *fillet of veal* and put it on a board.

7. We take a sharp knife, cut away all the skin and fat, and cut up the *meat* into small pieces.

8. We put these pieces of *veal* into a mortar, and pound them well with the pestle.

9. We place a wire sieve over the plate; we take this

pounded *meat* and pass it through the sieve, rubbing it with a wooden spoon.

10. When the *panada* on the plate is cold, we put half of it and *one egg* in the mortar and pound it to a *cream*.

11. We then add half the *meat*, and *salt* and *pepper* to taste, and pound all well together with the pestle.

12. We put into the mortar the remainder of the *panada*, and break in another *egg* and add the rest of the *meat*.

13. We pound these well together again with the pestle.

14. We turn the mixture from the mortar into a basin.

15. We take a sauté-pan and *butter* it inside.

16. We take a dessertspoon and fill it with the mixture, shaping it to the form of an oval with a knife, which we must dip occasionally into *hot water* to prevent the mixture from sticking.

17. We take another dessertspoon and dip it into *boiling water*.

18. We scoop the *quenelle* from the first spoon into the second spoon, and put it into the sauté-pan, and continue doing this till we have used up all the mixture.

19. We must now make the *sauce* to be served with the quenelles.

20. We take a stewpan, and put in *half an ounce of butter* and *three quarters of an ounce of flour*.

21. We put the stewpan on the fire, and mix them together with a wooden spoon.

22. We take *one dozen of button mushrooms*, cut off the end of the stalks and wash them well in cold water.

23. We take them out of the water, put them upon a board, and peel them carefully with a sharp knife.

24. We pour in *half a pint of second white stock* to the mixture in the stewpan, and add the *mushroom peelings* for flavouring.

25. We must stir well until it boils and thickens.

26. We stand the stewpan by the side of the fire with the lid half on, and let it boil for *a quarter of an hour*.

Cooking Meat.—(*Entrées.*) *Quenelles of Veal.* 67

27. We then take a spoon, and skim off all the *butter* from the top of the *sauce*.

28. We now stir into the *sauce one gill of cream*, and stand the stewpan aside to keep warm, until required for use.

29. We take the *peeled mushrooms* and put them in a stewpan with a piece of butter the size of a nut.

30. We squeeze over them *a teaspoonful of lemon juice* and pour in *one tablespoonful of cold water*.

31. We put the stewpan on the fire and just bring them to the boil.

32. We now pour *boiling water* carefully into the sauté-pan, enough to cover the *quenelles*.

N.B.—We must be careful to pour the water very gently into the sauté-pan or the quenelles will be spoiled.

33. We put the sauté-pan on the fire to poach the *quenelles* for *ten minutes*.

N.B.—We must watch them and occasionally turn them carefully with a spoon.

34. When the *quenelles* are done, we lift them carefully out of the water, and lay them on a cloth to drain off the water.

35. For serving we must arrange them tastily in a circle on a hot dish.

36. We fill in the centre of the dish with the *boiled mushrooms*.

N.B.—Peas (see "Vegetables," Lesson No. 9) or spinach (see "Vegetables," Lesson No. 8) may be served with them instead, according to taste.

37. We take the stewpan off the fire, and pour the *sauce* through a strainer over the *quenelles*.

Now it is finished.

ENTRÉES.

LESSON No. 3.

BRAISED FILLETS OF BEEF.

Average cost of "*Braised Fillets of Beef.*"

INGREDIENTS.

	s.	d.
1 lb. of fillet of beef	1	4
A piece of the fat of bacon	0	3
A bouquet garni of parsley, thyme, and bay leaf	0	0½
2 young carrots	0	1
1 onion, and ¼ of a stick of celery	0	1
A pint of good stock	0	7½
	2	4½

Time required (the stock should be made the day before), about one hour and a half.

Now we will show you how to lard and braise *Fillets of Beef*.

1. We take *one pound of fillet of beef* (cut from the under-cut of the sirloin), and put it on a board.

2. We take a sharp knife, and cut the *beef* into small round *fillets*, to about the size of the top of a breakfast cup, and about three quarters of an inch in thickness, and trim them neatly.

3. We take a strip of the *fat of bacon* (nearest the rind is best, as it is harder), about *one inch* wide.

4. We take a sharp knife and cut up this piece of *bacon* into little strips, *an inch* long, and the *one-eighth of an inch* in width and thickness.

5. We take each *fillet* and hold it in a clean cloth.

6. We take a larding needle with a little strip of *bacon* in it, and lard each *fillet* neatly in regular rows; until one side of the *fillet* is entirely covered with strips of *bacon*.

7. When we have larded all the *fillets*, we lay them carefully in a clean sauté-pan.

8. We add a *bouquet garni*, consisting of a sprig of *parsley, thyme*, and a *bay leaf*, all tied neatly and tightly together.

Cooking Meat.—(Entrées.) Braised Fillets of Beef.

9. We take *two young carrots*, scrape them clean with a knife, and cut them in halves.

10. We take an *onion* and peel it carefully.

11. We add these *vegetables* and a *quarter of a stick of celery* to the *fillets* in the sauté-pan.

12. We now pour in a *pint* of good *stock*, put the sauté-pan on the fire, and baste the *fillets* continually.

N.B.—The stock must not cover the meat.

13. We take a piece of kitchen paper, and cut a round to the size of the sauté-pan and butter it.

14. As soon as the *stock* boils, we lay this round of paper on the *fillets* in the sauté-pan.

N.B.—This paper is to prevent the meat browning too quickly.

15. We must lift the paper every now and then, when we require to baste the *fillets*.

16. We should put the sauté-pan into a very hot oven, to brown the *fillets*.

17. We let the *pint of stock* reduce to a half glaze, which will take about *half an hour*.

18. We must watch it, frequently raise the paper, and baste the *fillets* with the *stock*.

N.B.—If the fillets are not brown enough, we take a salamander and heat it in the fire.

19. We hold the salamander over the *fillets*, to brown them a nice colour.

20. For serving, we take the *fillets* carefully out of the sauté-pan, and arrange them on a hot dish in a circle, on a border of *mashed potatoes*. (See "Vegetables," Lesson No. 2.)

N.B.—We must stand this dish on the hot plate, or near the fire to keep warm until the sauce is ready.

21. We put the sauté-pan on the fire, and let the sauce reduce to a half glaze.

22. We then strain the glaze round the meat.

N.B.—The centre of the dish may be filled in with mixed vegetables, *i.e.*, peas and beans, which should be cut in the shape of dice, carrots and turnips cut with a cutter, to the size of the peas.

Now it is finished.

ENTRÉES.

Lesson No. 4.

MUTTON CUTLETS.

Average cost of "*Mutton Cutlets.*"

INGREDIENTS.

	s.	d.
3 lbs. of the best end of the neck of mutton..	3	0
Bread crumbs	0	1
1 egg	0	1
Salt and pepper	0	0½
3 ounces of clarified butter.............	0	3
	3	5½

Time required, about three-quarters of an hour.

Now we will show you how to fry *Mutton Cutlets.*

1. We take *three pounds* of the best end of the *neck of mutton* and put it on a board.

2. We take a saw and saw off the end of the *rib bone*, leaving the *cutlet bone three inches* in length.

3. We saw off the *chine bone*, which lies at the back of the *cutlets.*

4. We joint each *cutlet* with the chopper.

5. We take a sharp knife and cut off each *cutlet* close to the bone.

6. We take a cutlet-bat, wet it, and beat each *cutlet* to about *half an inch* in thickness.

7. We trim the *cutlet* round, leaving about *half an inch* of the *rib bone* bare.

8. We form the *cutlets* to a good shape.

> N.B.—The trimmings of the cutlets should be put aside, as the fat may be clarified and used as dripping.

9. We take a wire sieve and stand it over a piece of paper.

10. We take some *crumb of bread* and rub it through the sieve.

Cooking Meat.—(*Entrées.*) Mutton Cutlets.

11. We take *one egg* and beat it on a plate with a knife.

12. We season the *cutlets* on both sides with *pepper and salt*.

13. We lay them in the *egg*, and egg them well all over with a brush.

14. We then put them in the *bread crumbs* and cover them well.

N.B.—We should be careful to finger them as little as possible, and lift them by the bare bone.

15. We take a sauté-pan, and pour in it *one ounce of melted clarified butter* or *lard* or *clarified dripping* (see Lesson "Frying.")

16. We now lay in the *cutlets* with the bones to the centre of the sauté-pan.

17. We pour over them *two more ounces of melted clarified butter* or *fat*.

18. We must now put the sauté-pan on a very quick fire for about *seven minutes*.

19. We must watch and turn the *cutlets* when they have become a light brown, so as to fry them the same colour on both sides.

20. We place a piece of whitey-brown paper on a plate.

21. When the *cutlets* are done we take them carefully out with a fork, and lay them on the paper on the plate to drain off the grease.

N.B.—We should be careful not to stick the fork into the meat (or the gravy will run out), but into the fat.

22. For serving, we arrange them nicely in a dish, in a circle, one leaning over the other; the centre may be filled with any *vegetable* according to taste.

Now it is finished.

ENTRÉES.

Lesson No. 5.

CHAUD FROID OF CHICKEN.

Average cost of "*Chaud Froid of Chicken.*"

INGREDIENTS.

	s.	d.
1 chicken	3	6
½ a pint of white sauce	1	0½
1 gill of cream	0	6
2 tablespoonsful of aspic jelly } Chopped pieces of aspic jelly }	1	0
Mixed vegetables	0	9
1 gill of mayonnaise sauce	0	5
	7	2½

Time required, about one hour and three-quarters.

Now we will show you how to make *Chaud froid of Chicken*.

1. We put *half a pint of white sauce* (see "Sauces," Lesson No. 1), in a stewpan.

2. We put the stewpan on the fire to boil, and stir well with a wooden spoon till the sauce is reduced to *one gill* (or *quarter of a pint.*)

3. We then add *one gill* (or *quarter of a pint*) of *cream*, and stir again until it just boils.

4. We take a tammy sieve and stand it over a basin.

5. We take the stewpan off the fire and pass the contents through the sieve into the basin.

6. When it is all passed through into the basin, we stir in *two tablespoonsful of aspic jelly* (see "Jelly," Lesson No. 2.)

    N.B.—This aspic jelly should be made with chicken as well as veal.

7. We take a *cold roast chicken* (see "Trussing a Fowl for Roasting"), and put it on a board.

    N.B.—The chicken must be young, as the flesh should be as white as possible.

8. We cut it up in the same way as for carving, taking

care that the pieces are all of one size. We must remove the *skin* and neatly trim each piece.

9. We take these pieces of *chicken* and dip them in the *sauce*, covering them well over.

10. We stand a drainer over a dish.

11. We place the pieces of *chicken* on the drainer, and let them remain until the *sauce* is set over each piece.

12. For serving we arrange the pieces of *chicken* on chopped *aspic jelly* (see "Jelly," Lesson No. 2,) in a circle on a dish.

13. The centre should be filled in with mixed *vegetables*, *i.e.*, cooked *potato*, *carrot*, and *beet-root*, stamped out with a vegetable cutter, cooked *French beans*, cut to the shape of dice, and *green peas*, all mixed together, with *two tablespoonsful of mayonnaise sauce*. (See "Sauces," Lesson No. 3.)

Now it is finished.

ENTRÉES.

LESSON No. 6.

VEAL CUTLETS.

Average cost of "*Grilled Veal Cutlets.*"

INGREDIENTS.

	s.	d.
3 lbs. of the best end of the neck of veal....	3	0
Savory thyme		
The rind of half a lemon	0	1
1 bunch of parsley		
1 ounce of butter	0	1½
1 teaspoonful of lemon juice	0	0¼
1 egg	0	1
Pepper and salt	0	1
Bread crumbs		
	3	4¼
½ lb. of bacon for rolls	0	6
	3	10¼

Time required, about half an hour.

Now we will show you how to grill *Veal Cutlets*.

1. We take *three pounds* of the best end of the *neck of veal*, or *veal cutlet*, and put it on a board.

2. We take a saw and saw off the end of the *rib bone*, leaving the *cutlet bone three inches* in length.

3. We saw off the *chine bone*, which lies at the back of the cutlets.

4. We joint each *cutlet* with the chopper.

5. We take a sharp knife and cut off each *cutlet* close to the bone, so as to get an extra *cutlet* between each bone.

6. We take a cutlet bat and beat each *cutlet* to about *half an inch* in thickness.

7. We trim the *cutlet* round, leaving about *half an inch* of the rib bone bare.

8. We form the *cutlets* to a good shape.

N.B.—The trimmings of the cutlets should be put aside, as the fat may be clarified, and used for dripping.

Cooking Meat.—(Entrées.) Veal Cutlets.

9. We take a little *savoury thyme*, put it on a board, and chop it up very finely (the thyme, when chopped, should fill a saltspoon.)

10. We take *half a lemon* and peel it very thinly.

11. We chop this *lemon rind* up very finely.

12. We take a small bunch of *parsley*, wash it in cold water, and dry it in a cloth.

13. We chop this *parsley* up very finely, on a board.

14. We put *one ounce of butter* on a kitchen plate, and put it in the oven to melt.

15. When the butter is melted, we add a *tablespoonful of lemon juice* and the *chopped thyme, lemon rind,* and *parsley.*

16. We add *one egg* and *pepper* and *salt* to taste, and beat all up together with a knife.

17. We take a wire sieve and stand it over a piece of paper.

18. We take some *crumb of bread* and rub it through the sieve.

19. We dip each *cutlet* into the plate, and cover them all over with the mixture.

20. We then put them in the *bread crumbs* and cover them well.

N.B.—We should finger them as little as possible.

21. We take a gridiron and hold it to the fire to warm.

22. We arrange the *cutlets* on the gridiron.

23. We place the gridiron in front of a bright fire, but not too near, or the *bread crumbs* will burn before the *cutlets* are sufficiently cooked.

24. We should then let them grill for about *ten minutes,* and when they have become a pale brown on one side, we should turn the gridiron so as to brown them on both sides alike.

25. For serving, we arrange the *cutlets* on a wall of *mashed potatoes,* (see "Vegetables," Lesson No. 2) in a circle on a hot dish, one leaning over the other; the centre may be filled in with *rolls of bacon*, (see below) and with a *thick brown sauce* (see "Sauces," Lesson No. 2).

Now it is finished.

For *Rolls of Bacon*.

1. We cut some *thin slices of bacon*, about *two inches* wide, and about *four inches* in length.

2. We roll up these *strips of bacon*.

3. We take a skewer and run it through the centre of each *roll of bacon*.

4. We place this skewer, with the *bacon*, on a tin and put it in the oven for *six minutes*.

5. For serving, we take the *rolls of bacon* off the skewer, and arrange them in the centre of the *cutlets*, as described above.

Now it is finished.

ENTRÉES.

Lesson No. 7.

FRICASSEE OF CHICKEN.

Average cost of a "*Fricassee of Chicken.*" Average cost of a "*Fricassee of Cold Chicken.*"

INGREDIENTS.	s.	d.	INGREDIENTS.	s.	d.
1 young chicken	3	6	Some cold chicken, ½ one	1	9
1 small carrot			½ a carrot		
½ an onion			¼ of an onion		
1 stick of celery			½ a stick of celery	0	1
2 or 3 sprigs of parsley			A bouquet garni, of parsley, thyme, and bay-leaf		
1 sprig of thyme	0	1½			
1 bay leaf			1 gill of cream	0	6
2 cloves			1 clove		
6 peppercorns			3 peppercorns	0	0¼
1 blade of mace			½ a blade of mace		
1½ pint of second white stock	0	5¾	1 pint of good white stock	0	7¼
1 oz. of butter	0	0¼	½ an oz. of butter	0	0¾
1½ oz. of flour	0	0¼	1 oz. of flour		
2 dozen of button mushrooms Fried bread	1	0	1 dozen button mushrooms	0	6
1 gill of cream	0	6	Fried bread Salt	0	0¼
	5	8¾		3	6½

Time required, about one hour and a half.   Time required, about forty minutes.

Now we will show you how to make a *Fricassee of Chicken.*

1. We take a young *chicken*, clean it, draw it (see "Trussing a Fowl for Roasting," from Note 1 to Note 12), and skin it.

2. We cut the *chicken* into joints, and put them in a basin of cold water for about *ten minutes.*

3. After that time we take the pieces of *chicken* out of the water and dry them in a clean cloth.

4. We take *one small carrot*, wash and scrape it clean, and cut it into slices.

5. We take *half an onion* and peel it.

6. We take *one stick of celery* and *two or three sprigs of parsley*, and wash them in cold water.

7. We put these vegetables into a stewpan.

8. We add to them *one sprig of thyme, one bay leaf, two cloves, six peppercorns,* and *one blade of mace.*

9. We now put in the pieces of *chicken*, and add *one and a half pint of second white stock.*

10. We put the stewpan on the fire to boil gently for about *half an hour.*

11. When the pieces of *chicken* are quite done, we take them out of the stewpan, wash them in a basin of cold water, and dry them in a cloth.

12. We strain the *stock* from the stewpan into the basin.

13. We take *two dozen of button mushrooms*, cut off the ends of the stalks, wash them in cold water, and peel them.

14. We take the *peeled mushrooms*, and put them into the stewpan with a *piece of butter the size of a nut.*

15. We squeeze over them a *teaspoonful of lemon juice,* and pour in a *tablespoonful of cold water.*

16. We put the stewpan on the fire and just bring them to the boil.

17. We then take the stewpan off the fire and turn them on to a plate.

18. We wash out the stewpan, and then put in it *one ounce of butter.*

19. We put the stewpan on the fire to melt the *butter.*

20. We then add *one and a half ounce of flour* to the *butter,* stirring it well with a wooden spoon.

21. We now remove all the *grease* from the *chicken stock*, and add it and the trimmings of the *mushrooms* to the stewpan, and stir well until it boils.

22. We must now move the stewpan to the side of the fire, and let it boil gently for *twenty minutes.* The cover of the stewpan should be half on.

23. After that time we take a spoon and carefully skim off all the *butter* that will have risen to the top of the *sauce.*

24. We now put the stewpan over the fire to boil, and

Cooking Meat.—(*Entrées.*) *Fricassee of Chicken.* 79

let the *sauce* reduce to about *one pint*, and then add *one gill of cream*.

25. We take the pieces of *chicken* and put them in another stewpan, with the *two dozen of button mushrooms*.

26. When the *sauce* is sufficiently reduced, we strain it over the *chicken*.

27. We then stand the stewpan in a saucepan of hot water over the fire until the *chicken* is quite hot.

28. For serving, we arrange the *fricassee of chicken* on a hot dish, with *fried bread* (as described in "Vegetables," Lesson No. 8, Note 13 to Note 17).

Now it is finished.

Now we will show you how to make a *Fricassee of Cold Chicken*.

1. We take some *cold roast* or *boiled chicken*.

2. We cut away all the *meat* from the *bone*, and cut it up into neat pieces.

3. We put *one pint* of good *white stock* (see "Lesson on Stock"), and the *chicken bones* into a stewpan.

4. We take *half a carrot*, wash and scrape it clean, and cut it into slices.

5. We take a *quarter of an onion* and peel it.

6. We take *half a stick of celery* and wash it in cold water.

7. We put these vegetables into the stewpan.

8. We add to them a *bouquet garni* (consisting of a *sprig of parsley*, *one sprig of thyme*, and *one bay leaf* tied tightly together), *one clove*, *three peppercorns*, and *half a blade of mace*.

9. We put the stewpan on the fire and let it boil for *twenty minutes*.

10. After that time we strain the *stock* into a basin.

11. We take *one dozen of button mushrooms*, cut off the end of the stalks, wash them in cold water, and peel them.

12. We take the *peeled mushrooms* and put them in a stewpan with a piece of *butter* the size of a nut.

13. We squeeze over them a *teaspoonful of lemon juice*, and pour in a *tablespoonful of cold water*.

14. We put the stewpan on the fire and just bring them to the boil.

15. We then take the stewpan off the fire and turn them on to a plate.

16. We put *half an ounce of butter* into a stewpan.

17. We put the stewpan on the fire. When the *butter* is melted we put in *one ounce of flour*, stirring it well with a wooden spoon.

18. We now add the *chicken stock*, and the *mushroom peelings*, and stir the *sauce* well until it boils.

19. We let it boil for *ten minutes* to cook the *flour*.

20. After that time we add *one gill of cream*, and *salt* to taste.

21. We put the pieces of *chicken* and the *button mushrooms* into another stewpan.

22. We strain the *sauce* over the *chicken*, and then stand the stewpan, in a saucepan of hot water, over the fire until the *chicken* is quite hot.

23. For serving, we arrange the *fricassee of chicken* on a hot dish, with some *fried bread* (as described in "Vegetables," Lesson No. 8, Note 13 to Note 17), put round the edge.

Now it is finished.

ENTRÉES.

LESSON No. 8.

BEEF OLIVES.

Average cost of "*Beef Olives.*"

INGREDIENTS.

	s.	d.
1½ lb. of beef or rump steak, or the fillet of beef	2	0
2 oz. of beef suet	0	1¼
3 oz. of bread crumbs	0	1
1 teaspoonful of chopped parsley	0	0½
¼ of a teaspoonful of chopped thyme and marjoram	0	0¼
A little grated lemon rind and nutmeg Salt and pepper	0	0¼
1 egg	0	1
1 pint of brown sauce or stock	1	0
	3	4¼

Time required, about one hour.

Now we will show you how to make *Beef Olives.*

1. We take *one and a half pound* of *beef* or *rump steak*, or the *fillet of beef*, and put it on a board.

2. We cut the *beef* in slices about *half an inch in thickness* and *four inches* in length, and beat them out with a wet cutlet bat.

  N.B.—We should be careful that all the slices are of the same size.

3. We take the *trimmings* that remain, chop them up very finely, and put them in a basin.

4. We take *two ounces of beef suet*, and put it on a board.

5. We take a knife and cut away all the skin, and chop the *suet* up very finely.

6. We stand a wire sieve over a piece of paper.

7. We take some *crumb of bread* and rub it through the sieve. (There should be *three ounces of bread crumbs.*)

8. We take a little *parsley* and chop it up finely. (There should be *one teaspoonful of chopped parsley.*)

9. We take a little *thyme* and *marjoram* and chop them up finely. (There should be about a *quarter of a teaspoonful of chopped thyme* and *marjoram.*)

10. We add all these things (*i.e.*, *suet, bread crumbs, parsley, thyme,* and *marjoram*) to the *chopped beef* in the basin.

11. We also grate about *half a teaspoonful of lemon rind,* and *nutmeg* (as much as would cover a *3d. piece*) into the basin.

12. We season it with *pepper* and *salt* according to taste, and add *one egg,* and mix all well together with a wooden spoon.

13. We take this mixture out of the basin, and form it into pieces the shape and size of a cork.

14. We roll up each *slice of beef,* placing a piece of *stuffing* in the centre.

15. We should tie each *roll* round with a piece of *twine* to fasten it securely together.

16. We place these *rolls* in a stewpan, with about *one pint of brown sauce* (see " Sauces," Lesson. No. 2), or *good stock* (see Lesson on " Stock.")

17. We put the stewpan on the fire and let them stew gently for *three quarters of an hour.*

18. For serving, we arrange the *beef olives* on a hot dish in a circle, pouring the *sauce* round the edge ; the centre may be filled in with *dressed spinach* (see " Vegetables," Lesson No. 8), or with *mashed potatoes* (see " Vegetables," Lesson No. 2.)

Now it is finished.

ENTRÉES.

LESSON No. 9.

IRISH STEW.

Average cost of an "*Irish Stew.*"

INGREDIENTS.

	s.	d.
3 lbs. of the best end of the neck of mutton or the scrag end	3	0
1 teaspoonful of salt 1 saltspoonful of pepper	0	0½
1 doz. of button onions or two moderate ones	0	1
6 large potatoes	0	2
	3	3½

Time required, about two hours.

Now we will show you how to make an *Irish Stew*.

1. We take the best end of the *neck of mutton* and cut and trim the *cutlets* in the same way as for "haricot mutton" (see "Entrées," Lesson No. 10, from Note 1 to Note 8).

2. We place the *cutlets* in a stewpan.

3. We sprinkle over them a *teaspoonful of salt* and a *saltspoonful of pepper*, and pour in *one and a half pint of cold water*.

4. We put the stewpan on the fire, and when it has come to the boil we should skim it.

5. We now draw the stewpan to the side of the fire, and let it simmer gently for *one hour*.

6. We must watch it and skim it occasionally and remove all *fat*.

7. We take *half a dozen of potatoes*, wash, scrub them, and peel them.

8. We cut these *potatoes* in halves.

9. We take *one dozen of button onions*, or two moderate-sized ones, and peel them carefully.

10. We add the *onions and potatoes* to the stew, and let it simmer for *one hour*.

11. After that time we should take a fork and feel if the *vegetables* are quite tender.

12. For serving we arrange the *cutlets* in a circle on a hot dish, and pour the *sauce* round, and the *vegetables* in the centre.

> N.B.—The scrag end of the neck of mutton might be used instead of the best end, but care should be taken in cleansing it before use.

Now it is finished.

ENTRÉES.

Lesson No. 10.

HARICOT MUTTON.

Average cost of "*Haricot Mutton.*"

INGREDIENTS.

	s.	d.
3 lbs. of the best end of the neck of mutton	3	0
1 onion	0	0½
Pepper and salt	0	0½
1 tablespoonful of flour		
1 pint of second stock	0	3¾
1 carrot	0	0¾
1 turnip	0	0½
1 dozen button onions	0	1
	3	6½

Time required, about one hour and a half.

Now we will show you how to make *Haricot Mutton.*

1. We take the best end of the *neck of mutton* and put it on a board.

2. We take a saw and saw off the end of the *rib bone,* leaving the *cutlet bone three inches in length.*

3. We saw off the *chine bone* which lies at the back of the *cutlets.*

4. We joint each *cutlet* with a chopper.

5. We take a sharp knife and cut off each *cutlet.*

6. We take a cutlet-bat and beat each *cutlet* to about rather more than *half an inch* in thickness.

7. We trim the *cutlet* round, leaving about *half an inch* of the rib bone bare.

8. We form the *cutlets* to a good shape.

N.B.—The trimmings of the cutlets should be put aside, as the fat may be clarified and used for dripping (see Lesson on "Frying").

9. We take *one onion,* peel it, and cut it in slices.

10. We put the *onion* and the *cutlets* in a stewpan, with *two ounces of butter.*

11. We put the stewpan on a quick fire to fry the *cutlets* a nice brown.

12. We must watch and turn the *cutlets* when they have become a light brown, so as to fry them the same colour on both sides :—We then remove the *cutlets* from the stewpan.

13. We should pour off the *grease* from the stewpan (and leave the *onion*), and then add *one tablespoonful of flour*, and pour in by degrees *one pint of second stock*, and stir well until it boils.

14. We strain this *sauce*, and return the *cutlets* with the *sauce* into the stewpan.

15. We take *one carrot*, wash it, and scrape it clean with a knife, and cut it in the shape of young carrots, or into fancy shapes with a cutter.

16. We take *two turnips*, peel them, and cut them in quarters.

17. We take *one dozen button onions* and peel them very carefully, so as not to break them in pieces.

18. We put the stewpan on the fire and let the *meat* stew gently for *half an hour*, then add the prepared *vegetables*, and let all simmer for *half an hour*.

19. After that time we should take a fork and feel if the *vegetables* are quite tender.

20. For serving we arrange the *cutlets* in a circle on a hot dish with the *vegetables* in the centre ; we remove all *grease* from the *sauce* and pour it round.

> N.B.—The scrag end of the neck of mutton might be used instead of the best end, but care should be taken in cleansing it before use.

Now it is finished.

ENTRÉES.

LESSON No. 11.

CROQUETTES OR RISSOLES OF CHICKEN.

Average cost of "*Croquettes or Rissoles of Chicken*" (about 15).

INGREDIENTS.

	s.	d.
½ a cold chicken	1	9
2 oz. of lean ham or bacon	0	6
6 mushrooms	0	3
1 oz. of flour }	0	2
1 oz. of butter }		
¼ a gill (1 gill is ¼ pint) of cream	0	3
1 gill of stock	0	2
Seasoning	0	0½
The juice of half a lemon	0	1
1 egg	0	1
¼ lb. of bread crumbs	0	2
	3	5½
If for rissoles with paste—		
4 oz. of flour and 3 oz. of butter	0	4½
	3	10

Time required, about one hour.

Now we will show you how to make *Croquettes or Rissoles of Chicken.*

1. We take the *half chicken* (either *roasted* or *boiled*), cut away all the *flesh* from the *bones*, and put it on a board.

2. We cut away the *skin*, and mince the *meat* up very finely.

3. We take the *mushrooms*, wash them, peel them, and mince them and the ham up finely on the board, mixing them with the *minced chicken.*

4. We put *one ounce of butter* in a stewpan, and put it on the fire.

5. When the *butter* is melted we stir in *one ounce of flour*, and mix it to a smooth *paste.*

6. We now add the *stock*, and stir again smoothly until it boils and thickens.

7. We move the stewpan to the side of the fire and stir in *half a gill of cream*.

8. We take *half a lemon* and squeeze the *juice* of it into the *sauce*.

  N.B.—We must be careful not to let any *pips* fall in.

9. We season the *sauce* with *pepper and salt* according to taste, and, if liked, we might grate about *half a saltspoonful of nutmeg* into it.

10. We now stir in the *minced chicken, ham, and mushrooms* until all are well mixed together.

11. We take a plate and turn the contents of the stewpan on to it.

12. We take a piece of *kitchen paper*, cut it to the size of the plate, *butter* it, and lay it on the top of the *mixture*, and stand the plate aside to cool.

13. When the *mixture is cold* we put *one pound and half of lard* or *clarified dripping* in a deep stewpan, and put it on the fire to heat.

14. We take some *crumb of bread* and rub it through a wire sieve on to a piece of paper.

15. If *rissoles* are required we put *four ounces of flour* on a board, and rub into it *three ounces of butter* until both are thoroughly mixed and there are no lumps remaining.

16. We mix the *flour and butter* into a stiff smooth *paste* with cold *water*.

17. We take a rolling-pin, *flour* it, sprinkle some *flour* over the board, and roll the *paste* out into as thin a sheet as possible.

18. We *flour* our hands, dip a knife in *flour* (to prevent any sticking), and form the *chicken mixture* into any fancy shapes for croquettes either in *balls* or long *rolls*, &c., or we can roll it in the *paste* for *rissoles*.

19. We break an *egg* on to a plate and beat it up slightly with a knife.

20. We dip the *croquettes* or *rissoles* into the *egg*, and *egg* them well all over with a paste brush.

21. We now roll them in the *bread crumbs*, covering them well all over.

N.B.—We must be careful to cover them smoothly and not too thickly.

22. We take a *frying basket* and arrange the *croquettes* or *rissoles* in it, but we must finger them as little as possible, and not allow them to touch each other.

23. When the *fat* on the fire is quite hot and smoking, we put in the *frying basket* for *two minutes* or so, to fry them a *pale yellow*.

24. We put a piece of *whity-brown paper* on a plate, and as the *rissoles* are fried we turn them on to the paper to drain off the *grease*.

25. For serving we arrange them tastily on a hot dish, with fried *parsley* in the centre.

N.B.—Cold veal or pheasant, &c., might be used for the rissoles and croquettes instead of chicken, if preferred.

Now it is finished.

ENTRÉES.

LESSON No. 12.

CURRIED RABBIT.

Average cost of "*Curried Rabbit or Veal.*"

INGREDIENTS.

	s.	d.
1 rabbit or 1½ lb. of veal cutlet	1	6
¼ lb. of butter	0	4
2 onions }	0	2
1 apple }		
2 tablespoonsful of curry powder	0	4
1 pint of good stock	0	8
1 gill (¼ pint) of cream	0	6
1 lemon }	0	2
½ a teaspoonful of salt }		
	3	8

Time required, about two hours and a half.

Now we will show you how to make a *Curry of rabbit or veal*.

1. We put a *quarter of a pound of butter* into a stewpan and put it on the fire to melt.

2. We take *two onions*, peel them, put them on a board, and chop them up as finely as possible.

3. We put the *chopped onions* into the *melted butter*, and let them fry a light brown.

N.B.—We must be careful that they do not burn.

4. We take a *rabbit* (which has been skinned and properly prepared for cooking), wash it well, and dry it in a cloth.

5. We put the *rabbit* on a board and cut it up in pieces of equal size.

6. If *veal* is used we should put it on a board and cut it into equal sized pieces.

N.B.—If preferred *chicken* can be used instead of *rabbit* or *veal*.

7. When the *onions* are fried we strain them from the *butter*.

8. We put the *butter* back into the stewpan.

9. We now put in the pieces of *meat*, put the stewpan over a quick fire, and let it fry for *ten minutes*.

10. We must watch it and turn the pieces of *meat* occasionally, so that they are fried on both sides alike.

11. We take an *apple*, peel it, cut out the core, and chop it up as finely as possible on a board.

12. When the *meat* is fried we add to it *two tablespoonsful of curry powder*, and *half a teaspoonful of salt*, and stir well over the fire for *five minutes*.

13. We then put in the *fried onions*, the *chopped apple*, and *one pint of good stock*.

14. We move the stewpan to the side of the fire and let it simmer gently for *two hours*.

15. After that time we stir in *one gill* (quarter of a pint) *of cream*.

16. We take a *lemon*, wipe it clean with a cloth, and peel it as thinly as possible with a sharp knife (the *peel* we should put aside as it is not required for present use).

17. We cut the *lemon* in half, and squeeze the *juice* of it through a strainer into the stewpan.

18. For serving we take the pieces of *meat* out of the stewpan and arrange them nicely on a hot dish, and pour the *sauce* over the *meat*.

N.B.—Boiled rice (see Lesson on "Rice") should be served with the *curry*.

Now it is finished.

RICE.

Average cost of "*Boiled Rice*," to be served with *Curry*, &c.

INGREDIENTS.

	d.
½ lb. of Patna rice	1½
¼ of a teaspoonful of salt	
	1½

Time required, about half an hour.

Now we will show you how to boil *Rice* to be served with curry, &c.

1. We take a large stewpan and pour in it *four quarts of water*.

2. We put the stewpan on the fire to boil the *water*.

3. We take *half a pound of Patna rice*, put it in a basin of cold water, and wash it well.

4. We drain off the water and rub the *rice* with our hands.

5. We must carefully pick out all the yellow grains and bits of black.

6. We must wash the *rice* in this manner four times.

7. Just before putting the *rice* on to boil we must pour some fresh cold water over it.

8. When the water in the stewpan is quite boiling, we throw the *rice* into it, stirring it round with a spoon.

9. We must add *one quarter of a teaspoonful of salt*, which will make the scum rise.

10. We must take a spoon and skim it occasionally.

11. The *rice* should boil fast from *fifteen to twenty minutes*.

N.B.—To test if the rice is sufficiently boiled, we should take out a grain or two, and press it between the thumb and finger, and if quite done, it will mash.

12. We now pour the *rice* out of the saucepan into a cullender to drain off the water.

Lessons on Cooking.—Boiled Rice.

13. We take the cullender which contains the *rice*, and hold it under the tap.

14. We turn the tap and let the cold water run on to the *rice* for *one or two seconds.* (This is to separate the grains of rice.)

15. We take a clean dry stewpan and put it at the side of the fire.

16. When the water is quite drained from the *rice*, we turn it from the cullender into the dry stewpan at the side of the fire.

17. We put the lid half on the stewpan.

18. We watch it, and stir it occasionally, to prevent the grains from sticking to the bottom of the stewpan.

19. When the *rice* is quite dry, we take it out carefully with a wooden spoon, and place it lightly on to a hot dish.

Now it is finished.

STEWS.

LESSON No. 1.

A-LA-MODE BEEF.

Average cost of "*A-la-Mode Beef.*"

INGREDIENTS.

	s.	d.
1 cow-heel	0	6
An ox-cheek	2	0
3 oz. of dripping	0	1½
3 carrots	0	1½
6 onions	0	2
1 bunch of herbs (marjoram, thyme, parsley, and bayleaf)	0	0½
2 tablespoonsful of flour	0	0½
Pepper and salt		
	3	0

Time required, three hours.

Now we will show you how to make *A-la-mode Beef.*

1. We take a *dressed cow-heel* and wash it thoroughly in water.

2. We put the *cow-heel* on a board, and cut off all the *flesh;* we cut the *flesh* into neat pieces.

3. We take an *ox-cheek* and wash it well in cold water.

N.B.—We must be sure it is quite clean and free from all impurities.

4. We put the *ox-cheek* on a board, and rub it well with *salt.*

5. We then rub it quite dry in a clean cloth.

6. We put *three ounces of clarified dripping* into a large saucepan, and put on the fire to melt.

7. We cut the *ox-cheek* up into neat pieces.

N.B.—We should weigh the flesh of the *ox-cheek and cow-heel*, so as to know how much *water* should be added, as 1 *pint* is allowed to each *lb. of meat.*

8. We *flour* each piece.

9. When the *dripping* is melted, we put in the floured pieces of *ox-cheek*, and let them fry a nice brown.

Lessons on Cooking Meat.—A-la-Mode Beef.

10. We must stir the *pieces* occasionally, and not let them stick to the bottom of the saucepan.

11. We take *three carrots*, wash them, scrape them clean, and cut them in slices with a sharp knife.

12. We take *six onions*, peel them, and cut them in slices.

13. We take a *sprig or two of parsley*, wash it, and dry it in a cloth.

14. We take *one sprig of marjoram, thyme, one bay-leaf*, and the *parsley*, and tie them tightly together with a piece of string.

15. We put these *vegetables* and the *bunch of herbs* into the saucepan.

16. We also pour in the proper quantity of *water*, namely, *one pint of water* to each *pound of meat*.

17. We put *two tablespoonsful of flour* into a basin, and mix it into a smooth *paste* with cold water.

18. We now put the pieces of *cow-heel* into the saucepan, and plenty of *pepper and salt* to taste.

19. We stir the *paste* smoothly into the saucepan.

20. We put the lid on the saucepan, and when it boils we should move the saucepan to the side of the fire, and let it stew gently for *three hours*.

21. We must watch it and skim it very often.

> N.B.—We must be always careful to skim anything that is cooking directly the *scum* rises, or it will boil down again into the *meat* and will spoil it—*scum* is the impurity which rises from the *meat* or *vegetables*.

22. When the *stew* is finished, we pour it into a large dish or a soup tureen; it is then ready for serving.

> N.B.—The *bones* of the *cowheel* should be put into the *stockpot*.

Now it is finished.

STEWS.

Lesson No. 2.

BRAZILIAN STEW.

Average cost of a "*Brazilian Stew.*"

INGREDIENTS.

	s.	d.
4 lbs. of shin or sticking of beef	2	0
2 carrots	0	1
2 turnips	0	1
4 onions	0	2
A bunch of herbs, *i.e.*, marjoram, thyme, and parsley } Pepper and salt }	0	0½
1 gill of vinegar	0	0½
	2	5

Time required, about three hours and ten minutes.

Now we will show you how to make a *Brazilian Stew*.

1. We take *four pounds of the shin or sticking of beef*, put it on a board, and cut all the *meat* off the bone.

2. We cut the *meat* up into neat pieces.

3. We put some *vinegar* into a basin; we dip each piece of *meat* into the *vinegar*.

> N.B.—Putting meat into vinegar will make in tender, therefore any tough pieces of meat may be used for this stew. The vinegar will not be tasted when the meat is cooked.

4. We take *two carrots*, wash them, scrape them clean, and cut them into slices with a sharp knife.

5. We take *two turnips* and *four onions*, peel them, and cut them up into slices.

6. We put the pieces of *meat* into a saucepan, arranging them closely together.

7. We should sprinkle some *pepper and salt* over the *meat*.

8. We now put in all the *vegetables*, and we also add a

Lessons on Cooking Meat.—Brazilian Stew.

small bunch of herbs, namely, a *sprig of marjoram, thyme,* and *parsley*, tied tightly together.

> N.B.—We put no *water* in this stew; the vinegar draws out the juices of the meat, and makes plenty of gravy.

9. We shut down the lid tight, put the saucepan by the side of the fire, and let it simmer gently for at least *three hours*.

10. For serving we turn the *stew* on to a hot dish, or in a soup tureen.

Now it is finished.

STEWS.

Lesson No. 3.

IRISH STEW.

Average cost of an "*Irish Stew.*"

INGREDIENTS.

	d.
2 lbs. of potatoes	2
1 lb. of the scrag end of mutton	8
1 lb. of onions	⎫
Pepper and salt	⎬ 1
	11

Time required, about three hours.

Now we will show you how to make an "*Irish Stew.*"

1. We take *two pounds of potatoes*, wash them well in cold water.

2. We take a sharp knife, peel them, carefully cut out the eyes or any black specks about the *potatoes*, and cut them in slices.

3. We take *one pound of onions*, peel them, and cut them in slices.

4. We take *one pound of the scrag end of the neck of mutton*, wash it in cold water, and scrape it clean with a knife.

5. We put the *meat* on a board, and cut it up in small pieces.

6. We take a large saucepan, put in a layer of *meat*, then a layer of *potatoes*, then a layer of *onions*.

7. We should sprinkle a little *pepper and salt* over each layer for seasoning.

8. We continue to fill the saucepan in this way till there is no *meat* or *vegetables* left.

9. We now pour in sufficient *cold water* to cover the bottom of the saucepan (about *half a pint*).

10. We put the saucepan on the fire, and when it has

come to the boil, we draw it to the side of the fire and let it stew gently for from *one hour and a half to two hours*.

11. We must watch it, and stir it occasionally to prevent its catching.

12. For serving we turn the stew out on a hot dish.

> N.B.—If a larger quantity of *potato* is required in the *stew*, the extra quantity of *potato* should be parboiled (see note below), and then cut in slices, and added to the *stew* ½ *an hour* before it is ready for serving. If all the *potatoes* were put in with the *meat* at first, so much water would be required that the stew would be spoiled.
>
> N.B.—For parboiling (or half boiling) *potatoes* we wash them, and peel them, put them in a saucepan with enough *cold water* to cover them, put the saucepan on the fire, and let the *potatoes* boil for about a ¼ *of an hour*.

Now it is finished.

STEWS.

Lesson No. 4.

STEWED BRISKET OF BEEF (cold).

Average cost of "*Stewed Brisket of Beef.*"

INGREDIENTS.

	s.	d.
7 lbs. of brisket of beef at 9*d.* per lb.	5	3
2 carrots	0	1
1 turnip	0	0½
2 onions	0	1
1 head of celery	0	2
1 leek	0	1
Bouquet garni (*i.e.*, sprig of thyme, marjoram, and bay leaf)		
6 cloves		
12 peppercorns	0	2
6 allspice		
1 tablespoonful of salt		
	5	10½

Time required, about four hours.

Now we will show you how to stew *Brisket of Beef*, to be served *cold*.

1. We take *seven pounds of brisket of beef* (not very fat), see that it is quite clean, and, if necessary, scrape it with a knife and wipe it with a clean cloth, and then put it into a large saucepan.

2. We take *two carrots*, wash and scrape them clean and cut them in halves.

3. We take *one turnip* and *two onions*, wash them and peel them, and cut the *turnip* in quarters.

4. We take *one leek* and *one head of celery*, wash them well in water, cut the long green leaves off the *leek*, and the green tops from the *celery*.

5. We add all these *vegetables* to the *meat* in the saucepan.

6. We also add a *bouquet garni*, of *thyme, marjoram*, and a *bay leaf* tied tightly together, *six cloves, twelve pepper-*

Lessons on Cooking Meat.—Stewed Brisket of Beef. 101

corns, six *allspice*, one *tablespoonful* of *salt*, and *three quarts* of *cold water*.

7. We put the saucepan on the fire, and when it comes to the boil we should skim it well.

8. We then move the saucepan to the side of the fire, and let the contents simmer gently for *three hours*, we must watch it and skim it occasionally.

9. After that time we take the *meat* out of the saucepan and put it on a dish.

10. We take a knife and carefully remove the flat bones at the side of the *beef*.

11. We place the *beef* between two dishes and some heavy weight on the top to press the *beef*.

12. We pour the *stock* through a strainer into a basin, and when it is cold we should remove every particle of *fat*.

13. We then put the *stock* in a stewpan, and put it on the fire to boil, without the lid, so as to reduce the *stock* to a *glaze*, about *a gill* (a quarter of a pint).

14. We now take the *beef* and with a paste brush cover the joint with the *glaze*, brushing it over several times until all the *glaze* is used up; as soon as the *glaze* is cold and set on the *beef*, it is ready for serving.

Now it is finished.

TRIPE.

Lesson No. 1.

CURRIED TRIPE.

Average cost of "*Curried Tripe.*"

INGREDIENTS.

	d.
1 lb. of tripe	8
¼ lb. of Patna rice	0¾
1 onion	0½
Flour, sugar, and curry powder	1½
	10¾

Time required, about three hours.

Now we will show you how to make a *Curry of Tripe.*

1. We take *one pound of tripe*, put it in a saucepan of cold water, and let it boil up. Immediately it boils take it out of the water.

   N.B.—This is called blanching.

2. After the *tripe* has been blanched, we scrape it with a knife to thoroughly cleanse it.

3. We cut the *tripe* up into small pieces.

4. We take a saucepan and lay the pieces of *tripe* in it, and pour in sufficient *cold water* to cover the *tripe.*

5. We take a *small onion* and peel it, and cut it partially through.

6. We put the *onion* into the saucepan of *tripe.*

7. We put the saucepan on the fire, and when it boils we must remove it to the side of the fire and let it simmer for not less than *two hours and a half.*

8. After that time we try the *tripe* with a fork, and if it is sufficiently cooked it will be very tender.

9. We take the saucepan off the fire and stand it on a piece of paper on the table.

10. We take the pieces of *tripe* out with a fork and put them on a dish.

Lessons on Cooking Meat.—Curried Tripe.

11. We take a small saucepan and put in it *one ounce of flour, one dessertspoonful of curry powder*, and *half an ounce of dripping*, and mix them all well together with a wooden spoon.

12. We add *cold water*, sufficient to make the above into a stiff *paste*.

13. We now pour in *half a pint of the liquor* in which the *tripe* was boiled.

14. We put the saucepan on the fire, and stir the mixture well until it boils and thickens. We must not let it get lumpy.

15. We stir in a *quarter of a teaspoonful of brown sugar and salt* according to taste. We must now stand the saucepan aside to get cool.

16. We take the *onion* which was boiled with the *tripe*, and cut it in shreds and add it to the *sauce*.

17. When the *sauce* is a little cool we put in the pieces of *tripe* and just let them warm through.

18. We take a dish and warm it, and pour the *tripe* and *sauce* on it, keeping it as much in the centre of the dish as possible.

19. We take a *teacupful of Patna rice*, wash it well in two or three waters, and put it in a saucepan full of boiling water. We must be sure the water is boiling. (N.B.—Rice should be boiled in plenty of water.) We add to it a *saltspoonful of salt*.

20. We must let it boil from a *quarter of an hour to twenty minutes*, after that time we must feel the *rice* to see if it is soft.

21. When the *rice* is sufficiently cooked we strain it off, and pour *cold water* over it.

22. We then put the *rice* back into the empty saucepan, and stand the saucepan by the side of the fire to dry the *rice*. The lid should be only half on the saucepan.

23. When the *rice* is quite dry we take it out of the saucepan and arrange it round the *tripe*.

Now it is finished.

TRIPE.

Lesson No. 2.

TRIPE IN MILK.

Average cost of "*Tripe in Milk.*"

INGREDIENTS.

	s.	d.
1 lb. of tripe	0	8
3 or 4 good sized onions	0	2
1 pint of milk	0	2
Seasoning and flour	0	0½
	1	0½

Time required, about two hours and a half.

Now we will show you how to cook *Tripe in Milk*.

1. We take *one pound of tripe*, put it into a saucepan of cold water to boil up and blanch. When it boils we take it off the fire.

2. After the *tripe* has been blanched, we take it out of the water and scrape it with a knife to thoroughly cleanse it.

3. We put the *tripe* on a board and cut it in small pieces.

4. We take *three or four good sized onions*, peel them and cut them partially through.

5. We put the *tripe and onions* into a saucepan with *one pint of milk*.

6. We put the saucepan on the fire to boil.

7. When it boils we should move the saucepan to the side of the fire, and let it simmer for not less than *two hours*.

8. After that time we should feel the *tripe* with a fork, and if it is sufficiently cooked it will be very tender.

9. We take the saucepan off the fire and stand it on a piece of paper on the table.

Lessons on Cooking Meat.—Tripe in Milk.

10. We take the *onions* out of the saucepan and put them on a board and chop them up finely.

11. We take the *tripe* out of the saucepan and arrange it on a warm dish.

12. We stand the dish near the fire to keep warm.

13. We take a *dessertspoonful of flour* and mix it to a smooth *paste* with *cold milk*.

14. We stir, by degrees, the *paste* into the *hot milk*, and let it boil and thicken.

15. We now stir the *onion* into the *milk* and let it warm through.

16. We season the *onion sauce*, according to taste, and pour it over the *tripe*.

Now it is finished.

TRIPE.

LESSON No. 3.
TRIPE À LA COUTANCE.

Average cost of "*Tripe à la Coutance.*"

INGREDIENTS.

	s.	d.
1 lb. of thin tripe	0	8
½ lb. of bacon	0	6
1 small carrot	0	0½
4 mushrooms	0	2
½ a large onion or 6 small green onions ⎫ Bouquet garni ⎬ 2 shalots and parsley ⎭	0	2¾
2 oz. of butter	0	2
1 tablespoonful of Harvey sauce ⎫ 1 tablespoonful of mushroom ketchup ⎬	0	2
1 oz. of flour	0	0½
1 pint of stock	0	7½
The juice of half a lemon	0	1
Salt and pepper	0	0½
	2	8¼

Time required, about two hours and a half.

Now we will show you how to cook *Tripe à la Coutance.*

1. We wash the *tripe* well in cold water.

2. We put the *tripe* in a stewpan with cold water enough to cover it.

3. We put the stewpan on the fire and bring it to the boil.

> N.B.—This is to blanch the *tripe.*

4. We then take the *tripe* out of the stewpan and dry it in a clean cloth.

5. We put the *tripe* on a board, and with a sharp knife cut it into *strips about two inches wide and four inches in length.*

> N.B.—Only the *thin part of the tripe* can be used for "*tripe à la Coutance;*" if there are any *thick* pieces they can be cooked with *milk and onions* (see "Tripe," Lesson No. 2).

6. We take the *half pound of bacon* and cut it in very thin slices, the same size as the *strips of tripe*.

7. We take *one shalot*, peel it, and *two or three sprigs of parsley*, and chop them up finely on a board.

8. We lay one *slice of bacon* on each *strip of tripe*, sprinkle a little *chopped shalot and parsley* over each *slice of bacon*, roll them up together, and tie them firmly round with a piece of string.

9. We take the *carrot*, wash it, scrape it clean with a knife, and cut it in slices.

10. We take the *half onion* and the other *shalot*, peel them, and cut them in slices.

11. We take a *sprig of marjoram, thyme, and a bay-leaf*, and tie them tightly together with a piece of string.

12. We take the *mushrooms*, wash them, and cut off the end of the stalks.

13. We arrange the *rolls of tripe and bacon* in a stewpan.

14. We also add all the *vegetables* and the *herbs*.

15. We pour in a *pint of stock*, and put the stewpan on the fire.

16. When it just boils we remove the stewpan to the side of the fire, and let the contents simmer gently for *two hours*.

17. After that time we take out the *rolls of tripe* and put them on a plate.

18. We take a strainer, hold it over a basin, and strain the *stock*.

19. We put *two ounces of butter* into another stewpan, and put it on the fire to melt.

20. When the *butter* is melted we add to it *one ounce of flour*, and mix them smoothly together.

21. We now add the *stock*, and stir it over the fire until it boils and thickens.

22. We take *half a lemon* and squeeze the *juice* of it into the *sauce*.

N.B.—We must be careful not to let any *pips* fall in.

23. We also stir in *one tablespoonful of Harvey sauce*, and *one tablespoonful of mushroom ketchup*, and season the *sauce* with *pepper and salt*.

24. We now place in the *rolls of tripe*, and let them warm through.

25. For serving we arrange the *rolls of tripe* in a circle on a hot dish, with some *purée of carrot*, or *spinach* (see "Vegetables," Lessons Nos. 6 and 8), or with a mixture of *vegetables* (according to taste), in the centre, and pour the *sauce* round the edge.

Now it is finished.

BRAISED FILLET OF VEAL.

Average cost of "*A Braised Fillet of Veal.*"

INGREDIENTS.

	s.	d.
3½ lbs. of the fillet of veal	3	6
½ lb. of the fat of bacon	0	6
A bouquet garni of parsley, thyme, and bayleaf	0	0½
1 onion	0	0½
3 pints of good stock	1	10
2 young carrots	0	1
Celery and turnip Salt	0	0½
	6	0½

Time required (the stock should be made the day before), about one hour and a half.

Now we will show you how to *Braise a Fillet of Veal.*

1. We take *three and a half pounds of the fillet of veal*, put it on a board, and cut off all the *skin* with a sharp knife.

2. We *lard* this *fillet* in the same way as for *fillets of beef* (see "Entrée," Lesson No. 3, from Note 3 to Note 7).

3. We place the *fillet* carefully in a clean braising pan.

4. We add a *bouquet garni*, consisting of a sprig of *parsley*, *thyme*, and a *bay-leaf*, all tied neatly and tightly together.

5. We take *two young carrots*, wash them, scrape them clean with a knife and cut them in halves.

6. We take an *onion* and a *quarter of a turnip*, and peel them carefully.

7. We add these *vegetables*, and *half a stick of celery*, to the *fillet* in the braising pan.

8. We now pour in about *three pints of good stock* (the *stock* must not cover the *meat*), put the stewpan on the fire, and baste the *fillet* continually.

9. We take a piece of *kitchen paper*, cut a round to the size of the braising pan and *butter* it.

10. As soon as the *stock* boils, we lay this round of paper on the *fillet* in the stewpan.

N.B.—This paper is to prevent the meat from browning too quickly.

11. We keep the lid of the braising pan on, and place it in a hot oven, and let it cook slowly for *one hour and a quarter*.

12. We must watch it, frequently raise the paper, and baste the *veal* with the *stock*.

13. We take the *veal* out of the braising pan, and place it on a hot dish.

>N.B.—We must stand this dish on the hot plate, or near the fire, to keep warm until the sauce is ready.

14. We put the braising pan on the fire and let the sauce reduce to a half glaze.

15. We then strain the glaze round the *meat*.

16. We serve it with dressed *spinach* (see "Vegetables," Lesson No. 8), or with dressed *carrots and turnips* (see "Vegetables," Lesson No. 6).

Now it is finished.

ROAST BULLOCK'S HEART.

Average cost of a "*Bullock's Heart stuffed*," and "*Brown Sauce.*"

INGREDIENTS.

"Bullock's Heart."	s.	d.	"Sauce."	s.	d.
1 bullock's heart .... 2s. or	2	6	1 small onion	0	0½
¼ lb. of suet................	0	2	Salt and pepper .... }	0	0¼
¾ lb. of bread crumbs	0	0½	½ oz. of flour .... }		
1 gill (¼ pint) of milk..........	0	0½	1 oz. of butter..............	0	1
Salt and pepper .... ⎫			1 dessertspoonful of mushroom ketchup	0	0¼
1 tablespoonful of chopped parsley................ ⎪					
1 dessertspoonful of chopped mixed herbs : thyme, lemon thyme, and marjoram .... ⎬	0	1½		0	2
¾ lb. dripping	0	2			
	3	0½			

Time required, about two hours and a half.

Now we will show you how to stuff a *Bullock's Heart* and roast it.

1. We must first prepare the fire for roasting, as described in "Roasting," Lesson No. 1.

2. We take a *bullock's heart*, and wash it thoroughly in *salt and water*.

3. We must be careful to cleanse all the cavities of the *heart*, and to remove all the blood.

4. We take it out of the *salt and water*, and put it into a basin of clean water and wash it again, until it is quite clean.

5. We now wipe it thoroughly dry with a cloth.

6. If the *heart* is not quite dry, it will not roast properly.

7. We put the *heart* on a board, and with a sharp knife cut off the *flaps*, or *deaf ears* (as they are called).

N.B.—These we should put aside for gravy.

8. We take *a quarter of a pound of suet*, put it on a board, cut away all the *skin*, and chop it up as finely as possible.

9. We should sprinkle a little *flour* over the *suet* to prevent it from sticking to the board or knife.

10. We grate some *bread crumbs* with a grater on to the board.

11. We take *two or three sprigs of parsley*, wash them in cold water and dry them in a cloth.

12. We put the *parsley* on a board and chop it up as finely as possible; when chopped there should be about *one tablespoonful*.

13. We take a *sprig of thyme, lemon thyme, and marjoram*, rub them through a strainer, or chop them up finely on a board; there should be about *one dessertspoonful of the mixed herbs*.

14. We now mix the chopped *suet and bread crumbs* well together.

15. We then add the *parsley* and the *herbs, one teaspoonful of salt*, and *pepper* to taste, and mix them thoroughly together.

16. We now mix it with *one gill* (a quarter of a pint) *of milk*.

17. We take the *heart* and fill all the cavities with the *stuffing*, pressing it in as firmly as possible.

N.B.—If there is any *stuffing* over, it can be put aside for the *sauce*.

18. We take a piece of kitchen paper, and grease it well with a piece of *butter* or *dripping*.

19. We place this piece of greased paper over the top of the *heart* where the cavities are, and tie it on tightly with string.

20. We put the roasting screen in front of the fire, to keep off the draught, and to keep in all the heat.

N.B.—A chair with a cloth over it, would answer the purpose if there was no screen.

21. We put the dripping-pan, or a large dish, down on a stand within the screen close to the fire, with the dripping ladle or a large spoon in it.

Lessons on Cooking Meat.—Roast Bullock's Heart.

22. We hang the roasting-jack up from the mantelpiece over the dripping-pan.
> N.B.—If there is no roasting jack, we can manage with a strong piece of worsted tied to a poor man's jack.

23. We must wind up the jack with its key, before we put the *meat* on.

24. We take the hook of the roasting-jack and pass it through the *heart*, and hang it on the jack or the worsted.
> N.B.—If the *heart* is hanging from a piece of worsted, we must twist the worsted occasionally to make it go round.

25. We put about *one ounce of clarified dripping* into the dripping-pan and baste the *heart* occasionally.

26. It will take about *two hours* to roast.

27. We now take the *deaf ears* out of the water and put them into a saucepan with *one pint of cold water*.

28. We put the saucepan on the fire to boil.

29. We take *one small onion*, peel it, and cut it in quarters.

30. When the water boils, we put in the *onion*, and a little *salt and pepper* to taste.

31. We now move the saucepan to the side of the fire, put the lid on, and let it stew gently until *five minutes* before the *heart* is done.

32. We must watch it and skim it occasionally.

33. After that time we strain the *liquor* into a basin.

34. We wash out the saucepan, and put in it *one ounce of butter* and put it on the fire to melt.

35. When the *butter* is melted, we add *one tablespoonful of flour*, and mix them smoothly together with a wooden spoon.

36. We now pour in by degrees the *liquor* and stir smoothly until it boils and thickens.

37. We then stand the saucepan by the side of the fire until required for use.

38. When the *heart* is roasted, we take it down, place the *heart* on a hot dish and draw out the hook.

39. We cut the string and take off the greased paper.

40. If there was any *stuffing* over, we now stir it into the *sauce;* we also add *one dessertspoonful of mushroom ketchup.*

N.B.—If the flavouring of *mushroom ketchup* is disliked, it may be omitted.

41. We pour the *sauce* round the *heart* on the dish, and it is then ready for serving.

Now it is finished.

CORNISH PASTIES.

Average cost of "*Cornish Pasties*" (*about* 12).

INGREDIENTS.

	s.	d.
½ lb. of buttock steak or beef skirt	0	5
½ lb. of potatoes	0	0½
1 onion	0	0½
1 lb. of flour	0	2¼
½ lb. of dripping	0	4
Salt and pepper }	0	0¼
1 teaspoonful of baking powder }		
	1	0½

Time required about one hour.

Now we will show you how we make *Cornish Pasties*.

1. We take *half a pound of buttock steak* or *beef skirt*, put it on a board, and cut it up into small pieces.

2. We take *half a pound of potatoes*, wash and peel them, put them on a board, and cut them up into small pieces.

3. We take *one small onion*, peel it, put it on a board, and chop it up as finely as possible.

4. We put *one pound of flour* into a basin with a little *salt*, and a *teaspoonful of baking powder*.

5. We put in *half a pound of dripping*, and rub it well into the *flour* with our hands.

6. We now add enough *cold water* to mix it into a stiff *paste*.

7. We *flour* a board and turn the *paste* on to it.

8. We take a rolling-pin, *flour* it, and roll the *paste* out into a thin sheet, about a *quarter of an inch* in thickness.

9. We cut the *paste* into pieces about *six or seven inches* square.

10. We place a little of the *meat* and *potato* in the centre of each square, sprinkle over it a little *pepper and salt*, and a very little of the *chopped onion*.

11. We fold the *paste* over the *meat*, joining it by pressing the edges together with our thumb and finger.

12. We grease a baking tin and put the *pasties* on it.

N.B.—If there is no baking tin we should grease the shelf in the oven to prevent the pasties from sticking.

13. We put the tin into the oven to bake for from *half an hour* to *three quarters of an hour*.

14. For serving, we put the pasties on a dish.

Now it is finished.

A GRILLED STEAK.

Average cost of —" *Grilled Steak.*"

INGREDIENTS.

	d.
½ lb. rump steak	8
Lemon, pepper, and salt	1
Butter and salad oil	1
	10

Time required about ten minutes.

Now we will show you how to *Grill a Steak* (either *beef* or *rump steak* will do, but the latter is more tender).

1. We take a small bunch of *parsley*, wash it, dry it well in a cloth, and put it on a board.

2. We must chop the *parsley* up very fine with a knife.

3. We take a *quarter of an ounce of butter* and mix it well with the *chopped parsley*.

4. We sprinkle over it *pepper and salt* (according to taste), and *six drops of lemon juice*.

5. We make it all up into a small pat.

6. We take *half a pound of rump steak, half an inch* in thickness.

7. We pour about a *tablespoonful of salad oil* on to a plate.

8. We dip both sides of the *steak* into the *oil*.

9. We take a gridiron and warm it well by the fire.

10. We place the *oiled steak* on the gridiron, and hang it on the bars of the stove close to the fire to cook quickly.

> N.B.—If the meat is at all frozen it must be warmed gradually through, before putting it quite near the fire, or it will be tough.

11. We must turn the gridiron with the *steak* occasionally; it will take from *ten to twelve minutes*, according to the brightness and heat of the fire.

12. When the *steak* is sufficiently cooked, we must place it on a hot dish; and we should be careful not to stick the fork into the *meat* (or the gravy will run out, but into the fat).

13. We take the pat of *green butter* and put it on the *steak*, spreading it all over with a knife.

Now it is finished.

LIVER AND BACON.

Average cost of "*Liver and Bacon.*"

INGREDIENTS.

	s.	d.
2 lbs. sheep's liver	1	4
1 lb. bacon	0	10
1 dessertspoonful of flour }	0	0¼
1 small onion }		
	2	2¼

Time required about half an hour.

Now we will show you how to cook *Liver and Bacon*.

1. We take *one pound of bacon*, put it on a board, and cut it in thin slices.

2. We cut the *rind* off each slice of *bacon*.

3. We put these slices of *bacon* into a frying-pan.

4. We put the frying-pan on the fire to fry the *bacon*. It will take about *ten minutes*.

N.B.—If the bacon is not very fat, we must put a small piece of dripping in the frying-pan with the bacon.

5. We should turn it when one side is fried.

6. We now take a *sheep's liver* (it will weigh about *two pounds*), put it on a board, and cut it in slices.

7. We put about *two tablespoonsful of flour* on a plate.

8. We dip the slices of *liver* into the *flour*, and *flour* them well on both sides.

9. When the *bacon* is fried we take it out of the frying-pan and put it on a warm dish.

10. We stand the dish near the fire to keep warm.

11. We put the *slices of liver* in the frying-pan, a few at a time, as they must not be on the top of each other.

N.B.—If the flavour of onion is liked, *a small onion*, peeled, and cut in slices, might be fried with the liver.

12. The *liver* will take about a *quarter of an hour* to fry.

13. We should watch it occasionally, and turn it once.

14. To see when the *liver* is sufficiently cooked we

should cut a slice; the inside should be of a brownish colour.

15. When the *liver* is all cooked we should place it on the dish with the bacon.

16. We put a *dessertspoonful of flour* in a cup, and mix it into a smooth *paste* with nearly a *gill* (quarter of a pint) *of water*.

17. We pour the *flour and water* into the frying-pan and stir it until it boils and thickens.

18. We pour this *sauce* over the *liver and bacon*.

Now it is finished.

MEAT PIE (BEEF STEAK).

Average cost of a "*Meat Pie*" (in a quart dish).

INGREDIENTS.

	s.	d.
1½ lb. buttock steak	1	3
½ lb. bullock's kidney	0	6
Seasoning	0	0½
1 lb. flour	0	2¼
½ lb. clarified dripping	0	4
1 teaspoonful baking powder	0	0½
	2	4

Time required about two hours and a quarter.

Now we will show you how to make a *Meat Pie*.

1. We take *one and a half pound of buttock steak*, put it on a board, and cut it in thin slices.

2. We should cut away all the skin.

3. We take *half a pound of bullock's kidney*, put it on a plate, and cut it in slices.

4. We put *one tablespoonful of flour, one teaspoonful of salt*, and a *teaspoonful of pepper* on to a plate, and mix them well together.

5. We dip each *slice* of *meat* and *kidney* into the seasoning, and roll them up into little rolls.

6. We arrange these rolls of *meat* and *kidney* in a quart pie dish, and fill up the dish *two-thirds with water*.

7. We put *one pound of flour* into a basin.

8. We add *one teaspoonful of baking powder* and *half a saltspoonful of salt* to the *flour*, and mix them well together.

9. We take *half a pound of clarified dripping*, cut it in small pieces, and rub it well into the *flour* with our hands.

N.B.—We should be careful that there are no lumps of dripping in the flour.

10. We then add by degrees enough *cold water* to make it into a stiff *paste*.

11. We take a rolling-pin and *flour* it. We also sprinkle *flour* on the board, and *flour* our hands to prevent the *paste* from sticking.

12. We take the *paste* out of the basin and put it on a board.

13. We roll out the *paste* once to the shape of the pie dish, only rather larger, and to the thickness of about *one-third of an inch.*

14. We wet the edge of the dish with *water.*

15. We take a knife, dip it in *flour*, and cut a strip of the *paste* the width of the edge of the pie dish, and place it round the edge of the dish.

> N.B.—We should cut this strip of paste from round the edge of the paste, leaving the centre piece the size and shape of the top of the pie dish.

16. We wet the edge of the *paste* with *water.*

17. We take the remaining *paste* and place it over the pie dish, pressing it down with our thumb all round the edge.

> N.B.—We must be very careful not to break the paste.

18. We take a knife, dip it in *flour*, and trim off all the rough edges of the *paste* round the edge of the dish.

19. We take a knife, and with the back of the blade we make little notches in the edge of the *paste*, pressing the *paste* firmly with our thumb to keep it in its proper place.

> N.B.—We can ornament the top of the pie with any remaining paste to our fancy.

20. We make a hole with the knife in the centre of the *pie* to let out the steam while the *pie* is baking.

> N.B.—If there was not an escape for the steam it would sodden the inside of the crust, and so prevent it from baking properly.

21. We put the *pie* into the *oven* to bake gently for *two hours.* We must watch it occasionally, and turn it to prevent its burning. It should become a pale brown.

> N.B.—Meat pies should be put in the hottest part of the oven first, which, in most ovens, is the top, to make the crust light, and then put in a cooler part to cook the meat thoroughly.
>
> N.B.—This pie could be made with veal or mutton instead of *steak.*

Now it is finished.

MEAT PUDDING.

Average cost of a "*Meat Pudding*" (a quart basin.)

INGREDIENTS.

	s.	d.
6 oz. of suet	0	3¾
1 lb. of flour	0	2¼
1 teaspoonful of baking powder	0	0¼
Seasoning	0	0¼
1½ lb. of buttock steak, 10*d*. per lb.	1	3
½ lb. bullock's kidney, 1*s*. per lb.	0	6
	2	3½

Time required about two hours and a half.

Now we will show you how to make a *Meat Pudding*.

1. We take a large saucepan full of *cold water*, and put it on the fire to boil.

2. We take *six ounces of suet* and put it on a board.

3. We take a knife and cut away all the *skin*, and chop up the *suet* as finely as possible, and sprinkle a little *flour* over the *suet* to prevent its sticking.

4. We put *one pound of flour* into a basin, and add to it a *teaspoonful of baking powder* and *half a saltspoonful of salt* and mix all well together.

5. We now add the chopped *suet* and rub it well into the *flour* with our hands.

N.B.—We should be careful not to leave any lumps of suet.

6. We then add by degrees about *half a pint of cold water* to make it into a paste; we should mix it well.

7. We put *one teaspoonful of salt* and *one teaspoonful of pepper* on a plate, and mix them together.

8. We take *one pound and a half of buttock steak*, put it on a board, and cut it in slices about *three inches long and two inches broad*.

N.B.—We should cut away all the skin.

9. We take *half a pound of bullock's kidney*, put it on a board, and cut it in slices.

10. We dip each slice of *meat* and *kidney* into the plate of seasoning.

11. We take a quart basin and grease it well inside with *dripping*.

12. We take a rolling pin and *flour* it; we also sprinkle a very little *flour* on the board to prevent the *paste* sticking.

> N.B.—In making paste we should always keep our hands well floured to prevent its sticking to them.

13. We take the *paste* out of the basin and put it on the board.

14. We cut off about *one-third* of the *paste* and lay it aside for the cover or top of the *pudding*.

15. We roll out the remainder of the *paste* to a round twice the size of the top of the basin; it should be about *one-third of an inch in thickness*.

16. We line the basin inside smoothly with the *paste*.

17. We place the slices of *meat* and *kidney* in the basin, fitting them neatly in.

18. We pour in about *one gill and a half of water*, so as to fill the basin to within *half an inch* of the top.

19. We roll the remaining pieces of *paste* to a round, the size of the top of the basin, to about a *quarter of an inch in thickness*.

20. We wet the edge of the *paste* in the basin with *cold water*, and cover over the top of the basin with the round of *paste*.

21. We must join the *paste* together at the edge of the basin, pressing the edges together with our thumb.

22. We take a knife, *flour* it, and trim the edges of the *paste* neatly round.

23. We take a small pudding cloth, wring it out in warm water, and *flour* it.

24. We put this cloth over the top of the basin, tying it on tightly with a piece of string under the rim of the basin.

25. We tie the four corners of the cloth together over the top of the *pudding*.

Lessons on Cooking Meat.—Beef Steak Pudding.

26. When the water in the saucepan is quite boiling, we put in the *pudding* and let it boil for *two hours*.

N.B.—The lid should be on the saucepan.

N.B.—We should keep a kettle of boiling water and fill up the saucepan, as the water in it boils away.

27. After that time we take the *pudding* out of the saucepan and take off the cloth.

28. We place a hot dish on the top of the *pudding*, turn the basin and dish quite over, and carefully raising the basin, we should leave the *pudding* in the middle of the dish unbroken.

N.B.—This pudding might be made of beef skirt or Australian beef.

Now it is finished.

PIG'S FRY.

Average cost of this dish, *i.e.*, "*Poor Man's Goose*" (1 quart dish)—

INGREDIENTS.

	d.
1 lb. of pig's fry	6
2½ lbs. of potatoes	2½
1 onion	0½
Sage and seasoning	0½
Total	9½

Time required about one hour and a quarter.

Now we will show you how to cook *Pig's Fry*—"*Poor Man's Goose.*"

1. We take *two and a half pounds of potatoes*, and put them in a basin of cold water.

2. We take a scrubbing brush and scrub and wash the *potatoes* well.

3. We put the *potatoes* into a saucepan of cold water.

4. We put the saucepan on the fire to boil.

5. As soon as it boils we take the *potatoes* out of the water (N.B.—This is called par-boiling *potatoes*), we peel them, and cut them in slices with a sharp knife.

6. We take *one onion* and peel it.

7. We take two or three *sage-leaves* and put them on a board.

8. We chop up the *onion* and *sage* together on the board with a sharp knife.

9. We take *one pound of pig's fry* and cut it in small pieces.

10. We take a quart pie-dish and grease the dish with *dripping or fat*.

11. We put a layer of sliced *potatoes* in the bottom of the pie-dish.

12. We sprinkle a little of the chopped *sage* and *onion*, *pepper* and *salt*, over the *potatoes*.

13. We now put a layer of the *pig's fry*.

14. We sprinkle a little of the chopped *sage* and *onion*, *pepper* and *salt*, over the *pig's fry*.

15. Now we add another layer of *sliced potatoes*, and sprinkle them with a little of the chopped *sage* and *onion*, *pepper* and *salt*.

16. We put in another layer of *pig's fry*, and sprinkle the remainder of the chopped *sage* and *onion*, and a little *pepper* and *salt* on the top.

17. We cover these *layers* with the rest of the sliced *potatoes*.

18. We now fill up the pie-dish with water for gravy.

19. We take the *skin* usually sent with the *pig's fry* and put it over the top of the pie-dish.

20. If the *skin* is not sent we must take a piece of whity-brown paper and grease it with some *dripping or fat*, and put that over the pie-dish instead.

21. We put the pie-dish into a moderate oven to bake for from *three quarters of an hour to one hour*.

Now it is finished.

BOILED PIG'S HEAD (salted) WITH ONION SAUCE.

Average cost of "*Pig's Head*" 5d. or 6d. per lb.

INGREDIENTS.

For "*Brawn.*"	s.	d.	For "*Onion Sauce.*"		d.
½ a pig's head	1	3	3 onions		1½
40 peppercorns	}		3 gills of milk		1½
2 blades of mace	}		A dessertspoonful of flour		0¼
4 cloves	} 0	1	½ oz. of butter	}	0½
12 allspice	}		Pepper and salt	}	
A bunch of herbs	}				
2 large onions	} 0	1			
	1	5			3½

Time required (after salting) for boiling pig's head about two hours; for making into brawn, two hours.

Now we will show you how to boil *Pig's Head*.

1. We take a *pig's head*, wash it thoroughly in plenty of tepid water.

2. We take out the *brains* and throw them away.

3. We cut out the little *veins* and all the *splinters of bone*.

4. We wash the *head* in all parts with plenty of *salt*, thoroughly cleansing it from blood.

5. We lay the *head* in *pickle* (see *Pickle for Meat*) for *three days*.

6. When the head is salted, we put it into a saucepan with cold water enough to cover it.

7. We put the saucepan on the fire to boil.

8. When it boils we draw the saucepan to the side of the fire, and let it simmer gently for from *one hour and a half to two hours*, according to the size and age of the pig.

N.B.—*Boiled pig's head* is eaten with *boiled rabbit*, or with *veal*, or with *onion sauce*.

N.B.—If preferred the *pig's head* can be made into *brawn* (see below).

For making *Onion Sauce*,

9. We take *three* or *four onions*, peel them, and cut them in quarters.

Lessons on Cooking Meat.—Pig's Head.

10. We put them into a saucepan with water enough to cover them.

11. We put the saucepan on the fire to boil until the *onions* are quite tender.

12. We then strain them off, throw the water away, put the *onions* on a board, and chop them up small.

13. We throw the *onions* into a saucepan with *three gills* (one gill is a quarter of a pint) of *milk*, put it on the fire, and let it come to the boil.

14. We put a *dessertspoonful of flour* into a basin and mix it with *half an ounce of butter* into a paste with a knife.

15. We stir this *paste* smoothly into the boiling *milk* and *onions*, and continue to stir it until it boils.

16. We season the *sauce* with *pepper* and *salt* to taste, and then move the saucepan to the side of the fire to keep warm till required for use.

17. We take a grater and grate some *bread crumbs* on to a plate.

18. We put the plate in the oven or in a Dutch oven to brown the *bread crumbs*.

19. When the *pig's head* is sufficiently boiled we take it out of the saucepan and put it on a hot dish.

20. We take out the *half tongue*, skin it, and put it back on the dish with the *head*.

21. We sprinkle the browned *bread crumbs* over the *pig's head*, and pour the *onion sauce* round it, or, if preferred, it may be served separately in a sauce boat.

For making the *pig's head* into *Brawn*.

1. We *salt* and boil the *pig's head* in the same way as above from Note 1 to Note 8.

2. When the *pig's head* is sufficiently boiled we take it out of the saucepan and put it on a board.

3. We cut all the *meat* off the bones, and cut it into small pieces the shape of dice; we also cut up the *ear* and the *tongue* (the *tongue* should be previously skinned).

4. We put the bones back into the saucepan with *a quart of the liquor* (in which the *head* was boiled), *forty peppercorns, two blades of mace, four cloves*, and *twelve allspice*.

5. We also add a *bunch of herbs*, namely, *a sprig of marjoram, thyme*, and *two bay leaves* tied tightly together.

6. We take *two onions*, peel them, cut them in quarters, and put them into the saucepan.

7. We put the saucepan on the fire and let it come to the boil, we should remove the lid and let the *liquor* reduce for about *half an hour*.

8. After that time we strain the *liquor* into a basin.

9. We pour *one pint and a half of the strained liquor* back into the saucepan and put it on the fire.

10. We now put the pieces of *meat* into the *liquor*, season it with *pepper* (and *salt* if necessary) to taste, and let it come to the boil.

11. We take a basin or tin mould, rinse it in cold water.

12. We then pour the *meat* and the *liquor* together into the wet basin or tin, and stand it aside to get cold and set.

13. For serving we turn the *brawn* out of the basin on to a dish.

Now it is finished.

PORK PIE.

Average cost of "*Pork Pie*" (1 lb.)

INGREDIENTS.

	s.	d.
¼ lb. lard	0	3
1 lb. pork (either loin or leg)	0	10
Seasoning	0	0¼
1 lb. of flour	0	2¼
1 egg	0	1
	1	4½

Time required two hours and a half.

Now we will show you how to make a *Pork Pie*.

1. We put *a quarter of a pound of lard* and *a quarter of a pint of cold water* into rather a large saucepan.

2. We put the saucepan on the fire to boil.

N.B.—We must watch it, as if it boils over it will catch fire.

3. We take *one pound of lean pork* (cut either from the *loin* or from the *leg*), put it on a board, and cut it up in pieces of about *one inch square*.

4. We put *one pound of flour* into a *basin*.

5. When the *lard and water* are quite boiling, we pour them into the middle of the *flour* and mix them well with a spoon.

6. When the *paste* is cool enough we should knead it well with our hands.

N.B.—More water must not be added, as the paste is required to be rather stiff.

7. We take the *paste* out of the basin, and put it on a floured board.

8. We cut off *a quarter of the paste*, and the remainder we mould into the shape of a *basin*, pressing it inside with one hand and supporting it outside with the other.

9. We should shape it as evenly as possible, and it should be about *one-third of an inch* in thickness all round.

10. We should take a knife, flour it, and cut the top of the shape level all round.

11. We dip the pieces of *pork* into cold water, then season them well with *pepper* and *salt*.

12. We should put these *pieces* inside the mould of *paste* as close together as possible.

> N.B.—The pie can be flavoured, if liked, with chopped sage, about a teaspoonful sprinkled well amongst the pieces of pork.

13. We take the remainder of the *paste* and roll it out (with a floured rolling pin), and cut it to the size of the top of the mould and to about the thickness of *one-third of an inch*.

14. We take *an egg* and break it into two cups, dividing the *yolk* from the *white*.

15. We take a paste brush, dip it into the *white of egg*, and *egg* the edge of the mould of *paste*.

16. We take the piece of *paste* and put it over the top of the *pie*, pressing the edges together with our thumb.

17. We cut little leaves out of the remaining paste, dip them in the *white of the egg*, and stick them on the top of the pie.

18. We wet the *pie* all over with the *yolk of egg*.

19. We put the *pie* in a moderate oven to bake for *two hours*.

Now it is finished.

SAUSAGE ROLLS.

Average cost of "*Sausage Rolls*." (about one dozen) made with cooked or uncooked meat.

INGREDIENTS.

	d.
½ lb. of cooked (or uncooked 5*d*.) meat	3½
1 lb. flour	2¼
½ lb. dripping	4
1 teaspoonful baking powder	⎫
Seasoning	⎪
½ a shalot	⎬ 1
1 small onion	⎪
4 sage leaves	⎭
1 egg	1
	11¾

Time required half an hour.

Now we will show you how to make *Sausage Rolls*.

1. We take *half a pound of meat* (*cooked* or *uncooked*), put it on a board, take away all the *fat*, and *mince* the *meat* up as finely as possible.

2. We take the *mince meat*, put it in a basin, and season it well with *pepper and salt*.

3. We take *four sage leaves*, put them on a board, and chop them up as finely as possible with a knife.

4. We take *half a shalot* and *one small onion*, peel them, and chop them up upon the board.

5. We mix the *chopped sage, shalot*, and *onion* well into the *mince meat* with a spoon.

6. We put *one pound of flour* into a basin.

7. We add to it *one teaspoonful of baking powder*, a *quarter of a saltspoonful* of *salt*, and *half a pound of clarified dripping*.

8. We rub the *dripping* well into the *flour* with our hands.

N.B.—We must mix it thoroughly and be careful not to leave any *lumps*.

9. We add enough *water* to the *flour* to make it into a stiff *paste*.

10. We flour the paste board.

11. We turn the *paste* out on the board.

N.B.—We should divide the *paste* in two, so as not to handle it too much.

12. We take a rolling pin, flour it, and roll out *each portion* into a thin sheet, about *one-eighth of an inch* in thickness.

13. We cut the *paste* into pieces about *six inches* square.

14. We should collect all the scraps of *paste* (so that none is wasted), fold them together, and roll them out and cut them into squares.

N.B.—There should be about *one dozen squares* of paste.

15. We should put about a *tablespoonful* of the *mince meat* and *herbs* into the centre of each square of *paste*.

16. We fold the *paste* round the *meat*, joining it smoothly down the centre, and pressing the *ends* of the *paste* together with our finger and thumb.

17. We take a baking tin, grease it well, and place the *sausage rolls* on it.

18. We break *one egg* on to a plate, and beat it slightly with a knife.

19. We take a paste brush, dip it in the *egg*, and paint over the tops of the *rolls*.

20. We place the tin in a hot oven to bake for *fifteen minutes* if the *meat* is already *cooked*, but if *raw meat* is used, then *half an hour* is required.

N.B.—We should look at them once or twice, and turn them if necessary, so that they shall be equally baked.

21. For serving we take the *rolls* off the tin and place them on a hot dish.

Now it is finished.

SEA PIE.

Average cost of a "*Sea Pie*" (about two quarts).

INGREDIENTS.

	s.	d.
2 lbs. of buttock steak at 10d.	1	8
2 onions	0	1
1 small carrot	0	0½
½ a turnip }		
Pepper and Salt }	0	0¼
¾ lb. of flour	0	1¾
¼ lb. of suet }		
1 teaspoonful of baking powder }	0	2
	2	1½

Time required about two hours.

Now we will show you how to make a *Sea Pie*.

1. We put *two pounds of buttock steak* on a board, and cut it in slices with a sharp knife.

2. We take *two onions*, peel them, and slice them as thinly as possible.

3. We take a *small carrot* and *half a turnip*, wash them, scrape the carrot clean with a knife, peel the turnips, and cut them in thin slices.

4. We season the *slices of meat* with *pepper* and *salt* to taste.

5. We put the *slices of meat* in layers in a two quart saucepan, sprinkling a little of the *sliced vegetables* on each layer of the *meat*.

6. We pour in enough *cold water* just to cover the *meat*.

7. We put the saucepan on the fire, just bring it to the boil, and then move it to the side of the fire to simmer.

N.B.—During this time we make the crust.

8. We take *a quarter of a pound of suet*, put it on a board, cut away all the *skin*, and chop it up as finely as possible.

9. We should sprinkle a little *flour* over the *suet*, to prevent it sticking to the board or knife.

10. We put *three quarters of a pound of flour* into a basin, and mix into it *half a saltspoonful of salt*, and *one teaspoonful of baking powder*.

11. We now put in the chopped *suet* and rub it well into the *flour* with our hands.

12. We add sufficient *cold water* to mix it into a stiff *paste*.

13. We flour a board and turn the *paste* out on it.

14. We take a rolling-pin, flour it, and roll out the *paste* to the size of the saucepan.

15. This quantity of *paste* will roll out to the size of a *two quart saucepan*, so that if a smaller saucepan is used less *paste* will be required.

16. We put this *paste* over the *meat* in the saucepan, and let it simmer gently for *one hour and half*.

N.B.—The lid should be on the saucepan.

17. We must watch it, and be careful to pass a knife round the sides of the saucepan, or the *paste* will stick.

N.B.—Sailors add *sliced potatoes* to the *pie* when they can get them.

18. For serving, we carefully remove the *crust*, turn the *meat, vegetables*, and *gravy* on to a hot dish, and place the *crust* over it.

Now it is finished.

SHEEP'S HEAD.

Average cost of "*Sheep's Head*," consisting of 1 *quart of broth* and 1 *dish of boiled sheep's head*, with *vegetables* or *browned sheep's head*.

INGREDIENTS.

	s.	d.
1 sheep's head	1	0
Salt .... } 4 peppercorns .... }	0	0¼
2 turnips................................	0	1
1 carrot	0	0½
1 onion	0	0½
½ small head of celery	0	1
1 sprig of thyme .... } 2 sprigs of parsley .... }	0	0½
Toasted crusts of bread	0	0¼
½ oz. of flour	0	0¼
1 oz. clarified dripping or ½ oz. butter......	0	0½
	1	4¾

Time required (after the sheep's head has been soaked for 2 hours) one and a half hours.

Now we will show you how to cook *Sheep's Head*.

1. We take a *sheep's head* (which has been previously chopped half way through by the butcher) and put it in a basin of warm water, with a *dessertspoonful of salt*.

2. We should wash the *head* thoroughly, carefully removing the *brains* (which should be put aside) and all the *splinters of the bones*.

3. We should wash away all the *blood* and *matter* from the *passages of the nose, throat,* and *ears,* and clean round the *gums*.

N.B.—If this is not thoroughly done the sheep's head will be spoiled.

4. We now put the *sheep's head* in a basin of *salt and water*, to soak for *two hours*.

5. After the *head* has been soaked, we take it out of the water and carefully cut the *tongue* out with a knife.

6. We tie the *head* together with a piece of string, to keep it in shape.

7. We put the *head* and the *tongue* in a large saucepan.

8. We pour in sufficient *lukewarm water* to cover the head.

9. We add a good *saltspoonful of salt* and 4 *peppercorns*.

N.B.—If liked, one ounce of pearl barley or rice, previously washed, may be now added.

10. We put the saucepan on the fire and let it boil very gently for 1 *hour*.

11. We must watch it and skim it occasionally with a spoon, removing as much of the *fat* as possible.

12. We take *two turnips*, wash them in cold water, peel them, and cut them in quarters with a sharp knife.

13. We take a *carrot*, scrape it clean with a knife, and cut it in pieces.

14. We take a *good-sized onion*, peel it, and cut it in quarters.

15. We take *half a small head of celery* and *two sprigs of parsley* and wash them in cold water.

16. When the *sheep's head* has boiled for *an hour* we should add all these *vegetables*.

17. We also add *one sprig of thyme*.

18. We now move the saucepan to the side of the fire and let it simmer gently for *one hour and a half*.

N.B.—The lid should be on the saucepan.

19. *Half an hour* before the *sheep's head* is finished, we wash the *brains* well in cold water (removing all the skin).

20. We tie the *brains* up in a piece of muslin and put them in the saucepan with the *head*, to boil for *ten minutes*.

21. We put *one ounce of clarified dripping*, or *half an ounce of butter*, into a small saucepan.

22. We put the saucepan on the fire to melt the *dripping*, and then add *half an ounce of flour* and mix them well together with a spoon.

23. We take *one gill* (a quarter of a pint) of *broth* from the saucepan in which the *head* is boiling, and add it by degrees to the *sauce*, stirring it as smoothly as possible until it boils and thickens.

24. We now move the saucepan to the side of the fire.

Lessons on Cooking Meat.—Sheep's Head. 139

25. When the *brains* have boiled for *ten minutes* we take them out of the saucepan, take them out of the muslin, and chop them up in small pieces with a knife.

26. We add the *brains* to the *sauce*.

27. When the *sheep's head* is sufficiently cooked we take it out of the saucepan, cut away the string, and place it on a warm dish.

28. We take the *tongue*, skin it carefully, and place it on the same dish.

29. We take out the *turnips*, put them in a basin, and mash them with a fork.

30. We take out the *carrot* and arrange it alternately with the *mashed turnips* round the *sheep's head*.

31. We take the *brain sauce* and pour it over the *sheep's head*.

32. We should pour the *broth* carefully into a basin, without the *bread* or *vegetables*.

> N.B.—Bread or vegetables should never be kept in broth, as they would turn it sour.

33. We put the basin of *broth* away until required for use.

> N.B.—All the fat should be removed from the broth before it is used.
> N.B.—When the broth is required for use, a few toasted crusts of bread might be added, and a little chopped parsley.
> N.B.—The fat from the broth should be melted down into dripping.

> N.B.—If the sheep's head be preferred browned.

1. We proceed as above (see from Note 1 to Note 17).

2. We then move the saucepan to the side of the fire, and let it simmer gently for *one hour*.

> N.B.—The lid should be on the saucepan.

3. We take a piece of *stale bread* and grate a *tablespoonful of bread crumbs* with a grater.

4. We mix with these *crumbs* a *teaspoonful of parsley*, and a *teaspoonful of mixed herbs*, chopped up finely.

5. When the *head* has simmered for *one hour*, we take it out of the saucepan.

6. We cut the string round it, and lay it on a dish.

7. We sprinkle the *bread crumbs* and *herbs* over the *head*, and put a few tiny pieces of *dripping* on it.

8. We put the dish in the oven, or in front of the fire, for *ten to fifteen minutes;* it will be then ready for serving.

9. We take the *brains* and wash them well in cold water (removing all the skin).

10. We tie the *brains* up in a piece of muslin and put them in the saucepan of *broth* (in which the *sheep's head* was boiled) to boil for *ten minutes.*

N.B.—For serving, the tongue should be skinned as above, and served separately with the brain sauce (see above from Note 21 to Note 27).

11. We proceed with the *broth* the same as above, from Note 32.

Now it is finished.

STEWED STEAK.

Average cost for "*Stewing a Steak.*"

INGREDIENTS.

	s.	d.
1 lb. of rump steak	1	4
1 carrot	0	1
1 turnip	0	1
2 sticks of celery		
1 onion	0	1
1 oz. of butter	0	1¼
1 tablespoonful of flour		
Pepper and salt	0	0¼
	1	8½

Time required about one hour.

Now we will show you how to *Stew a Steak* (either beef or rump steak will do, the latter is more tender).

1. We take *one pound of rump steak, one and a half inch in thickness*, and put it on a board.

2. We cut off all the skin and fat from the *steak*.

3. We take *one carrot, one turnip*, and a few *celery leaves*, and wash them well in cold water.

4. We take a sharp knife and scrape the *carrot* clean.

5. We take the *turnip*, cut it in half (as not all will be required), and peel off the outside skin.

6. We take a sharp knife and peel the *carrot* and *turnip* very thinly into ribbons, leaving just the centre part of each vegetable.

7. We take *one onion*, peel it, and put it on a board.

8. We shred the *onion* and *celery*.

9. We put *one ounce of butter* in a stewpan, and we put the *steak* in it to brown.

10. We put the *onion* and *celery*, and the *insides* of the *carrot* and *turnip* (left after peeling), into the stewpan with the *steak*.

11. We put the stewpan on the fire.

12. We must look occasionally at the *steak*, and when it is sufficiently browned on one side we must turn it carefully over to brown the other.

13. When the *steak* is sufficiently browned on both sides, then put in the vegetables.

14. We take a basin and put in it a *tablespoonful of flour*, *half a teaspoonful of salt, half a saltspoonful of pepper*, and mix them together with a wooden spoon, and *one pint of water or stock*.

15. We stir them all well together into a smooth *sauce*.

16. We pour this *sauce* into the stewpan, with the *steak* and vegetables, and stir all together until it boils and thickens.

17. We let it gently simmer *one hour*.

18. We take the fat which we have cut off the *steak* and cut it into small pieces.

19. We put the pieces of fat on a tin dish.

20. We put the fat in the oven to cook till brown.

 N.B.—It is better for stewed steak to cook the fat separately as it keeps the gravy of the steak free from grease.

21. We take the thin pealings from the *carrot* and *turnip*, and put them on a board and shred them finely with a sharp knife.

22. We put these *shredded vegetables* into a small saucepan with about a *gill of cold water*.

23. We put the saucepan on the fire and let it boil until the *vegetables* are quite tender; we must feel them with a fork.

24. When the *steak* is sufficiently stewed, we must put it on a hot dish.

25. We take a strainer and strain the gravy, in which the *steak* has been stewed, over the *steak*.

26. The *stewed vegetables* must be thrown away, as all the goodness is out of them.

27. We take the tin dish out of the oven, and place the pieces of fat about on the *steak*.

28. We take the boiled *shredded vegetables* and garnish the *steak* with them.

 N.B.—Any other vegetables can be used for garnishing, *i.e.*, peas, French beans, asparagus, &c.

Now it is finished.

TOAD IN THE HOLE.

Average cost of "*Toad in the Hole.*"

INGREDIENTS.

	s.	d.
6 ozs. of flour	0	1
1 egg	0	1
1 pint of milk	0	2
1½ lbs. of meat (either beef or mutton) Seasoning	1	0
	1	4

Time required about one hour and three quarters.

Now we will show you how to make *Toad in the Hole*.

1. We put *six ounces of flour* into a basin, with *half a saltspoonful of salt*.

2. We break *one egg into the flour* and stir in smoothly and by degrees *one pint of milk*.

N.B.—We must be careful that it is not lumpy.

3. We should beat it up as much as possible, as it will make the *batter* lighter.

4. We take *one pound of meat*, put it on a board, and cut it in neat pieces.

N.B.—*Buttock steak, beef skirt*, or any pieces of *mutton* might be used; for instance, the *short bones* from the *neck of mutton*. *Sausages* or *cold meat* might very well be used.

5. We take a pie dish or a tin and grease it inside with *clarified dripping*.

6. We season the pieces of *meat* with *pepper and salt*, and place them in the greased dish.

7. We pour the *batter* over the *meat*, and put the dish in the oven to bake for *one hour*.

8. After that time it is ready for serving.

Now it is finished.

TRUSSING A FOWL FOR BOILING.

Average cost of a "*Boiled Fowl*" and "*Egg Sauce.*"

INGREDIENTS.

	s.	d.
1 fowl	3	6
1½ oz. of butter	0	1¼
Stock or water }		
1 carrot }		
1 small onion }	0	1
A bouquet of herbs }		
2 eggs	0	2
1 oz. of flour }		
½ pint of milk }	0	1¼
Gill of cream	0	6
	4	5¾

Time required about one hour and a quarter.

Now we will show you how to prepare a *Fowl*, and truss it for boiling.

1. We take a *fowl* that has been already plucked, and put it on a board.

2. We prepare it and clean it in the same way as described in "Trussing a Fowl for Roasting," from Note 1 to Note 12.

3. We take a sharp knife and cut off the claws, and the end of the legs of the *fowl* to the first joint.

4. We take a twist of paper or taper and light it.

5. We take the *fowl* up by its legs, and hold the lighted paper under it to singe off the little hairs.

6. We then hold the *fowl* up by its wings and singe the other end.

N.B.—We must be careful in singeing not to blacken or mark the fowl in any way.

7. We turn the *fowl* on its back with the tail towards us.

8. We put our hands through the incision (made for drawing the *fowl*), and pass two fingers round the inside of the leg, so as to loosen the outside skin.

9. We draw this outside skin right off the legs, and press the legs well into the sides of the *fowl*, forcing the breast up to give the *fowl* a good shape.

Cooking Poultry.—Trussing Boiled Fowl. 145

10. We pull this outside skin and turn it neatly inside the *fowl* over the joints of the legs.

11. We turn the *fowl* on its breast, and draw tightly the breast skin over the incision on to the back of the neck.

12. We cross the ends of the wings over the back of the neck.

13. We now turn the *fowl* on its back with the neck towards us.

14. We take a trussing needle and thread it with fine twine.

15. We take the threaded trussing needle, and pass it through the bottom of one thigh, through the body, and out on the other side through the other thigh.

16. We must now turn the *fowl* on its breast, and take the threaded trussing needle again, and pass it through the middle of the pinion or wing, through the little bone, called the sidesman or stepmother's wing, catching up the skin which folds over the incision, and out through the other little bone and wing.

17. We must pull this twine very tightly and tie it as firmly as possible at the side of the *fowl*.

18. We turn the *fowl* over on its back, keeping the neck still towards us.

19. We put our finger in the incision (made for drawing the *fowl*), and lift up the end of the breast bone.

20. We take the threaded trussing needle and pass it through the skin over the bottom of the breast bone, over one leg, back through the body close to the back bone, and tie it firmly over the other leg at the side.

21. We take a piece of kitchen paper and butter it well.

22. We take this piece of buttered paper and wrap it well round the *fowl*.

23. We take a large saucepan half full of hot *second white stock or water*, and put it on the fire.

N.B.—The reason why second white stock should be used is that the goodness which comes from the fowl after boiling adds to the goodness of this stock, which can afterwards be used for soup.

N.B.—If hot water be used, the goodness which comes from the fowl after boiling is only wasted, as it is not of sufficient strength to make the large quantity of water of any use,

K

24. When the water is quite boiling, we place the *fowl* in the saucepan with its breast downwards.

25. We also put into the saucepan *one carrot*, which has been scraped, a small *onion*, which has been peeled, and a *bouquet of herbs* for flavouring.

26. The *fowl* will take from *three-quarters of an hour* to *one hour* to boil, according to its size.

> N.B.—We must not allow it to *boil fast*, only to *simmer*. The saucepan should be at the side of the fire.

Now we must make the *Egg Sauce* to be served with the *boiled fowl*.

1. We take a small saucepan full of *hot water*, and put it on the fire to boil.

2. When the water is quite boiling, we put in *two eggs* to boil for *ten minutes*.

3. We take a stewpan and put in it *one ounce of butter* and *one ounce of flour*.

4. We mix them well together with a wooden spoon.

5. We pour in *half a pint of milk*.

6. We put the stewpan on the fire, and stir the mixture with a wooden spoon until it boils and thickens.

7. We must then remove the stewpan to the side of the fire until required for use.

8. When the *eggs* are sufficiently boiled, we take them carefully out of the saucepan with a spoon.

9. We take the *eggs* and knock them against the edge of a basin to break off all the shell.

10. We take a small basin of *cold water*.

11. We cut the *eggs* in half and take out the *yolks*.

12. We put the *whites* into *cold water* to prevent their turning yellow.

13. We take the *whites of the eggs* out of the water and cut them to the shape of small dice.

14. We add the pieces of *white of egg* to the *sauce* in the stewpan.

Cooking Poultry.—Trussing Boiled Fowl. 147

15. We now add *one gill of cream* to the *sauce*.

16. We move the stewpan to the centre of the fire, and stir well till it boils again.

N.B.—We must be careful in stirring not to break the pieces of egg.

17. When the *fowl* is sufficiently boiled we take it out of the saucepan ; we take off the buttered paper, and place the *fowl* on a hot dish.

18. We take a knife and cut the twine, and draw it all out of the *fowl*.

19. We take the stewpan off the fire and pour the *sauce* over the *fowl*.

20. We take a wire sieve with the hard boiled *yolks* of the *eggs*, place it over the *fowl*, and rub the *yolks* through on to the breast.

N.B.—The neck, gizzard, liver, heart, and claws of the fowl (namely the *Giblets*), should be put aside, and when properly prepared can be used for soup (see "Soups," Lesson No. 6), or should be put in the *stock pot*.

N.B.—To clean and prepare the *giblets* for use.

   A. We take the *gizzard*, cut it very carefully with a knife down the centre, where there is a sort of seam (we must be sure only to cut the first or outer skin), and draw off the outer skin without breaking the inside, which should be thrown away.

   B. We take the *outer skin* of the *gizzard*, the *heart*, and *liver*, wash them well in water, and dry them in a cloth.

   C. We take the *neck*, cut off the *head*, which is of no use, draw the skin off the *neck*, and wash the latter well in water, so as to remove the blood and any impurities.

   D. We put the *claws* and ends of *legs* in a basin of boiling water for some minutes, then take a knife, cut off the *nails*, and draw off the outer *skin*, which can be pulled off like a glove.

Now it is finished.

TRUSSING A FOWL FOR ROASTING.

Average cost of "*Roasting a Fowl*" and making "*Bread Sauce.*"

INGREDIENTS.

	s.	d.
1 fowl	3	6
1 oz. of butter	0	1½
1 penny roll	0	1
1 onion	0	0½
½ pint of milk	0	1
5 peppercorns		
Salt	0	0½
1 tablespoonful of cream	0	1½
	3	11½

Time required, about three quarters of an hour.

Now we will show you how to prepare a *Fowl* and truss it for roasting.

1. We take a suitable *fowl* that has been already plucked, and put it on a board.

2. We turn the *fowl* on its breast, and make an incision of an *inch* long down the neck, *three inches* below the head.

3. We pass our thumb round this incision and loosen the *skin*.

4. We take a sharp knife and put it under the *skin*, and cut off the neck as near the body as possible.

5. We must be careful in cutting off the neck to leave a piece of *skin* to fold over on to the back of the neck and cover the opening.

6. We take out the crop which lies in the front of the neck.

7. Then with our finger we loosen the *liver* and the other parts at the breast end.

8. We must now turn the *fowl* round, and make an incision at the vent, about *one inch and a half* wide.

9. We must put our hand through this incision into the body and draw out all the interiors carefully, so as not to mess the *fowl*.

Cooking Poultry.—Trussing Roast Fowl. 149

10. We must be very careful not to break the gall bag, or the *liver* will be spoiled.

> N.B.—We take the *liver, heart,* and *gizzard,* and put them in a basin of water, with about half a teaspoonful of salt; the other interiors should be thrown away.
>
> N.B.—We should look through the fowl from one end to the other and see it is perfectly cleared out.

11. We take a damp cloth and wipe out the inside of the *fowl* to clean it thoroughly.

> N.B.—If the fowl is not quite fresh, we should use a little vinegar and water on the cloth we use for cleaning it, and then take a clean cloth and wipe it quite dry.

12. We take a sharp knife and cut off the claws from the legs of the *fowl*.

13. We take a basin of boiling water, and hold the end of the legs of the *fowl* in the water for a minute or two.

14. We then take off the outside *skin* as far as to the first joint.

15. We take a twist of paper or a taper and light it.

16. We take the *fowl* up by its legs and hold the lighted paper under it to singe off the little hairs.

17. We then hold the *fowl* up by its wings and singe the other end.

> N.B.—We must be careful in singeing not to blacken or mark the fowl in any way.

18. We turn the *fowl* on its breast, and draw tightly the breast skin over the incision on to the back of the neck.

19. We cross the ends of the wings over the back of the neck.

20. We now turn the *fowl* on its back with the neck towards us.

21. We take a trussing needle and thread it with fine twine.

22. We hold the legs up and press the thighs well into the sides of the *fowl*, forcing the breast up to give the *fowl* a good shape.

23. We take the threaded trussing needle, and pass it through the bottom of one thigh, through the body, and out on the other side through the other thigh.

> N.B.—If liked, a part of the *gizzard* and *liver* (when cleaned, see Note at the end of "Trussing a Fowl for Boiling") can be put into the *wings* of the *fowl*.

24. We must now turn the *fowl* on its breast, and take the threaded trussing needle again, and pass it through the middle of the pinion or wing, through the little bone called the sidesman or stepmother's wing, catching up the skin which folds over the incision, and out through the other little bone and wing.

25. We must pull this twine very tightly and tie it as firmly as possible at the side of the *fowl*.

26. We turn the *fowl* over on its back, keeping the neck still towards us.

27. We put our finger in the incision (made for drawing the *fowl*) and lift up the end of the breast bone.

28. We take the threaded trussing needle and pass it through the skin over the bottom of the breast bone, over the end of one leg, back through the body close to the backbone, and tie it firmly over the other leg at the side.

> N.B.—If there is no gravy ready for serving with the *roast fowl*, we should prepare it now (see Note at the end).

29. We now put the screen with the jack and dripping-pan before the fire.

30. We must make up the fire in the same manner as described in *Roasting*.

> N.B.—We do not require such a large fire as for roasting meat.

31. We take the *trussed fowl* and pass the hook of the jack through the back of the *fowl*, and hang it up on the jack.

> N.B.—If the fire is very fierce, we should take a piece of whity brown paper, butter it, and tie it over the fowl so as to prevent it from burning.

32. We put *one ounce of butter* in the dripping-pan to melt.

33. We use this melted *butter* to baste the *fowl*, as the *fowl* is not very fat, there will not be much dripping from it.

34. The *fowl* will take from *half an hour to three-quarters of an hour* to roast, according to its size.

35. We must baste the *fowl* frequently.

> N.B.—While the fowl is roasting, we should make the *bread sauce* (see below).
> N.B.—If liked, the *roast fowl* can be garnished with rolls of *bacon* (see the end of "Veal Cutlets," Entrées, Lesson No. 6).

Cooking Poultry.—Trussing Roast Fowl.

36. When the *fowl* is quite done, we take it off the jack, and put it on a hot dish.

37. We take a knife and cut the twine, and draw it all out of the *fowl*, and take off the paper before serving.

For making *Bread Sauce*.

1. We take a *French penny roll*, and cut it in half.

2. We pull out all the inside *crumb*, and put it on a plate.

3. We pull this *crumb* apart into small pieces.

> N.B.—If a French roll cannot be procured, bread crumbs can be used instead, about 1½ ounce.

4. We take a small *onion*, and peel it with an onion knife.

5. We take a small stewpan and put in it the peeled *onion*.

6. We pour in *half a pint of milk*.

7. We now put in the *crumb* of the *roll*.

8. We add *five peppercorns*, and salt to taste.

9. We stand the stewpan aside with the lid on, for a *quarter of an hour*, to soak the *crumb*.

10. After that time we put the stewpan on the fire, and stir the *sauce* smoothly with a wooden spoon, until it boils.

11. We now add a *tablespoonful of cream*, and stir the *sauce* until it just boils again.

12. Before serving the *sauce*, we must take out the *onion*, and pour the *sauce* into a sauce tureen.

> N.B.—The *neck, gizzard, liver, and claws* of the fowl, when properly prepared (see Note at the end of "Trussing a Fowl for Boiling"), can be used for soup, or gravy, to be served with the *Roast Fowl*. For making the gravy, we put the *giblets* into a saucepan with enough water to cover them (about ½ *a pint*), we also add *half on onion* (peeled), 6 *peppercorns*, and *salt* to taste. We put the saucepan on the fire, and when it comes to the boil, we move it to the side to simmer while the *fowl* is roasting.
>
> For serving, we strain the gravy into a basin and colour it, if necessary, by stirring in a quarter of a teaspoonful of "*Liebig's Extract*," or ten or twelve drops of *caramel* (see Note at the end of "Australian Meat," Lesson No. 2, "Brown Purée"), we then pour it in a sauce tureen, or round the *fowl*.

Now it is finished.

SOUPS.

Lesson No. 1.

CLEAR SOUP.

Average cost for making "*Clear Soup,*" (*to be served*) with Vegetables or Savoury Custard (*about 3 pints*).

INGREDIENTS.

	s.	d.
2 quarts of stock	2	4½
¾ lb. of gravy beef	0	9
2 carrots	0	1
2 turnips	0	1
1½ leek	0	0¾
1 cabbage lettuce	0	1
1 tablespoonful of young peas	0	1
Salt		
	3	6½

For "Savoury Custard."

1 lump of sugar		
2 eggs	0	2
Butter	0	0¼
	0	2¼

Time required (*the stock should be made the day before*), *about one hour and a half.*

Now we will show you how to make *Clear Soup.*

1. We take *two quarts of stock* (see Lesson on "Stock"); we must be careful to remove from it all fat.

2. We put the *stock* into a stewpan.

3. We take *three quarters of a pound of gravy beef* (from the shin of beef), put it on a board, and cut off all the fat and skin with a sharp knife.

4. We chop the *beef* up very fine.

> N.B.—The proportion of beef for clarifying stock is one pound to every five pounds of meat with which the stock is made.

5. We put the chopped *gravy beef* into the stewpan.

6. We take *one carrot, one turnip,* and *one leek,* and wash them well in cold water.

7. We take the *vegetables* out of the water and put them on a board.

Lessons on Making Soup.—Clear Soup. 153

8. We take a sharp knife, and scrape the *carrot* quite clean, and slice it up.

9. We take the *turnip*, peel it, and cut it in small pieces.

10. We take the *leek* and cut off part of the long green leaves, and the little straggling roots, and chop up the remainder finely.

11. We put all these vegetables into the stewpan, and stir them all well with an iron spoon, until they are well mixed with the *beef* and *stock*.

12. We put the stewpan on the fire, and stir the contents until it boils.

13. We now take a large spoon and skim it carefully.

14. We must stand the stewpan by the side of the fire, and let it simmer gently for *twenty minutes*.

15. We take a clean soup cloth and fix it on the soup stand.

16. We take a large basin and place it below the cloth.

17. We take the stewpan off the fire and pour the contents carefully into the cloth, and let it all pass into the basin.

> N.B.—The chopped gravy beef acts as a filter to the soup.

18. After the *soup* has all passed through, we remove the basin and put a clean one in its place.

19. We take a soup ladle and pour a little of the *soup* (at a time) over the *meat* in the cloth, and let it pass through very slowly.

> N.B.—We must be careful not to disturb the deposit of chopped beef, which settles at the bottom of the cloth.
>
> N.B.—If *savoury custard* should be preferred in the *soup* instead of *shredded vegetables*, see No. 31.

20. We take a small *carrot, turnip, half a leek, cabbage lettuce,* and a *tablespoonful of young peas*, and wash them in cold water.

21. We put the vegetables on a board, scrape the *carrot* clean, and peel the *turnip* with a sharp knife, and cut off all the outside leaves of the *lettuce* and the long green leaves of the *leek*.

22. We must shred the *carrot, turnip, leek*, and *cabbage lettuce* very finely in equal lengths.

23. We put the shredded *carrot, turnip,* and *leek* into a small saucepan of cold water with *half a saltspoonful of salt.*

24. We put the saucepan on the fire and let it just come to the boil.

>N.B.—This is to blanch the vegetables.

25. We take the saucepan off the fire and strain the water from the vegetables.

26. We take a stewpan, and put in the blanched vegetables and *cabbage lettuce and peas;* we add a *lump of sugar* and *half a pint* of the *clear soup.*

27. We put the stewpan on the fire to boil fast, and reduce the *soup* to a glaze over the vegetables.

28. We take the basin of strained *soup* and pour the *soup* on the vegetables in the stewpan, and let it just boil.

29. We then remove the stewpan to the side of the fire, and let it boil gently for half an hour.

30. For serving we pour the *soup* into a hot soup tureen.

For *Savoury Custard.*

31. We take the yolks of *two eggs* and the white of *one,* and put them in a small basin.

32. We add *one gill* of the *clear soup,* and a *quarter of a saltspoonful of salt.*

33. We whisk up the *eggs* and the *stock* well together.

34. We take a small gallipot and butter it inside.

35. We pour the mixture into the gallipot.

36. We take a piece of whity-brown paper and butter it.

37. We put this buttered paper over the top of the gallipot and tie it on with a piece of string.

38. We take a saucepan of hot water and put it on the fire.

39. When the water is quite boiling, we stand the little gallipot in it.

>N.B.—The water must not quite reach the paper with which the gallipot is covered.

Lessons on Making Soup.—Clear Soup. 155

40. We draw this saucepan to the side of the fire, and let it simmer for a *quarter of an hour*.

<small>N.B.—It must not boil or the custard will be spoiled.</small>

41. We take the gallipot out of the saucepan, take off the buttered paper, and turn the *custard* out on to a plate to cool.

42. We cut the *custard* into small pieces the shape of diamonds.

43. Just before serving, we pour the *soup* into the hot tureen, and add the savoury *custard* to the *soup*.

Now it is finished.

SOUPS.

Lesson No. 2.

TAPIOCA CREAM.

Average cost of "*Tapioca Cream*" (*about* 1 *pint*).

INGREDIENTS

	s.	d.
1 pint of white stock	0	7¼
1 oz. of tapioca	0	1
Yolks of 2 eggs	0	2
2 tablespoonsful of cream or good milk	0	3
Pepper and salt		
	1	1¼

Time required for making (*the stock should be made the day before*), *about a quarter of an hour.*

Now we will show you how to make *Tapioca Cream*.

1. We take *one pint of white stock* (see "Lesson on Stock,") and pour it in a stewpan.

2. We put the stewpan on the fire to boil.

3. We take *one ounce of prepared crushed tapioca*.

4. When the *white stock* boils, we stir in gradually the *tapioca*.

5. We move the saucepan to the side of the fire, and let it all simmer until the *tapioca* is quite clear.

6. Now we must prepare the *liaison*.

7. We put the *yolks of two eggs* in a basin, and add to them *two tablespoonsful of cream or good milk*.

8. We just stir it with a wooden spoon, and then pour the mixture through a strainer into another basin.

9. We now take the stewpan with the *white stock*, off the fire, and stand it on a piece of paper or wooden trivet on the table.

10. When the *stock* is cooled a little we add by degrees *two or three tablespoonsful* of it to the *liaison*, stirring well all the time.

N.B.—We must be careful that the eggs do not curdle.

11. We now add this mixture to the remainder of the *stock* in the stewpan and stir well.

12. We add *pepper* and *salt* to the *soup* according to taste.

13. We place the stewpan of *soup* on the fire to warm before serving.

    N.B.—It must not boil. For serving we pour it into a hot soup tureen.

    Now it is finished.

SOUPS

Lesson No. 3.

BONNE FEMME SOUP.

Average cost of *"Bonne Femme Soup"* (one pint and a half).

INGREDIENTS.

	s.	d.
2 lettuces	0	2
2 leaves of sorrel	0	1
4 sprigs of tarragon	0	1
4 sprigs of chervil	0	1
½ a cucumber	0	2
½ oz. of butter	0	0¼
Salt	} 0	0¼
1 saltspoonful of sugar		
1½ pint of white stock	0	10½
The yolks of 3 eggs	0	3
1 gill of cream or milk	0	6
The crust of a French roll	0	1
	2	4½

Time required, about half an hour. (The stock should be made the day before.)

Now we will show you how to make *Bonne Femme Soup.*

1. We take *two lettuces, two leaves of sorrel, four sprigs of tarragon, four sprigs of chervil,* and wash them well in cold water.

2. We take these *vegetables* and *herbs* out of the water, put them upon a board, and shred them finely.

3. We take a *cucumber* and cut it in half.

4. We peel half the *cucumber,* and cut it up in thin slices, and then shred it with a sharp knife.

5. We put *half an ounce of butter* in a stewpan, and put it on the fire to melt.

6. We place all the shredded *vegetables* and *herbs* in the stewpan to sweat for *five minutes.*

7. We sprinkle over them *half a saltspoonful of salt,* and a *saltspoonful of castor sugar.*

8. We must watch it occasionally, as the *vegetables* must not burn or in any way discolour.

Lessons on Making Soup.—Bonne Femme Soup.

9. We take a *pint and a half of white stock* (see "Lesson on Stock") and put it in another saucepan.

10. We put the saucepan on the fire to boil.

11. We must now make a "*liaison.*"

12. We take the *yolks of three eggs*, put them in a basin, and beat them well.

13. We stir in *one gill* (quarter of a pint) of cream or milk.

14. When the *stock* is quite boiling, we pour it into the stewpan with the *vegetables*, and let all boil gently for *ten minutes* until the *vegetables* are quite tender.

15. After that time we take the stewpan off the fire, and stand it on a piece of paper on the table.

16. We take a *French roll* and cut off all the *crust*.

17. We put the *crust* on a tin, and put it in the oven to dry for a minute or two.

18. When the *stock* has cooled a little, we stir in the *liaison*, straining it through a hair-sieve into the stewpan.

19. We stand the stewpan by the side of the fire to keep warm until required for use.

N.B.—We must not let it boil as, now the "*liaison*" is added, it would curdle.

20. We take the tin out of the oven and turn the dried *crust* on to a board.

21. We cut this *crust* up into small pieces, and in any fancy shape, according to taste.

22. We place these pieces of crust in a hot soup tureen and pour the soup over them.

Now it is finished.

SOUPS.

Lesson No. 4.

PURÉE OF POTATOES.

Average cost for making a "*Purée of Potatoes*" (about 1 *pint and a half.*)

INGREDIENTS.

	s.	d.
1 lb. of potatoes	0	1
1 small onion	0	0½
2 leaves of celery	0	1
1 oz. of butter	0	1½
1½ pint of white stock	0	10½
Salt		
1 gill of cream	0	6
Fried bread	0	2
	1	10½

Time required (the stock should be made the day before), about three-quarters of an hour.

Now we will show you how to make a *Purée of Potatoes*.

1. We take *one pound of potatoes*, put them in a basin of cold water and scrub them clean with a scrubbing brush.

2. We take a sharp knife and peel the *potatoes*, and cut them in thin slices.

3. We take a *small onion*, wash it well in cold water, and peel it.

4. We take *two leaves of celery* and wash them.

5. We take a stewpan and put in it *one ounce of butter*.

6. We now add the sliced *potatoes*, the *onion*, and the *celery*.

7. We put the stewpan on the fire and let the *vegetables* sweat for *five minutes;* we must take care that they do not discolour.

8. We pour into the stewpan *one pint of white stock* and stir frequently with a wooden spoon to prevent it from burning.

Lessons on Making Soup.—Purée of Potatoes.

9. We let it boil gently till the *vegetables* are quite cooked.

10. We put *half a pint of white stock* into a stewpan and put it on the fire to heat.

11. We now place a tammy-sieve over a basin and pass the contents of the stewpan through the sieve with a wooden spoon, adding by degrees the *half pint of hot white stock*, which will enable it to pass through more easily.

12. We take the stewpan and wash it out.

13. We pour the *Purée* back into the stewpan.

14. We add *salt* according to taste, and *one gill* (quarter of a pint) *of cream* and stir smoothly with a wooden spoon until it boils.

15. For serving we pour it into a hot soup tureen.

N.B.—Fried bread cut in the shape of dice should be served with the purée (see "Vegetables," Lesson No. 8, from Note 13 to 17).

Now it is finished.

SOUPS.

LESSON No. 5.

SPRING VEGETABLE SOUP.

Average cost of "*Spring Vegetable Soup*" (two quarts).

INGREDIENTS.

	s.	d.
2 lbs. of the shin of beef	1	0
2 lbs. of the knuckle of veal	1	0
Salt }	0	1
2 young carrots }		
1 young turnip	0	0½
1 leek	0	0½
½ of a head of celery	0	1
1 cauliflower	0	4
1 gill of peas }	0	3
¼ of a saltspoonful of carbonate of soda }		
	2	10

Time required for making, about five hours.

Now we will show you how to make *two quarts of Spring Vegetable Soup*.

1. We take *two pounds of shin of beef*, and *two pounds of knuckle of veal*, and put them on a board.

2. We must cut off all the *meat* from the *bone* with a sharp knife.

3. We cut off all the *fat* from the *meat* (the *fat* we put aside for other purposes).

4. We take a chopper and break the *bones* in halves.

5. We take out all the *marrow* inside the *bones*, and put it aside for other uses.

> N.B.—If the fat and marrow were to go into the soup they would make it greasy.

6. We take a stockpot or a large stewpan, and put the *meat* and *bones* into it.

7. We pour in *five pints of cold water*.

8. We put in a *teaspoonful of salt*. This will assist the *scum* to rise.

Lessons on Making Soup.—Spring Vegetable Soup.

9. We put the stockpot on the fire, with the lid on, and let it come to the boil quickly.

10. We take a spoon and remove all the *scum* as it rises.

11. We now draw the stockpot rather to the side of the fire and let it simmer gently for *five hours*.

12. We take *two young carrots*, scrape them clean with a knife, and cut them in *slices*.

13. We take *one young turnip*, peel it, and cut it in *slices*.

14. We take *half a head of celery* and *one leek*, wash them well in cold water, and cut them in *squares* with a knife.

15. We take *one cauliflower*, wash it in cold water, and put it in a basin of cold water, with a *dessertspoonful of salt*, for two or three minutes.

16. We then take the *cauliflower* out of the water, and squeeze it dry in a cloth.

17. We take a knife and cut off all the green leaves and the stalk from the *cauliflower*, and pull the flower into sprigs.

18. We must watch and skim the *soup* occasionally, and we should add a little cold water to make the *scum* rise.

19. One hour before serving the *soup* we should add the *vegetables*.

20. We must first put in the sliced *carrots*, and the cut up *celery* and *leek*. (These vegetables take the longest to boil.)

21. In half an hour we should add the sliced *turnips*, and fifteen minutes after that the cut up flower of the *cauliflower*.

22. We take a saucepan full of hot water, and put it on the fire to boil.

23. When the water is quite boiling, we put in *one gill of shelled peas*, a *teaspoonful of salt*, and a *quarter of a saltspoonful of carbonate of soda*, and let it boil from *fifteen to twenty minutes*, according to the age of the peas.

N.B.—The cover should be off the saucepan

24. After that time we should feel the *peas*, and if they are quite soft we take them out of the saucepan and drain them in a cullender.

25. For serving, we put the boiled peas into a hot soup tureen, and ladle the *soup* and the other *vegetables* from the stockpot out into the tureen.

Now it is finished.

SOUPS.

Lesson No. 6.

GIBLET SOUP.

Average cost of "*Giblet Soup*" (about three pints).

INGREDIENTS.

	s.	d.
2 sets of giblets............................	2	0
¼ of a head of celery........................	0	1
1 carrot	0	0½
1 turnip	0	0½
2 small onions	0	0½
2 cloves		
1 blade of mace............................		
A bouquet garnie of parsley, thyme, lemon-thyme, basil, marjoram and bay leaf ..	0	1
2 quarts of second white stock	1	2½
1½ oz. of clarified butter	0	1¾
1 oz. of flour	0	0¼
½ a pint of Madeira	1	8
30 drops of lemon juice	0	1
A few grains of Cayenne pepper		
Salt	0	0¼
	5	5

(*Stock made the day before*). *Time required, about three hours and a half.*

Now we will show you how to make *Giblet Soup.*

1. We take *two sets of goose* or *four of ducks' giblets*, scald and skin the *claws, ends of legs,* &c., and wash them clean in cold water (see Note for "Cleaning Giblets" at the end of "Trussing a Fowl for Boiling").

2. We should put them into boiling water to blanch them, for *five minutes.*

3. We then lay them in a basin of cold water, and wash and scrape them clean.

4. We take them out of the water and drain them.

5. We take a knife and cut the *giblets* in pieces to about *one and a half inch* in length.

6. We put the pieces of *giblet* into a stewpan.

7. We take a *quarter of a head of celery* and wash it well in cold water.

166. National Training School for Cookery.

8. We take *one carrot*, wash it in cold water, and scrape it clean with a knife.

9. We take *one turnip* and *two small onions*, wash them in cold water and peel them.

10. We add these *vegetables* to the *giblets* in the stewpan.

11. We also put in *two cloves, one blade of mace*, and a *bouquet garni*, consisting of *parsley, one sprig of thyme, lemon-thyme, basil, marjoram*, and *one bay-leaf*, all tied tightly together.

12. We pour in *two quarts of second white stock*.

13. We put the stewpan on the fire, and let it boil gently for *two hours;* we must skim it occasionally.

14. After that time, we take out the best pieces of the *giblets*, and trim them neatly.

15. We put these pieces aside until required for use.

16. We leave the stewpan on the fire to boil for *half an hour*.

17. We put *an ounce and a half of clarified butter*, and *one ounce of flour* into a stewpan.

18. We put the stewpan on the fire, and let the *flour* and *butter* fry for a few minutes, stirring it well with a wooden spoon.

19. We now add the *stock* and stir it well until it boils.

20. We must now remove the stewpan to the side of the fire, and let it boil gently for *twenty minutes* (the cover of the saucepan should be only half on).

21. After that time, we take a spoon and carefully skim off all the *butter* that will have risen to the top of the *soup*.

22. We now strain the *soup* into a basin, add to it *half a pint of Madeira, thirty drops of lemon juice*, a few grains (just enough to cover thinly a *threepenny piece*) of Cayenne pepper, and *salt* according to taste.

23. For serving, we pour the *soup* into a hot soup tureen, and add to it the pieces of *giblet* that were put aside.

N.B.—If the *wine* is disliked, it may be omitted.

Now it is finished.

SOUPS.

Lesson No. 7.

MOCK TURTLE SOUP.

Average cost of "*Mock Turtle Soup*" (about two quarts).

INGREDIENTS.

	s.	d.
½ a calf's head	5	0
3 oz. of butter .... ⎱ ½ a tablespoonful of salt .... ⎰	0	4
¼ lb. of lean ham	0	4
1 shalot .... ⎱ 1 clove of garlic .... ⎰	0	0½
6 mushrooms	0	4
1 carrot .... ⎱ ½ head of celery .... ⎥ 1 leek .... ⎥ 1 onion .... ⎥ ½ a turnip .... ⎬ Bouquet garni (*i. e.* sprig of thyme, marjoram, parsley, and a bay leaf) .... ⎥ 1 blade of mace .... ⎥ 6 cloves .... ⎥ 3 oz. of flour .... ⎰	0	4
2 wine glasses of sherry	0	8
The juice of ½ a lemon	0	1
1 dozen forcemeat balls (see "Entrées," Lesson No. 8)	0	4¼
	7	5¾

Time required, about six hours.

N.B.—If the soup is required to be made in one day, the stock should be made early in the morning, so as to give time for it to get cold to have the fat removed.

Now we will show you how to make *Mock Turtle Soup*.

1. We take *half a calf's head*, and wash it well in water, to remove all blood and impurities.

2. We cut all the *flesh* from the *bones*, and tie the *flesh* up in a very clean cloth or napkin.

3. We put it in a large stewpan with the *bones* and *four quarts of cold water*, and *half a tablespoonful of salt*.

4. We put the stewpan on the fire, and let it come to the boil.

5. As soon as it boils, we should skim it carefully with a spoon, and move the stewpan to the side of the fire to stew gently for *three hours*.

N.B.—We should watch it and skim it occasionally.

6. After that time we take out the *calf's head*, and pour the *stock* through a strainer into a basin.

7. We stand the basin of *stock* aside to get cold, when we should carefully remove every particle of *fat* from the top of the *stock*.

8. We must now make some *forcemeat* (see "Beef Olives," Entrées, Lesson No. 8, from Note 4 to Note 12). and make it up into little balls, about *one dozen*.

9. We take *six mushrooms* (cut off the end of the stalks), *one onion*, and *half a turnip*, wash them, peel them, and cut them up in slices.

10. We take *one carrot*, wash it, scrape it clean, and cut it in slices.

11. We take *half a head of celery*, and *one leek*, wash them, cut off the long green leaves (to be thrown away), and cut them in slices.

12. We put a *quarter of a pound of lean ham* on a board, and cut it up in small pieces.

13. We put *one ounce of butter* in a stewpan, and put it on the fire to melt.

14. We add the *ham* and all the *sliced vegetables* to the *butter* in the stewpan.

15. We also add one *shalot* (peeled), *one clove of garlic*, *one blade of mace, six cloves*, and a *bouquet garni* (consisting of a *sprig of thyme, marjoram, parsley*, and a *bay leaf*, tied tightly together).

16. We let all these *vegetables* and *herbs*, &c., fry in the *butter* for *ten minutes*. We must stir them occasionally.

17. After that time we add *three ounces of flour*, and stir well.

18. We now add the *stock* and stir it until it boils, then move the stewpan to the side of the fire, and let it simmer for about *ten minutes*.

19. We must then take a spoon and remove every particle of scum.

20. We now strain the *soup* into another stewpan.

21. We take the *calf's head* out of the cloth, and cut it up in small and neat pieces.

22. We add the pieces of *calf's head* to the *soup*, also *two wine glasses of sherry*, the *dozen forcemeat balls*, and squeeze in through a strainer the *juice of half a lemon*.

23. We let the *soup* just come to the boil, and then pour it in a hot soup tureen for serving.

Now it is finished.

SOUPS.

Lesson No. 8.

POT-AU-FEU OR SOUP.

And use of Meat from which the Soup has been made.

Average cost of "*Pot-au-feu,*" consisting of about *five quarts of soup*, and a *dish of meat with vegetables.*

INGREDIENTS.

	s.	d.
4 lbs. of beef, or 4 lbs. of the meat off the ox cheek	2	0
Sago or tapioca for soup	0	0½
½ oz. salt, 2 turnips	0	1
2 carrots	0	1
2 leeks	0	1
1 parsnip	0	1
1 small head of celery	0	2
2 or 3 sprigs of parsley	0	0½
1 cabbage	0	1
1 bay-leaf, thyme and marjoram, and 1 onion, stuck with 3 cloves	0	1
	2	9

Time required, about four hours.

Now we will show you how to make *Pot-au-feu.*

1. We put *six quarts of water* in a large pot.

2. We take *four pounds of the sticking piece of beef*, or *four pounds* of the meat off the *ox cheek*, without any bone, tie it up firmly into a shape with a piece of string, and put it into the pot.

3. We put the pot on the fire to boil.

4. When the water is quite boiling we put in *half an ounce of salt*, and then move the pot to the side of the fire to simmer.

5. We take *two carrots, two leeks, two turnips, one parsnip, one small head of celery*, and wash them well in cold water.

6. We scrape the *carrots* and the *parsnip*, and cut them in quarters with a knife.

Lessons on Making Soup.—Pot-au-Feu or Soup.

7. We take the *leeks* and cut off the long *green leaves*, as only the *white part* is required.

8. We take the *head of celery* and cut off the *green tops* of the *leaves*.

9. We tie the *leeks*, the *celery*, and the *parsnip* and *carrot* together with a piece of string.

10. We take a *cabbage*, cut it in two, and wash it thoroughly in cold water, and tie it firmly together with string.

11. We should skim the *Pot-au-feu* occasionally with a spoon.

12. When the *Pot-au-feu* has boiled very gently for *one hour*, we add to it all the *vegetables*, except the *cabbage*.

13. We take *one bay-leaf*, a *sprig of parsley*, a *sprig of thyme*, a *sprig of marjoram*, and tie them together with a piece of string.

14. We put these *herbs* into the pot.

15. We take *one onion*, peel it, and stick *three cloves* in it.

16. We put the *onion* into the pot.

17. When the *vegetables* have been *two hours* in the pot we put in the *cabbage*.

18. When the contents of the pot has simmered gently for *four hours*, we take out the *meat* and put it on a hot dish.

19. We garnish the *meat* with the *carrots*, *turnips*, and *parsnips*, and pour over it about half a pint of the *liquor* for gravy.

20. We take out the *cabbage* and serve it in a hot vegetable dish.

21. We strain the *liquor* through a cullender or cloth into a basin, and put it by to cool.

22. We do not remove the fat until the liquor is required for use; it keeps the air from it.

To make a soup of the *liquor*.

23. We put *two quarts* of the *liquor* in a saucepan, and put it on the fire to boil.

24. We take *two ounces of crushed tapioca* or *small sago*, and when the *liquor* boils we sprinkle in the *tapioca* or *sago*, and let it boil for *fifteen minutes*, stirring occasionally.

25. We then pour it into a soup-tureen, and it is ready for use.

N.B.—If liked, *Beef à-la-mode*, or *rissoles* (see "Cooked Meat," Lesson No. 6), can be made with the *meat* from the *pot-au-feu*.

For "*Beef à-la-mode.*"

1. We put *two ounces of dripping* into a saucepan and put it on the fire to melt.

2. We then stir in *one tablespoonful of flour*.

3. We take *one pound and a half* of the *meat* and cut it in neat pieces.

4. We put these *pieces* of *meat* into the saucepan.

5. When it comes to the boil we turn over the *slices* of *meat* and pour in *half a pint of cold water*.

6. We take *one carrot*, wash it, scrape it clean and cut it in slices.

7. We put the *carrot* into the saucepan; we also add a *bunch of herbs*, namely, a sprig of *marjoram* and *thyme*, and a *bay-leaf*, tied tightly together.

8. We let it just come to the boil and then move the saucepan to the side of the fire and let it simmer gently for *three hours*.

9. We should watch it and stir it occasionally.

10. For serving, we turn the *meat* on to a hot dish, and place the *carrot* on the top of the *meat*.

Now it is finished.

SOUPS.

Lesson No. 9.

DR. KITCHENER'S BROTH.

Average cost of "*Dr. Kitchener's Broth*" (about 5 quarts).

INGREDIENTS.

	d.
4 oz. of Scotch barley	1
4 oz. of sliced onions	1
2 oz. of dripping	1
3 oz. of bacon	1½
4 oz. of oatmeal	
Pepper and salt	} 1
5 quarts of liquor	
	5½

Time required, about two hours.

Now we will show you how to make *Dr. Kitchener's Broth*.

1. We take *four ounces of Scotch barley*, wash it well, and let it soak in a basin of cold water for *two hours*.

2. We put *five quarts of liquor* into a saucepan, and put it on the fire to boil.

3. We take *two or three onions*, peel them, and cut them in slices. (There should be about *four ounces*.)

4. We drain off the *barley* and put it and the *onions* into the *liquor*, and let it boil gently for *one hour*.

5. We put *three ounces of bacon* into another saucepan with *two ounces of clarified dripping*.

6. We put the saucepan on the fire to fry the *bacon* brown.

7. We then add by degrees *four ounces of oatmeal*, stirring it well until it is a paste.

8. We now stir in by degrees the *broth*, and season it with *pepper* and *salt* according to taste.

9. We move the saucepan to the side of the fire, and let it simmer gently for at least *half an hour*.

10. For serving we pour the *broth* into a hot soup tureen or basin.

Now it is finished.

SOUPS.

LESSON No. 10.

CROWDIE.

Average cost of "*Crowdie*" or "*Scotch Broth*," made with liquor from boiled meat.

INGREDIENTS.

	d.
2 gallons of liquor from meat	
½ pint of oatmeal	0½
2 onions	1
Salt and pepper	0¼
	1¾

Time required, half an hour.

Now we will show you how to make *Crowdie*, or *Scotch Broth*.

1. We take *two gallons* of any *meat liquor*, either *salt* or *fresh*, remove all the *fat* from it, and put it into a saucepan.

2. We put the saucepan on the fire to boil.

3. We take *half a pint of oatmeal*, put it in a basin, and mix it into a smooth paste, with about *a gill* (a quarter of a pint) of the *liquor*.

N.B.—*Half a pint of oatmeal* is sufficient to thicken *two gallons of liquor*.

4. We take *two onions*, peel them, put them on a board, and chop them up as finely as possible.

5. We stir the *chopped onions* into the *paste*, and add *salt* and *pepper* to taste.

N.B.—If *salt liquor* is used, *salt* should not be added.

6. When the *liquor* in the saucepan is quite boiling, we stir in the *paste* smoothly.

7. We let it boil for *twenty minutes;* we should stir it occasionally; it must not get lumpy.

8. For serving, we pour it into a soup tureen or basin.

Now it is finished.

SOUPS.

Lesson No. 11.

MILK SOUP.

Average cost of "*Milk Soup*" (about two quarts).

INGREDIENTS.

	d.
4 potatoes	2
2 leeks or onions	1
2 oz. butter	2
¼ oz. salt	} 0¼
Pepper	
1 pint of milk	2
3 tablespoonsful of tapioca	1½
	8¾

Time required, about two hours and a half.

Now we will show you how to make *Milk Soup*.

1. We put *two quarts of water* into a large saucepan, and put it on the fire to boil.

2. We take *four large potatoes*, wash and scrub them clean in cold water, peel them, and cut them in quarters.

3. We take *two leeks*, cut off the *green tops* of the *leaves*, wash them well in cold water, and cut them up.

> N.B.—*Onions* can be used instead of *leeks*, only they would give a stronger flavour.

4. When the water is quite boiling we put in the *potatoes* and *leeks*.

5. We put in *two ounces of butter, a quarter of an ounce of salt*, and *pepper* to taste.

6. We let it boil till done to a mash.

7. We then strain off the *soup* through the cullender.

8. We rub the *vegetables* through the cullender with a wooden spoon.

9. We return the *pulp* and the *soup* to the saucepan, add *one pint of milk* to it, and put it on the fire to boil.

10. When it boils we sprinkle in by degrees *three table-spoonsful* of *crushed tapioca*, stirring it well the whole time.

11. We let it boil gently *fifteen minutes*.

12. For serving, we pour the *soup* in a hot tureen.

Now it is finished.

SOUPS.

Lesson No. 12.

CABBAGE SOUP.

Average cost of making "*Cabbage Soup*" (about one quart and a half).

INGREDIENTS.

	d.
1 cabbage..................................	2
2 oz. butter	2¼
¾ of a pint of milk	2
Pepper and salt .... }	0½
A slice of bread .... }	
	6¾

Time required, about one hour and a quarter.

Now we will show you how to make *Cabbage Soup*.

1. We put *three pints* of water into a saucepan, and put it on the fire to boil.

2. We take a good sized *cabbage*, wash it well in cold water, and trim off the outside dead leaves.

3. We cut the *cabbage* up, as we cut a lettuce up for a salad, but not into small pieces.

4. When the water in the saucepan is quite boiling we put in the *cabbage*.

5. We also add *two ounces of butter*, and *pepper* and *salt* for seasoning, and let it boil for *one hour*.

6. After that time we pour in *three quarters of a pint of milk*, and let it boil up.

7. We take a *slice of bread*, stick it on a toasting fork, and toast it slightly on both sides in front of the fire.

8. We cut the *toasted bread* up in pieces, the size of dice, and put them into a hot soup tureen or basin.

9. We pour the *cabbage soup* on to the *bread* in the soup tureen, and it is ready for serving.

Now it is finished.

SOUPS.

Lesson No. 13.

PEA SOUP.

Average cost of "*Pea Soup*" (about 2 quarts).

INGREDIENTS.

	d.
1 quart of split peas	5
2 onions	1
1 turnip	0½
1 carrot	0½
1 head of celery	2
Teaspoonful of salt ½ a teaspoonful of pepper	0½
Cooked or uncooked bones	2
	11½

Time required (after the peas have been soaked all night), about two hours and a half.

Now we will show you how to make *Pea Soup*.

1. We put a *quart* of *split peas* into a basin with cold water to cover them, and let them soak for *twelve hours*.

N.B.—This should be done over night.

2. We put *two quarts* of cold water and the *split peas* into a saucepan, and put it on the fire to boil.

N.B.—If there is any liquor from boiled meat it would of course be better than water for the soup.

3. We take *two onions* and *one turnip*, wash them in cold water, peel them, and cut them in halves.

4. We take *one carrot*, wash it, and scrape it clean with a knife.

5. We take *one head of celery*, cut off the ends of the root, and wash it well in cold water.

6. When the water in the saucepan is boiling we put in all the *vegetables*.

7. We add *twopennyworth* of *cooked or uncooked bones*, and season it with *one teaspoonful of salt* and *half a teaspoonful of ground pepper*.

N.B.—If some liquor (in which meat or pork has been boiled) is used the addition of bones will not then be necessary.

Lessons on Making Soup.—Pea Soup. 179

8. We let it all boil slowly for *two hours*, and we must watch it and skim it occasionally.

9. After that time we take the *bones* out of the saucepan.

10. We place a cullender or wire sieve over a basin.

11. We pour the contents of the saucepan into the cullender, and rub them through into the basin with a wooden spoon.

12. The *pea soup* is then ready for serving.

13. *Powdered* (*dried*) *mint*, and *toasted bread*, cut to the shape of dice, should be handed with the *soup*, either put in, or served separately on plates.

Now it is finished.

SOUPS.

LESSON No. 14.

GERMAN PEA SOUP.

Average cost of "*German Pea Soup*" (about three pints) made without Meat.

INGREDIENTS.

¼ of a stick of German pea soup sausage (to be bought at 8*d*. the stick).................... 2*d*.
3 pints of water

Time required, about a quarter of an hour.

Now we will show you how to make *Pea Soup* from the German *pea soup sausage*.

1. We put *three pints* of warm water into a saucepan, and put it on the fire to boil.

2. We take *a quarter of a stick of German pea soup sausage*, and scrape it into a basin.

3. We add to it a very little warm water, let it soak, and then mix it into a smooth paste.

N.B.—We must be very careful that there are no lumps in the *paste*.

4. When the water in the saucepan is quite boiling, we should stir the *paste* in smoothly.

5. It is now ready for use and should be poured into a hot soup tureen.

N.B.—If the soup is preferred thinner, more water might be added.

N.B.—*A dessert-spoonful of chopped mint* might be added to the *soup*, if the flavour is liked.

Now it is finished.

SOUPS.

Lesson No. 15.

MACARONI SOUP.

Average cost of "*Macaroni Soup*" *made from Bones*
(about 3 pints).

INGREDIENTS.

	d.
Bones (if bought)	2
1 tablespoonful of salt and peppercorns .... ⎫ 1 good-sized turnip and 4 leeks .... ⎭	$1\frac{1}{2}$
2 carrots	1
4 onions, 2 cloves, and a blade of mace	2
A bunch of herbs, *i.e.* marjoram, thyme, lemon ⎫ thyme, and parsley...................... ⎭	$0\frac{1}{2}$
¼ lb. of macaroni............................	$1\frac{1}{4}$
	$8\frac{1}{4}$

Time required, about two and a half hours.

Now we will show you how to make *Soup* from *Bones*.

1. We take the *bones* and cut off all the *meat* that can be used.

N.B.—Cooked or uncooked bones can be used.

2. We break up the *bones* in pieces and put them into a saucepan, with *cold water* enough to cover them, and *one quart* more.

3. We put the saucepan on the fire to boil.

4. When it just boils, we put in a *tablespoonful of salt*, to help the scum to rise.

5. We take *one good-sized turnip*, peel it, and cut it in quarters.

N.B.—When turnips are used only for flavouring, they can be peeled thinner than if for eating.

6. We take *two carrots*, wash them, scrape them, and cut them in quarters; we take *four leeks*, wash them, and shred them up finely.

N.B.—As these vegetables are prepared, they should be thrown into cold water to keep them fresh.

7. We take *four onions*, peel them, and stick *two cloves* into the *onions*.

> N.B.—The outer skins of the onions can be put into a saucepan by the side of the fire to brown; when browned, they are useful for colouring gravies and soups.

8. We should skim the *soup* well and then put in the *vegetables;* we also add a blade of *mace* and a *teaspoonful of peppercorns*.

9. We must move the saucepan to the side of the fire, and let it simmer gently for *two hours and a half*.

10. We should raise the lid slightly to let out the steam.

> N.B.—The soup can be thickened with macaroni, vermicelli, barley or rice.

11. If the *soup* is thickened with *macaroni*, we take *a quarter of a pound of macaroni* and wash it well in two or three waters.

12. We put the *macaroni* into a saucepan with plenty of cold water, and sprinkle a little *salt* over it.

13. We put the saucepan on the fire, and let it boil until the *macaroni* is quite tender; it will take about *half an hour*.

14. We should feel the *macaroni* with our fingers to see that it is quite soft and tender.

15. When it is sufficiently boiled, we strain the water off and pour some cold water on it, and wash the *macaroni* again.

16. We put the *macaroni* on a board, and cut it into small pieces about *a quarter of an inch* in length, it is then ready to be put into the *soup*.

> N.B.—If barley is used instead of macaroni, it will take a much longer time to boil, but if vermicelli is used, it takes a very short time to boil.

17. When the *soup* is ready for use, we should put the *macaroni* into a soup tureen and strain the hot *soup* over it.

> N.B.—It is better to boil macaroni separately as the first water is not clean.

Now it is finished.

STOCK.

Average cost of *brown or white " Stock" for soup* (about two quarts).

INGREDIENTS.

	s.	d.
4 lbs. of shin of beef, or 2 lbs. of knuckle of veal and 2 lbs of beef	2	0
4 young carrots or 2 old ones	0	2
1 turnip	0	0½
1 onion	0	0½
1 leek	0	0½
Half a head of celery	0	1
Salt		
	2	4½

Time required, about five hours.

Now we will show you how to make *Stock* for soup. It should be made the day before it is required for use.

1. We take *four pounds of shin of beef* and put it on a board.

2. We must cut off all the *meat* from the bone with a sharp knife.

3. We cut off all the *fat* from the *meat*. (The *fat* we put aside for other purposes.)

4. We take a chopper and break the bone in half.

5. We take out all the *marrow* inside the bone, and put it aside for other uses.

> N.B.—If the fat and marrow were to go into the stock it would make it greasy.

6. We take a stockpot or a large stewpan, and put the *meat* and *bone* into it.

7. We pour in *five pints of cold water*.

> N.B.—*One pint of water* is allowed for *each pound of meat* and *one pint* over.

8. We put in *half a teaspoonful of salt*. This will assist the scum to rise.

9. We put the stockpot on the fire with the lid on, and let it come to the boil quickly.

10. We take *four young carrots*, scrape them clean with a knife, and cut them in pieces.

11. We take *one turnip* and *one onion*, peel them and cut them in quarters.

12. We take a *leek* and *half a head of celery* and wash them well in cold water.

13. We take a spoon and remove the scum from the *stock* as it rises.

14. Now we put in all the *vegetables*, and let it simmer gently for *five hours*.

15. We must watch and skim it occasionally, and we should add a little *cold water* to make the scum rise.

16. We take a clean cloth and put it over a good-sized basin.

17. We put a hair-sieve on the top of the cloth over the basin.

18. When the *stock* has been simmering for *five hours* we take the stockpot off the fire.

19. We pour the contents into the sieve, which contains the *meat, bone,* and *vegetables ;* and the cloth very effectually strains the *stock*.

> N.B.—The meat and bone can be used again for second stock, with the addition of fresh vegetables and water.

20. We take the basin (into which the *stock* has been strained), and put it in a cool place till the next day, when it will be a stiff jelly.

21. When this *stock* jelly is required for use, we must take off the *fat* from the top with a spoon.

22. We take a clean cloth and dip it in hot water, and wipe over the top of the jelly so as to remove every particle of fat.

23. Now we must take a clean dry cloth and wipe the top of the jelly dry.

> N.B.—For some soups, vegetable soups, or purées, white stock is required. White stock is made in the same way, only with veal instead of beef, and it can also be made of veal and beef mixed, or rabbit and beef, but veal alone is considered best.

Now it is finished.

VEGETABLE STOCK.

Average cost of "*Vegetable Stock*" (about two quarts).

INGREDIENTS.

	d.
1 cabbage	1
3 large or 6 small onions	1½
2 carrots	1
1 turnip	0½
2 oz. of butter	2¼
3 cloves	
30 peppercorns	
A bunch of herbs (thyme, marjoram, and a bay-leaf)	0¼
Salt	
	6½

Time required, about two hours and a quarter.

Now we will show you how to make *Vegetable Stock*.

1. We take *one cabbage*, wash it well in cold water, and cut it in quarters.

2. We take *two carrots*, wash them, scrape them clean, and cut them in quarters.

3. We take *one turnip*, peel it, and cut it in quarters.

4. We take *three large* or *six small onions*, and wash them clean (the *skins* are to be left on).

5. We put all these *vegetables* into a saucepan, with *two ounces of butter*.

6. We also add a *bunch of herbs* (namely, a *sprig of thyme, marjoram*, and a *bay-leaf*) tied tightly together, *three cloves* and *thirty peppercorns*.

7. We put the saucepan on the fire, and let the *vegetables* and *herbs* sweat in the *butter* for *ten minutes*. We must stir them and not let them burn.

8. We now pour in *three quarts of cold water*, and add *salt* according to taste.

9. When the *water* boils we move the saucepan to the side of the fire and let it simmer gently for *two hours*. We must watch it and skim it occasionally.

10. After that time we strain the *stock* into a basin, and it is ready for use. It is now reduced to *two quarts and half a pint*.

N.B.—This *stock* can be used for *thick vegetable soups*.

Now it is finished.

FISH.

Lesson No. 1.
BOILED TURBOT AND LOBSTER SAUCE.

<small>Turbot varies in price considerably.</small>

Average cost of ingredients for "*Lobster Sauce.*"

INGREDIENTS.

	s.	d.
Lobster	2	0
2 oz. of butter	0	2¼
1 tablespoonful of cream.................	0	1½
½ an oz. of flour........................	0	0¼
	2	**4**

Time required, about half an hour.

Now we will show you how to boil *Turbot* and make *Lobster Sauce.*

1. We take the *turbot.*

2. We put it in a basin of cold water and wash it well.

3. We get a fishkettle and fill it with cold water, add to it as much *salt* as will make the water taste salt, and put it on the fire to boil.

4. We take the *turbot* out of the basin.

5. We put it on the drainer of the fishkettle, and put it in the kettle of boiling water, so that it is well covered with water.

6. We let it boil for *twenty minutes or half an hour.*

7. We must watch it and skim the water if necessary.

<small>N.B.—While the *turbot* is boiling, we should make the *lobster sauce* (see below).</small>

8. When the *fish* is sufficiently boiled, the flesh will divide from the bone.

9. Now we take the drainer carefully out of the fishkettle, stand it across the kettle a *minute* to drain, and slip the fish carefully on to a hot dish for serving.

For *Lobster Sauce.*

1. We take a small *lobster*—it should be a hen *lobster* if possible.

2. We put the *lobster* on a board.

3. We take a chopper and break the shell of the *lobster* by hitting it with the blade of the chopper, not with the edge; 1st because it would cut the *lobster* in pieces, and 2nd because it would spoil the edge of the chopper.

4. We break all the shell off the claws and back with our fingers and take out all the flesh.

5. We cut this flesh up with a sharp knife to the size of small dice.

6. If the *lobster* is a hen *lobster* we shall find a bit of *coral* in the neck, and a strip of it down the back.

7. We take all this *coral* out of the *lobster* and wash it carefully in cold water in a small basin.

8. We take the *coral* out of the basin and put it in a mortar with *one ounce of butter*.

9. We pound the *coral* and the *butter* well with the pestle.

10. We take it out of the mortar, and scrape the mortar out quite clean with a palette knife, for none must be lost.

11. If we have not a palette knife we can manage as well with a piece of uncooked potato cut into the shape of a knife blade with a thick back, with this we can scrape all out of the mortar.

12. We take a hair sieve and put it over a plate.

13. We rub the pounded *mixture* through the sieve with the back of a wooden spoon.

14. We must turn up the sieve when all the *mixture* has passed through, and we shall find some sticking on the underneath part.

15. We scrape all this carefully off with the spoon.

16. We make it all into a little pat.

17. We take a stewpan and put in it *one ounce of butter* and *half an ounce of flour*.

Lessons on Cooking Fish.—Lobster Sauce.

18. We mix them well together with a wooden spoon.

19. We add *one gill and a half* (one gill is quarter of a pint) of *cold water*.

20. We put the stewpan on the fire.

21. We stir the *mixture* smooth with a wooden spoon until it boils and thickens. We add a large *tablespoonful of cream*, and stir well till it boils again.

22. We then take the stewpan off the fire and stand it on a piece of paper on the table.

23. We add to the *mixture* in the stewpan the pat of *coral butter* by degrees to colour it.

N.B.—If there is no coral, the sauce might be coloured with *half a teaspoonful of essence of anchovy*.

24. We stir it quite smoothly with a wooden spoon, it must not be lumpy.

25. We now add *pepper* and *salt* and a *few grains of cayenne pepper*, according to taste.

26. We take the chopped *lobster* and mix it into the *sauce*, and add a little *lemon juice*.

27. We pour the *sauce* into a sauceboat, and serve it with the *turbot*.

Now it is finished.

FISH.

LESSON No. 2.

FISH PUDDING.

Average cost of "*Fish Pudding and Egg Sauce.*"

INGREDIENTS.

"Haddock."	s.	d.	"Sauce."	d.
Haddock	1	0	2 oz. of butter	2½
2 lbs. of potatoes	0	2	½ oz. of flour..................	0¼
3 oz. butter	0	3¼	½ gill of cream	3
1 egg	0	1	2 eggs and salt..................	2
	1	6¼		7¾

Time required, about one hour and a half.

Now we will show you how to make a *Fish Pudding* of a *Haddock*.

N.B.—Any *cold boiled fish* can be used for the *fish pudding*, instead of *haddock*.

1. We take a fishkettle of warm water, and we put in it a little *salt*, and put it on the fire to boil.

2. We take a *haddock*, and put it into a basin of cold water and wash it well.

3. We take the *haddock* out of the basin and put it into the fishkettle of boiling water, laying it carefully on the drainer so that it is well covered with water.

4. We let it simmer for *fifteen minutes*.

5. We take *six potatoes*, put them into a basin of cold water, and scrub them well with a scrubbing-brush.

N.B.—Any *cold potatoes* can of course be used instead of boiling fresh ones.

6. We take the *potatoes* out of the basin, and dry them with a cloth.

7. We take a sharp knife and peel the *potatoes*.

8. We take a saucepan of cold water, and lay the *potatoes* in it.

9. We put the saucepan on the fire to boil. It must not boil less than *twenty minutes*, or more than *three-quarters of an hour*, according to the size of the *potatoes*.

Lessons on Cooking Fish.—Fish Pudding.

10. When we think the *potatoes* are sufficiently done, we take a steel fork and try the *potatoes*, to see if they are tender all through.

11. When they are quite boiled, we drain off all the water from the saucepan, and sprinkle the *potatoes* with a little *salt*.

12. We put on the lid of the saucepan, and stand it by the side of the fire to steam the *potatoes* until they have become quite mealy and dry.

13. We should shake the saucepan every now and then, to prevent the *potatoes* from sticking to the bottom.

14. When the *haddock* is sufficiently boiled, we take it carefully out of the fishkettle.

15. We take a sharp knife, and cut off the head and tail of the *fish*.

16. We skin the *fish* from the head to the tail.

17. We cut up the *fish* and take out all the *bones*.

18. We cut the *fish* up into small pieces the size of dice, and put them in a large basin.

19. When the *potatoes* are steamed, we take them out of the saucepan with a spoon.

20. We have a wire sieve ready standing over a large plate.

21. We rub the *potatoes* quickly through the sieve with a wooden spoon.

N.B.—The *potatoes* when sifted should be of the same weight as the *fish*.

22. We add the sifted *potatoes* to the *haddock*, and mix them well together with a wooden spoon.

23. We add *salt* and *pepper*, and a few grains of *Cayenne pepper* to taste.

24. We put in *two ounces of butter*.

25. We take *one egg*, and beat it slightly in a basin.

26. We pour the *egg* into the above mixture, and mix all together to a thick paste.

27. We take a large-sized flat tin, and *butter* it well with our fingers.

28. We put the mixture on to this tin, and shape it as well as we can like a *haddock*.

    N.B.—If preferred, the mixture can be formed into cutlets, or croquette shapes, or as fish cakes, and egged and bread crumbed and fried in dripping, as for *lobster cutlets* (see "Fish," Lesson No. 7, Note 34 to Note 40).

29. We put some little bits of *butter* all about on the shape.

30. We put the tin into a quick oven for a *quarter of an hour*. It should become a pale-brown colour.

Now we will make the *Sauce*.

1. We take a stewpan, and put in it *two ounces of butter* and *one ounce and a half of flour*.

2. We mix them well together with a wooden spoon.

3. We add *half a teaspoonful of salt*.

4. We pour in *half a pint of cold water*.

5. We put the stewpan on the fire, and stir all smooth with a wooden spoon until it boils.

6. We now add *two tablespoonsful of cream*, and let it boil, stirring all the time.

7. We stand the stewpan by the side of the fire. The mixture must not boil again, but only keep warm.

8. We take a saucepan of warm water and put it on the fire to boil.

9. When the water boils we put *two eggs* in to boil for *ten minutes*.

10. We put the *eggs* into cold water for a minute, and then shell them.

11. We cut the *eggs* with a sharp knife into little square pieces.

12. We take the stewpan of *sauce* off the fire, and stand it on a piece of paper on the table.

13. We add the cut-up *eggs* to the *sauce*, and stir them lightly in, not to break the pieces of *egg*.

14. For serving we move the *fish pudding* carefully on to a hot dish, and pour the *egg-sauce* round.

        Now it is finished.

FISH.

Lesson No. 3.

WHITEBAIT.

Whitebait varies in price; it is in season from July to September.

Now we will show you how to fry *Whitebait*.

1. We take the *whitebait*, wash them in *iced water*, pick them over carefully, and dry them well in a cloth.

2. We take a sheet of paper and put on it a good *teacupful of flour*.

3. We take the *whitebait*, and sprinkle them in the *flour*. They must not touch each other, and we must finger them as little as possible.

4. We take up the paper and shake the *whitebait* well in the *flour*, so that they are well covered with *flour*.

5. We turn the *whitebait* from the paper of *flour* into a *whitebait* basket, and sift all the loose *flour* back on to the paper.

6. We take a saucepan and put in it *one pound and a half of lard or clarified dripping*.

7. We put the saucepan on the fire to heat the *fat*. When the *fat* smokes it will then be hot enough.

    N.B.—The fat requires to be much hotter for frying whitebait than for anything else.

    N.B.—If possible the fat should be tested by a frimometer, and the heat should rise to 400 *degrees* Fahrenheit.

8. We then turn the *whitebait* a few at a time into the frying basket and put it into the *fat* for *one minute*. The *whitebait* should be quite crisp.

9. We put a piece of whitey-brown paper on a plate, stand the plate near the fire and turn the *fried whitebait* on to the paper to drain off the grease. (We serve them on a napkin on a hot dish. *Lemon* cut, and thin slices of *brown bread* and *butter* should be served with the *whitebait*.)

Now it is finished.

FISH.

LESSON No. 4.

SOLE AU GRATIN.

Average cost of "*Sole au Gratin.*"

INGREDIENTS.

	s.	d.
1 sole	1	0
Parsley and ¼ of shalot	0	0½
4 mushrooms	0	2
A teaspoonful of lemon juice } Salt and pepper }	0	0½
2 tablespoonsful of glaze	0	3
½ oz. butter	0	0½
Crumbs	0	0½
	1	7

Time required, about one hour.

Now we will show you how to cook *Sole au Gratin*.

1. We take a small *sole* and cut off with a sharp knife the outside *fins*.

2. We cut through the *skin* only, across the head and the tail, on both sides of the *fish*.

3. We take the *skin* off from the tail to the head.

4. We wash the *sole* in cold water and dry it with a cloth, and nick it with a knife on both sides.

5. We can cook the *sole* in fillets, if required, or whole. (N.B.—If in fillets, we fillet the *sole* the same as for the *fried fillets* in Lesson No. 6.) We are going to cook the *sole* whole.

6. We take a small *bunch of parsley* and dry it well in a cloth.

7. We chop the *parsley* up finely on a board.

8. We chop a *quarter of a shalot* up finely and mix it with the *parsley*.

9. The *chopped parsley* and *shalot* should fill a *tablespoon*.

10. We take *four small mushrooms*, cut off the roots, and then wash the *mushrooms* well in a basin of cold water.

Lessons on Cooking Fish.—Sole au Gratin.

11. We take them out of the water, dry them in a cloth and peel them.

12. We chop them up finely.

13. We take a dish, and spread a little *butter* on it with our fingers.

14. We sprinkle half of the *chopped parsley, shalot, and mushroom* over the bottom of the buttered dish.

15. We pour *half a teaspoonful of lemon juice* over the chopped parsley, shalot, and mushroom in the dish, also sprinkle *half a saltspoonful of salt* and *a quarter of a saltspoonful of pepper*.

16. We lay the *sole* carefully in the dish, and sprinkle over it the remainder of the *chopped parsley, shalot,* and *mushroom*.

17. We sprinkle over the *sole pepper and salt* (enough to cover a *threepenny piece*), and squeeze over it *half a teaspoonful of lemon juice*.

18. We take *half an ounce of butter* and cut it in small pieces and put them over the *sole*.

19. We pour over it *two tablespoonsful of half glaze*.

<small>N.B.—*Glaze* can be bought, or it can be made by reducing some strong stock over the fire.</small>

20. We take a wire sieve and put it over a piece of paper.

21. We take some *crumb of bread* and rub it through the sieve.

22. We take these *bread crumbs* and put them on a flat tin. We put this tin into the oven to dry, and slightly brown, the *bread crumbs*.

23. When the *crumbs* are done we sift them over the *sole*.

24. We now put the dish into a brisk oven for *ten minutes*. We must take a fork and feel in the thick part of the *sole* if the *fish* is tender.

25. We carefully move the *sole* with a slice on to a clean dish, and pour the *sauce* round.

Now it is finished.

FISH.

Lesson No. 5.
FILLETS OF SOLES À LA MAÎTRE D'HÔTEL.

Average cost of "*Fillets of Soles à la Maître d'Hôtel.*"

INGREDIENTS.	s.	d.
Sole....................................	1	0
Lemon juice...........................	0	0½
½ oz. of butter	0	1
¾ oz. of flour	0	0½
½ gill of cream	0	3
	1	4¾

Time required about half an hour.

Now we will show you how to cook *Fillets of Soles à la Maître d'Hôtel.*

1. We take *one sole* and *fillet* it in the same way as for *fried fillets* (see "Fish," Lesson No. 6).

2. We take the *bones* and *fins* of the *sole* and put them into a stewpan, with *half a pint of water* and put it on the fire to boil.

3. We take a flat tin pan and *butter* it with our fingers.

4. We fold the *fillets* loosely over and lay them in the buttered tin.

5. We sprinkle *a quarter of a saltspoonful of salt* over the *fillets* and squeeze *six drops of lemon juice*, and cover them with a piece of buttered paper.

6. We put the tin with the *fillets* into a sharp oven for *six minutes.*

Now we will make the *Sauce.*

1. We take a small bunch of *parsley*, wash it, dry it, and chop it finely with a knife on a board.

2. We take a stewpan and put in it *one ounce of butter and three-quarters of an ounce of flour.*

3. We mix them smoothly together with a wooden spoon.

4. We take the saucepan of *fish stock* and pour it by degrees through a strainer into the stewpan of *butter* and *flour*, stirring well.

5. We put the stewpan on the fire and stir the mixture smoothly with a wooden spoon; we now add *two tablespoonsful of cream* and stir it well until it boils.

6. We take the stewpan off the fire and stand it on a piece of paper on the table.

7. We add the *chopped parsley* to the mixture.

8. We add *half a teaspoonful of lemon juice*, **salt**, and **pepper** to taste, and stir the *sauce* well.

9. Now we take the *fillets* out of the oven and arrange them on a hot dish for serving; we add the liquor from the *fillets of soles* out of the tin, to the *sauce*.

10. We pour the *sauce* over the *fillets of soles*.

N.B.—If there is no cream, the sauce can be made with milk; the bones of the fish should therefore be boiled in half a pint of milk instead of water.

Now it is finished.

FISH.

Lesson No. 6.

FRIED FILLETS OF SOLE.

Average cost of "*Fried Fillets of Sole* and *Anchovy Sauce.*"

INGREDIENTS.

For " Fried Sole."	s.	d.	For " Anchovy Sauce."	d
Sole	1	0	1 oz. butter	1¼
1 egg	0	1	¼-oz. flour	¼
Crumbs	0	0½	Anchovy sauce	¼
	1	1½		1¾

Time required about half an hour.

Now we will show you how to *Fry Filleted Soles.*

1. We take *one sole*, wash it well, and lay it on a board.

2. We take a sharp knife and cut off all the outside *fins*, the *head*, and the *tail*.

3. We take the *skin* off the *sole*, from the *tail* to the *head*.

4. We cut down the centre of the *fish*.

5. We slide the knife along carefully between the flesh and the bones, holding the flesh in one hand and drawing it gently away as the knife cuts it away from the bone.

6. We do both sides of the fish alike, and it will make *four fillets*.

7. We put each *fillet* separately on a plate, and rub it over with *flour*.

8. We take a wire sieve and stand it over a piece of paper.

9. We take some crumb of *bread* and rub it through the sieve.

10. We take *one egg* and beat it on a plate with a knife.

11. We lay the *fillets* in the *egg*, and *egg* them well all over with a brush.

Lessons on Cooking Fish.—Fried Fillets of Sole. 199

12. We then put them in the *bread crumbs* and cover them well. We should be careful to finger them as little as possible.

13. We take a saucepan and put in it *one pound and a half of lard or clarified dripping*.

Now we must make the *Butter Sauce* with *Anchovy* (see below).

14. We put the saucepan on the fire to heat the *fat*. Test the heat of it by throwing in a piece of *bread*, and if it makes a fizzing noise it is ready.

> N.B.—The heat is tested best by a frimometer ; the heat should rise to 345°.

15. We take a frying basket and place in it the *fillets*.

16. The *fillets* should be slightly bent, or folded over, to prevent their being quite flat when fried.

17. When the *fat* is quite hot we put in the frying basket with the *fillets* for *three minutes*.

18. We put a piece of whitey-brown paper on a plate.

19. When the *fillets* are done, they should be a pale brown ; we turn them out on to the paper on the plate to drain off the grease.

20. We serve them in a hot dish on a napkin, garnished with a little fried *parsley* [Refer to " Fish," Lesson No. 7, Note 41].

---

1. We take a stewpan, and put in it *one ounce of butter and half an ounce of flour*.

2. We mix them well with a wooden spoon.

3. We add *one gill and a half of cold water*.

4. We put the stewpan on the fire, and stir well with a wooden spoon until the mixture is quite smooth and boils.

5. We take the stewpan off the fire, and stand it on a piece of paper on the table.

6. We now add *one tablespoonful of anchovy sauce*, and stir it well into the *butter sauce*.

7. For serving we pour it into a sauceboat.

Now it is finished.

FISH.

Lesson No. 7.

LOBSTER CUTLETS.

Average cost of "*Lobster Cutlets*" (*about seven*).

INGREDIENTS.

	s.	d.
1 Lobster from 2s. to	3	0
1½ oz. of butter	0	2¼
¼ a gill of cream	0	3
Seasoning and flavouring	0	1
1 oz. of flour	0	0¼
1 egg	0	1¼
Bread	0	0¼
Parsley	0	0¼
	3	9¼

Time required about three hours.

Now we will show you how to make *Lobster Cutlets*.

1. We take a small *lobster*—it should be a hen *lobster* if possible.

2. We put the *lobster* on a board.

3. We take a chopper and break the *shell* of the *lobster* by hitting it with the blade of the chopper, not with the edge; 1st, because it would cut the *lobster* in pieces, and 2nd, because it would spoil the edge of the chopper.

4. We break all the *shell* off the *claws* and *back* with our fingers and take out all the *flesh*.

5. We cut this *flesh* up in pieces with a sharp knife to the size of small dice.

6. If the *lobster* is a hen *lobster* we shall find a bit of *coral* in the neck, and a strip of it down the back.

7. We take all this *coral* out of the *lobster* and wash it carefully in cold water in a small basin.

8. We take the *coral* out of the basin and put it in a mortar with *one ounce of butter*.

9. We pound the *coral* and the *butter* well with the pestle.

Lessons on Cooking Fish.—Lobster Cutlets.

10. We take it out of the mortar and scrape the mortar out quite clean with a palette knife or a slice of raw *potato*, for none must be lost.

11. We take a hair sieve and put it over a plate.

12. We pass the pounded mixture through the sieve with a wooden spoon.

13. We must turn up the sieve when all the mixture has passed through, and we shall find some sticking inside.

14. We scrape all this carefully off with the spoon.

15. We make it all into a little *pat*.

16. We take a stewpan and put in it *one ounce of flour* and *half an ounce of butter*. We mix them well together with a wooden spoon.

17. We add *one gill of cold water* (one gill is a quarter pint). We put the stewpan on the fire and stir the mixture with a wooden spoon till it boils and thickens.

18. We add *one tablespoonful of cream* and stir smoothly until it boils.

19. We take the stewpan off the fire and stand it on a piece of paper on the table.

20. We now stir in by degrees the *pat of coral butter*. We must be sure the *sauce* is quite smooth and not lumpy.

21. We add *salt and pepper* and a few grains of *cayenne pepper*, according to taste, and about *six drops of lemon juice*, and mix well.

22. We add the chopped *lobster* and stir lightly, not to break up the *lobster*, but only to mix it with the *sauce*.

23. We take a clean plate and pour the mixture from the stewpan on to it, smoothing it with a knife.

24. We take a piece of paper and cut it round to the size of the plate. We *butter* it with a knife.

25. We put the buttered paper over the mixture which is in the plate, to prevent the dust from getting in.

26. We take the plate and stand it on ice (if possible), or put it in a cold place to cool.

27. We take a wire sieve and put it over a piece of paper.

28. We take a piece of *crumb of bread* and rub it through the wire sieve.

29. We take *one egg* and beat it slightly with a knife on a plate.

30. We take a saucepan and put in it *one pound and a half of lard or clarified dripping.*

31. We put the saucepan on the fire to heat the *fat.* It must not burn.

32. We take the plate of *lobster mixture,* which should by this time be cold and rather stiff.

33. We shape the *mixture* into *cutlets.* This quantity will make seven.

34. We dip the *cutlets* into the *egg,* and *egg* them well all over with a brush.

35. We take them carefully out of the *egg* and cover them well with the *bread crumbs.*

N.B.—If the cutlets are not well covered with egg and bread-crumbs they will burst in the frying.

36. We take a frying basket and lay in it the *lobster cutlets,* a few at a time, so as not to touch each other.

37. When the *fat* is quite hot we should test it by a frimometer if possible, and the heat should rise to 345°, or by throwing into it a piece of *bread.* If it makes a sharp fizzing noise it is ready.

38. We put the frying basket into the *fat* for *three minutes,* or perhaps less. The *cutlets* should become a pale brown.

39. We get a plate with a piece of whitey-brown paper on it, ready to receive the *cutlets* when they come out of the boiling *fat.* This is to drain all the *grease* from them.

40. We take the small *claws* of the *lobster* and stick them into the end of each *cutlet* to represent the bone.

41. We take a few *sprigs of parsley,* wash them, and dry them in a cloth, and put them into the frying basket.

42. We just toss the basket with the *parsley* into the boiling *fat* for a second.

43. We arrange the *cutlets* on a napkin on a hot dish, and garnish them with the *fried parsley*.

Now it is finished.

FISH.

LESSON No. 8.

BOILED COD FISH AND OYSTER SAUCE.

Cod-fish varies in price considerably.

It is in season from October to February.

Average cost of "*Oyster Sauce.*"

INGREDIENTS.

	s.	d.
1 dozen oysters	1	6
½-oz. butter	0	0¾
¼-oz. flour		
1 tablespoonful of cream	0	1½
Lemon-juice and cayenne pepper	0	0¼
	1	8½

Time required about twenty minutes.

Now we will show you how to cook *Cod Fish*, and make *Oyster Sauce*.

1. We take a slice of *cod* weighing *one pound*.

2. We put it in a basin of cold water and wash it well.

3. We take a small fish-kettle of boiling water, and add to it as much *salt* as will make the water taste salt.

4. We put the fish-kettle on the fire.

5. We take the *cod* out of the basin and place it on the drainer in the fish-kettle, and let it boil for *fifteen minutes*.

    N.B.—It must not boil fast.

6. When the slice of *cod* is sufficiently cooked the flesh will leave the bone.

    N.B.—The bone is usually left in or the fish would break to pieces.

7. We serve the slice of *cod* on a folded napkin on a hot dish with *oyster sauce*.

Lessons on Cooking Fish.—*Oyster Sauce.*

For *Oyster Sauce.*

1. We take *one dozen oysters* and the liquor that is with them, and put them into a small saucepan.

2. We put the saucepan on the fire and bring them to the boil, this is to blanch the *oysters*.

3. We take the saucepan off the fire as soon as it boils.

4. We take a basin and pour into it the *oyster liquor* through a strainer.

5. We take the *oysters* out of the saucepan and lay them on a plate.

6. We take off the *beards* and all the hard parts of the *oysters*, leaving only the soft part.

7. We take a stewpan and put in *half an ounce of butter*, and a *quarter of an ounce of flour*.

8. We mix the *flour* and the *butter* well together with a wooden spoon.

9. We now add to the contents of the stewpan the *oyster liquor* which is in the basin.

10. We put the stewpan on the fire and stir the mixture well with a wooden spoon until it boils and thickens.

11. We now add *one tablespoonful of cream*, and stir again until it boils.

12. We take the stewpan off the fire and stand it on a piece of paper on the table.

13. We add *six drops of lemon juice* and a few grains of *cayenne pepper* according to taste.

14. We take the trimmed *oysters* and cut them into small pieces.

15. We add the pieces of *oyster* to the mixture in the stewpan and mix all together with a wooden spoon.

Now it is finished.

FISH.

Lesson No. 9.

GRILLED SALMON AND TARTARE SAUCE.

Salmon varies in price considerably.

It is in season from May to August.

Average cost of "*Tartare Sauce.*"

INGREDIENTS.

	d.
2 eggs	2
Salt and pepper	
A tablespoonful of French vinegar	1
Parsley	
Gherkins or capers	1
1 gill of oil	6
	10

Time required about fifteen minutes.

Now we will show you how to cook *Salmon* and make *Tartare Sauce*.

1. We take a thick slice of *salmon* weighing *one pound*.

2. We cut the *salmon* into two thin slices as it will cook better than in a thick piece.

3. We put the *salmon* in a basin of cold water and wash it well.

4. We take it out of the basin and dry it well with a cloth.

5. We take a plate and pour on it about *a gill of salad oil*.

6. We dip the slices of *salmon* into the *oil* on both sides, the *oil* will prevent the fish from drying whilst cooking.

7. We season the slices on both sides with *pepper and salt*.

8. We take a gridiron and heat it on both sides by the fire. This is to prevent the fish sticking.

9. When the gridiron is hot, we place on the slices of *salmon* and let them grill for *a quarter of an hour*.

10. We must turn the gridiron occasionally so as to cook the *fish* on both sides, which should become of a pale brown colour.

11. When the *fish* is quite done we can remove the bone in the centre of each slice. We serve the *salmon* on a napkin on a hot dish.

For *Tartare Sauce.*

1. We take *two eggs* and put the *yolks* in one basin, and the *whites* (which will not be wanted) into another basin.

2. We take a wooden spoon and just stir the *yolks* enough to break them.

3. We add to them a *saltspoonful of salt*, and *half a saltspoonful of pepper*, and a *tablespoonful of French vinegar*.

4. We take a *bottle of salad oil*, and, putting our thumb half over the top, pour in drop by drop, the *oil*, stirring well with a whisk the whole time; *a gill of oil* will be sufficient.

5. If the *sauce* is not sharp enough to taste we add about a *teaspoonful* more of *vinegar*, stirring it in smoothly.

6. We might now stir in a *teaspoonful* of ready-made *mustard* or *tarragon vinegar* if it is liked.

7. We take a small bunch of *parsley*, and put it in a small saucepan of boiling water with a little *salt and soda* (enough to cover a *threepenny piece*) for *two or three seconds*. (N.B.—Soda is to keep the parsley green).

N.B.—This is called blanching or parboiling Parsley.

8. We take the *parsley* out and dry it thoroughly by squeezing it in a cloth. We put it on a board and chop it up finely. There should be a teaspoonful.

9. We take a few *gherkins* or *capers* and chop them up finely on a board, there should be enough to fill a tablespoon.

10. We take these *chopped gherkins* or *capers* and the *chopped parsley* and put them all into the *sauce* and mix them in with a spoon.

11. We serve the *sauce* in a sauce tureen.

Now it is finished.

FISH.

Lesson No. 10.

BAKED MACKEREL OR HERRING.

Average cost of "*Mackerel or Herring*" (baked with bread crumbs and herbs).

INGREDIENTS.

	d.
2 mackerel 6d. or herrings 2d.	
1 dessertspoonful of chopped herbs and onions	1
1 dessertspoonful of chopped parsley	0½
1 dessertspoonful of bread crumbs	0½
Pepper and salt	
2 oz. of dripping	1
	3

With Herrings, 5d.
With Mackerel, 9d.

Time required about forty minutes.

Now we will show you how to bake *Mackerel or Herrings* with *herbs and bread crumbs*.

1. We wash the *mackerel or herrings* in cold water, dry them in a cloth, and put them upon a board.

2. We take a sharp knife, cut off the *heads* of the *fish* and carefully split open each *fish* and take out the *back bone*.

3. We lay one *fish* open flat on a tin (skin downwards).

4. We take a *sprig of parsley*, wash it in water, and dry it in a cloth.

5. We put the *parsley* on a board and take away the *stalks* and chop it up as finely as possible (there should be about a *dessertspoonful*).

6. We take *half an onion*, peel it, put it on a board, with a *sprig of thyme and marjoram*, and chop it up finely (there should be about a *dessertspoonful*).

7. We take a grater, stand it on the board and grate a few *bread crumbs* (there should be about a *dessertspoonful*).

8. We mix the *onion, herbs, and bread crumbs* together.

9. We sprinkle *pepper and salt* to taste, over the *fish* in the tin.

10. We then sprinkle over the *fish* the mixture of *herbs and bread crumbs*.

11. We take the other *fish* and lay it over the one in the tin (skin upwards).

12. We put *two ounces of clarified dripping* in a saucepan, and put it on the fire to melt.

13. We pour the *melted dripping* over the *fish* in the tin.

14. We cover the tin with a dish, and stand it on the hot plate or in the oven to bake for *half an hour*.

15. We must watch it and baste it occasionally with the *dripping*.

16. For serving, we turn the *fish* carefully out of the tin on to a hot dish.

Now it is finished.

FISH.

LESSON NO. 11.

BAKED STUFFED HADDOCK.

Average cost of a "*Stuffed Haddock*" (baked).

INGREDIENTS.

	d.
1 Haddock	6
Bread crumbs	1
1 dessertspoonful of chopped parsley	0½
1 teaspoonful of chopped herbs	0½
Pepper and salt	} 1
2 oz. of suet	
1 egg	1
2 oz. of dripping	1
	11

Time required, about three-quarters of an hour.

Now we will show you how to *Stuff a Haddock and Bake it.*

1. We take a *haddock*, wash it, clean it carefully in cold water, and dry it in a cloth.

2. We stand a grater on a piece of paper and grate some *bread crumbs*.

3. We take a *sprig of parsley*, wash it in cold water, and dry it in a cloth.

4. We put the *parsley* on a board, and chop it up finely. (There should be about a *dessertspoonful*.)

5. We take a small *sprig of thyme* and *marjoram*, take away the *stalks*, and chop the *herbs* up finely on a board. (There should be about a *teaspoonful*.)

> N.B.—The *stalks* will do for flavouring, but they cannot be eaten as they are bitter.

6. We mix all the *herbs* together with *two tablespoonsful* of the *bread crumbs*.

> N.B.—The remainder of the bread crumbs we shall require for rolling the fish in.

7. We add *pepper and salt* to taste, and mix the *stuffing* together with *two ounces of suet*.

8. We stuff the *belly* of the *fish* with the *stuffing* and sew it up.

9. We break an *egg* into a plate, and brush the *fish* over with it, then roll it in the *bread crumbs*, covering it well all over.

10. We *grease* a dish or tin with a piece of *dripping*.

11. We lay the *fish* on the dish or tin and put it into the oven to bake for from *half to three-quarters of an hour*, basting it frequently with *dripping*.

Now it is finished.

FISH.

LESSON NO. 12.

FISH BAKED IN VINEGAR.

Average cost of "*Fish Baked in Vinegar.*"

INGREDIENTS.

	d.
6 Herrings	6
30 peppercorns .... ⎫	
1 blade of mace .... ⎪	
1 shallot .... ⎬	1
1 bay leaf .... ⎪	
1 gill (¼ pint) of vinegar .... ⎫	
Salt .... ⎬	0½
	7½

Time required, about six hours.

Now we will show you how to *Bake Fish* (such as *herrings* or *mackerel*), *in Vinegar*.

1. We take the *fish*, wash them, and clean them thoroughly in cold water.

2. We put the *fish* on a board, and cut them into thick pieces.

3. We lay these pieces close together in a stone jar, with *thirty peppercorns* and *half a teaspoonful of salt*.

4. We add *one blade of mace* and *a bay-leaf*.

5. We take *one shallot*, peel it, and add it, or part of it (according to taste), to the *fish*.

6. We pour in *one gill* (a quarter of a pint) *of vinegar*, and tie a piece of brown paper tightly over the top of the jar with a piece of string.

7. We put the jar into a very slow oven to bake for *six hours*, or it may stand in a baker's oven all night.

N.B.—*The fish* is to be eaten cold.

Now it is finished.

FISH.

Lesson No. 13.
FRIED PLAICE.

Average cost of "*Plaice*" (fried).

INGREDIENTS.

	d.
1 Plaice	9
1 egg	1
Bread crumbs }	0½
Dripping for frying }	
	10½

Time required, about half an hour.

Now we will show you how to fry *Plaice in Egg and Bread Crumbs, or Batter.*

1. We put about *half a pound of clarified dripping* into a saucepan, and put it on the fire to heat.

2. We take the *plaice*, wash it in cold water, and dry it in a cloth.

3. We put the *plaice* on a board, and with a sharp knife carefully remove the *skin* from the back side of the *fish*, and cut off the *head* and the *tail*.

4. We hold a grater over a piece of paper and grate some *bread crumbs*.

5. We cut up the *fish* into slices or fillets.

6. We break an *egg* on to a plate and beat it lightly with a knife.

7. We dip the slices of *fish* into the *egg*, and *egg* them well all over.

8. We then roll them in the *bread crumbs*, covering them well.

N.B.—We must shake off the loose *crumbs*.

9. When the *dripping* is quite hot and smoking we carefully put in the *fish*, fingering it as little as possible, so as not to take off any of the *egg* or *bread crumbs*.

N.B.—We should not put too many pieces at a time into the dripping, as they must not touch each other.

10. We put a piece of whitey-brown paper on to a plate, and as the *fish* is fried we take it out of the *dripping* carefully with a slice, and lay it on the paper to drain off the *grease*.

N.B.—Soles or any fish can be fried in the same way.

N.B.—For frying fish in batter, we dip each piece of fish in the batter, made as for meat fritters (see Cooked Meat, Lesson No. 2), and fry it in the same way as above.

Now it is finished.

FISH.

LESSON No. 14.

BOILED FISH.

Average cost of the *Sauce* to be served with boiled fish (about half a pint).

INGREDIENTS.

	d.
1 dessertspoonful of cornflour or arrowroot....	0¼
1 teaspoonful of vinegar or lemon juice	0¼
	0½

Time required for boiling fish, about twenty minutes to three-quarters of an hour, according to the size of the fish.

Now we will show you how to *Boil Fish* and make the *Sauce*.

1. We put a saucepan or fish-kettle of water on the fire to boil.

2. We take the *fish* and clean it thoroughly in cold water.

3. When the water is quite boiling, we put in the *fish* on a strainer or a plate (there should be sufficient water just to cover the *fish*).

4. We also put in some *salt*, enough to make the water taste salt.

5. We put the lid on the saucepan, and move it to the side of the fire to simmer gently for *from twenty minutes to three-quarters of an hour* (according to the size of the *fish*).

6. We must watch it and skim it occasionally.

7. When we find that the skin of the *fish* is cracking, we shall know that it is sufficiently boiled.

While the *fish* is boiling we make the *sauce*.

8. We put a *dessertspoonful of corn flour* or *arrowroot* into a small saucepan, and mix it into a smooth *paste* with cold water.

9. We now add to it *half a pint of the water* in which the *fish* was boiled.

10. We put the saucepan on the fire and stir it until it boils and thickens.

11. We then take the saucepan off the fire, and stand it on a piece of paper on the table.

12. We flavour the *sauce* with a *teaspoonful of vinegar* or *lemon juice*, and season it with *pepper and salt* according to taste.

> N.B.—If liked, the *sauce* can be coloured with *half a teaspoonful of caramel* (burnt sugar). See Note at end of "Brown Purée" (Australian Meat, Lesson No. 2).

13. For serving, we take the *fish* carefully out of the saucepan and place it on a hot dish, we pour the *sauce* into a sauce boat or a basin, or round the *fish*.

Now it is finished.

VEGETABLES.

Lesson No. 1.

BOILED AND STEAMED POTATOES.

Time required for boiling:—
Old potatoes, about half an hour.
New potatoes, about twenty minutes.
Steamed potatoes, half an hour.

Now we will show you how to dress *Potatoes*.

For boiling *Old Potatoes*.

1. We wash *two pounds* of *potatoes* well in cold water, and scrub them clean with a scrubbing brush.

> N.B.—If the *potatoes* are diseased then we take a sharp knife, peel them, and carefully cut out the eyes and any black specks about the *potato*, but it is much better to boil them in their skins.

2. We put them in a saucepan with cold water, enough to cover them, and sprinkle over them a *teaspoonful* of *salt*.

3. We put the saucepan on the fire, to boil the *potatoes* for *from twenty minutes to half an hour*.

4. We should take a fork and put it into the *potatoes*, to feel if the centre is quite tender.

5. When they are sufficiently boiled, we drain off all the water, and place a clean cloth over the *potatoes* in the saucepan.

6. We stand the saucepan by the side of the fire, with the lid on, to steam the *potatoes*.

7. When the *potatoes* have become quite dry, we take them carefully out of the saucepan, peel them without breaking them, and place them in a hot vegetable dish for serving.

Now it is finished.

For boiling *New Potatoes*.

1. We wash *two pounds* of *potatoes* in cold water.
2. We take a knife and scrape them.
3. We take a saucepan of warm water, and put it on the fire to boil.
4. When the water is quite boiling, we put in the *new potatoes*, and sprinkle over them *a teaspoonful of salt*.
5. We let them boil for *a quarter of an hour*; we should take a fork and put it in the *potatoes*, to feel if the centre is quite tender.
6. We then drain off all the water, and place a clean cloth in the saucepan, over the *potatoes*, and stand the saucepan by the side of the fire with the lid on.
7. When they have become quite dry, we take them out of the saucepan, and arrange them on a hot vegetable dish for serving.

Now it is finished.

For *Steamed Potatoes*.

N.B.—Old potatoes only, can be steamed.

1. We wash the *potatoes* well in cold water, and scrub them clean with a scrubbing brush.

N.B.—It is best to steam the potatoes in their skins, but they can be peeled if preferred.

2. We take a potato steamer, fill the saucepan with hot water, and put it on the fire to boil.
3. When the water is quite boiling, we put the *potatoes* in the steamer, and sprinkle them over with *salt*.
4. We place the steamer on the saucepan of boiling water, and cover it down tight to keep the steam in.
5. We let the *potatoes* steam for *half an hour*.
6. We should take a fork and put it in the *potatoes*, to feel if the centre is quite tender.

7. When they are sufficiently steamed, we take them carefully out of the steamer, peel them without breaking them, and arrange them on a hot vegetable dish for serving.

Now it is finished.

VEGETABLES.

Lesson No. 2.

MASHED, SAUTÉ, AND BAKED POTATOES.

Average cost of a dish of "*Potatoes.*"

INGREDIENTS.

For "*Mashed Potatoes.*"	d.	For "*Sauté Potatoes.*"	d.
2 lbs of old potatoes	2	New potatoes	2
1 oz. of butter	1½	2 oz. of butter	⎫
1 gill of milk	⎫	Salt	⎬ 2½
Pepper and salt	⎬		⎭
	3¾		4½

Time required, about forty minutes. Time required, about half an hour.

Time required for Baked Potatoes, about three-quarters of an hour.

Now we will show you how to dress *Potatoes*.

For a dish of *Mashed Potatoes*.

1. We take *two pounds* of *old potatoes*, wash them, and steam them as for steaming *potatoes* (see "Vegetables, Lesson No. 1").

2. We take a stew-pan and put in it *one ounce of butter*, *one gill of milk*, and *pepper* and *salt* to taste.

3. We put the stew-pan on the fire to boil.

4. We place a wire sieve over a plate.

5. We take the steamed *potatoes*, one at a time, out of the steamer, put them on the sieve, and pass them through on to the plate as quickly as possible, rubbing them with a wooden spoon.

6. We take the sifted *potato* and stir it into the *boiling milk*, in the stew-pan.

7. We must now beat it all lightly together, and then turn it into a hot vegetable dish for serving.

Now it is finished.

Lessons on Cooking Vegetables.—Baked Potatoes.

For *Sauté Potatoes*—

1. We take some *new potatoes*, as small as possible, wash them in cold water, and scrape them clean.

> N.B.—If the potatoes are large, they should be cut in halves, or even in quarters, and trimmed.

2. We put them in a saucepan, with cold water.

3. We put the saucepan on the fire, and only just bring them to the boil.

4. We then drain off the water, and wipe the *potatoes* dry in a clean cloth.

5. We take a thick stewpan and put in it *two ounces of butter*, and the *potatoes*.

6. We put the stewpan on a quick fire for about *twenty minutes*, to brown the *potatoes*; we must watch them, and when they have begun to brown we should toss them occasionally in the stewpan, so as to brown them on all sides alike.

7. We then strain off the *butter*, sprinkle them over with *salt*, and serve them on a hot vegetable dish.

Now it is finished.

For *Baked Potatoes*—

1. We take the *potatoes*, wash, and scrub them well with a scrubbing-brush in a basin of cold water.

2. We take them out of the water, and dry them with a cloth.

3. We put them in a brisk oven to bake; they will take from *half an hour to three-quarters of an hour*, according to the heat of the oven, and the size of the *potatoes*.

4. We take a steel fork or skewer, and stick it into the *potatoes*, to see if they are done. They must be soft inside.

5. We take a table napkin and fold it.

6. We place the folded napkin on a hot dish.

7. When the *potatoes* are sufficiently baked, we take them out of the oven, and arrange them on the napkin for serving.

Now it is finished.

VEGETABLES.

LESSON No. 3.
FRIED POTATOES.

Average cost of "*Potato Chips or Fried Slices of Potato.*"

INGREDIENTS.

	d.
1 lb. of Potatoes............	1
Salt	

The use of 1½ lb. of clarified fat or lard for frying.

Time required, about eight minutes for either.

Now we will show you how to dress *Potatoes*.

For *Potato Chips—*

1. We wash the *potatoes* well in cold water, and scrub them clean with a scrubbing-brush.

2. We take a sharp knife, peel them, and carefully cut out the eyes and any black specks about them.

3. We must now peel the *potatoes* very thinly in ribbons, and twist them into fancy shapes.

4. We take a saucepan and put in it *one pound and a half of clarified fat or lard.*

5. We put the saucepan on the fire to heat the *fat.* We must test the heat of it with a piece of *bread* (see Lesson on "Frying").

6. We take a frying-basket and put the ribbons of *potato* in it.

7. When the *fat* is quite hot we put in the frying-basket with the *potatoes* for about *six minutes.*

8. We place a piece of whitey-brown paper on a plate.

9. When the chips are done, they should be quite crisp and of a pale brown colour. We turn them out on to the paper, to drain off the *grease*, and sprinkle over them a little *salt.*

10. We serve them on a hot dish.

Now it is finished.

For *Fried Slices of Potato*—

1. We take the *potatoes*, wash them clean, and peel them with a sharp knife.

2. We put the *potatoes* on a board, and cut them in slices, about *one-eighth of an inch* in thickness.

3. We take a saucepan and put in it *one and a half pound of clarified dripping or lard*.

4. We take a frying-basket and place in it the sliced *potatoes*.

5. We put the saucepan on the fire to warm the *fat*.

6. When the *fat* is warm, but not very hot, we place in the frying-basket with the slices of *potatoes*, and let them boil in the *fat*, until they are quite tender.

> N.B.—We should take out a piece of potato and press it between the thumb and finger, to feel that it is quite tender.

7. We must now take out the frying-basket with the *potatoes* and place it on a plate.

8. We leave the *fat* on the fire to heat.

9. When the *fat* is quite hot, we place in the frying-basket with the *potatoes* for about *two minutes*.

10. We put a piece of whitey-brown paper on a plate.

11. When the *potatoes* are fried, they should be a pale brown; we turn them out on to the paper to drain off the *grease*. .

12. We should sprinkle a little *salt* over them.

13. For serving we arrange them on a hot dish.

Now it is finished.

VEGETABLES.

Lesson No. 4.

POTATO CROQUETTES.

Average cost of "*Potato Croquettes*" (*about* 18).

INGREDIENTS.

	d.
2 lbs. potatoes	3
1 oz. butter .... } 1 tablespoonful of milk .... }	1½
3 eggs...	3
A small bunch of parsley	1
Bread crumbs .... } Pepper and salt .... }	2
	10½

Time required, about one hour.

Now we will show you how to make *Potato Croquettes*.

1. We take *two pounds of potatoes*, wash, scrub, and boil or steam them (see "Vegetables," Lesson No. 1).

   N.B.—Any remains of *cold potatoes* could be used up in this way, instead of boiling fresh ones.

2. We place a wire sieve over a plate.

3. We take the *potatoes*, one at a time, place them on the sieve and rub them through with a wooden spoon as quickly as possible on to the plate.

   N.B.—The *potatoes* can be passed through the sieve much quicker while they are hot.

4. We put 1 *oz. of butter* and *a tablespoonful of milk* into a stewpan, and put it on the fire.

5. When the *milk and butter* are hot, we stir in smoothly the *sifted potato*.

6. We take the stewpan off the fire, and stand it on a piece of paper on the table.

7. We break *two eggs*, put the *whites* in a cup (as they are not required for present use), and stir the *yolks*, one at a time, into the *potato* in the stewpan.

8. We take *two or three sprigs of parsley*, wash them in cold

Lessons on Cooking Vegetables.—Potato Croquettes.

water, dry them in a cloth, and chop them up finely on a board (there should be about *a teaspoonful*).

9. We sprinkle the *parsley* into the stewpan, and season the *potato* according to taste with *pepper and salt*.

10. We turn the *potato mixture* on to a plate and stand it aside till cold.

11. We put 1 *lb. of clarified dripping* into a deep stewpan, and put it on the fire to heat; we must be careful it does not burn.

12. We take some *crumb of bread*, and rub it through a wire sieve on to a piece of paper.

13. When the *potato mixture* is cold, we form it into *croquettes* or *balls*, according to taste.

14. We break an *egg* on to a plate and beat it up slightly with a knife.

15. We dip the *croquettes* into the *egg*, and *egg* them well all over with a paste brush.

16. We now roll them in the *bread crumbs*, covering them well all over.

    N.B.—We must be careful to cover them smoothly and not too thickly.

17. We take a frying basket and arrange the *croquettes* in it; but we must finger them as little as possible, and not allow them to touch each other.

18. When the *fat* on the fire is quite hot and smoking (we should test the heat by throwing in a piece of *bread* which should fry brown directly), we put in the frying basket for *two minutes* or so to fry the *croquettes* a pale yellow.

19. We put a piece of whitey-brown paper on a plate, and as the *croquettes* are fried we turn them on to the paper to drain off the *grease*.

20. We put *three or four small sprigs of parsley* (washed and dried) into the frying basket, and just toss the basket into the *boiling fat* for a *second* or so.

21. For serving, we arrange the *croquettes* tastily on a hot dish, with the *fried parsley* in the centre.

Now it is finished.

VEGETABLES.

Lesson No. 5.

BRUSSELS SPROUTS.

Average cost of dressing "*Brussels Sprouts.*"

INGREDIENTS.

	d.
Brussels sprouts	6
Salt	⎫
¼ of a saltspoonful of carbonate of soda	⎬ 1½
1 ounce of butter	⎪
Pepper	⎭
	7½

Time required, about half an hour.

Now we will show you how to dress *Brussels Sprouts*.

1. We take the *Brussels sprouts*, wash them well in two or three waters, and trim them.

2. We take a saucepan with plenty of warm water in it.

3. We put the saucepan on the fire to boil.

4. When the water is quite boiling, we add a *tablespoonful of salt*, and a *quarter of a saltspoonful of carbonate of soda*.

5. We put in the *sprouts*, and let them boil quickly for from *ten to twenty minutes*, according to their age.

N.B.—Young sprouts take the shortest time to boil.

6. We must keep the lid off the saucepan the whole time.

7. After that time, we pour the *sprouts* into a cullender to drain.

8. When the *sprouts* are quite dry, we put them in a sautépan with *one ounce of butter*.

9. We sprinkle over them a little *pepper and salt*, and toss them over the fire for a few minutes, but they must not fry.

10. For serving, we arrange them tastily on a hot vegetable dish.

Now it is finished.

VEGETABLES.

Lesson No. 6.

CARROTS AND TURNIPS.

Average cost of dressing "*Carrots and Turnips.*"

INGREDIENTS.

	d.
Carrots or Turnips .... ⎫ 2 tablespoonsful of salt .... ⎭	6
Half a pint of good stock	3¾
Dessertspoonful of castor sugar	0¼
Half an ounce of butter	0½
	10½

Time required, about three-quarters of an hour.

Now we will show you how to dress *Carrots and Turnips.* For *Carrots—*

1. We take a saucepan of water, and put it on the fire to boil.

2. When the water is quite boiling, we add a *tablespoonful of salt.*

3. We take the *carrots*, and if they are quite young, we put them into the saucepan of boiling water, to boil for *twenty minutes.*

4. We must take a fork and stick it in the *carrots* to feel that they are quite tender all through.

5. After that time we take them out of the saucepan, and rub them clean with a cloth.

> N.B.—If the carrots are old we should wash, scrape them clean with a knife, and cut them to the shape of young carrots, or cut them in quarters, or in fancy shapes, with a cutter, before boiling.

6. We should let them boil for from *half an hour to three-quarters of an hour.*

7. We take a stewpan and put the boiled *carrots* in it.

8. We pour in some good *stock*, enough to cover them.

9. We put in a piece of *butter*, the *size of a nut*, and sprinkle about a *teaspoonful* of white *castor sugar* over them.

10. We put the stewpan on the fire to boil, and reduce to a glaze over the *carrots*.

11. We then take them out of the stewpan, and they are ready for serving.

For *Turnips—*

1. We take the *turnips* and wash them well in cold water.

2. We take them out of the water, put them on a board, peel them with a sharp knife, and cut them in quarters, or cut them out with a round cutter.

3. We take a saucepan of water and put it on the fire to boil.

4. When the water is quite boiling we add a *tablespoonful of salt*.

5. We now put in the cut up *turnips*, and let them boil for from *ten to fifteen minutes*.

6. When they are sufficiently boiled, we take them out of the saucepan, and put them into a stewpan with some good *stock*, enough to cover them.

7. We add to them a piece of *butter*, the *size of a nut*, and sprinkle over them about a *teaspoonful* of white *castor sugar*.

8. We put the stewpan on the fire to boil, and reduce to a glaze over the *turnips*.

9. We then take them out of the stewpan, and they are ready for serving.

N.B.—The turnips and the carrots, as described above, can be served with *braised veal* (see Braised Fillet of Veal) or separately as a vegetable.

Now it is finished.

VEGETABLES.

LESSON No. 7.
BOILED CAULIFLOWER AND CAULI-FLOWER AU GRATIN.

Average cost of dressing "*Cauliflower au Gratin.*"

INGREDIENTS.

	d.
Cauliflower	6
Salt	
Half an ounce of butter	1
1 ounce of flour	
Tablespoonful of cream	1½
2 ounces of Parmesan cheese	
Cayenne pepper	3
	11½

Time required, about an hour.

Now we will show you how to dress a *Cauliflower*.

1. We take a *cauliflower* and wash it well in two or three waters, and take a knife, and cut off the end of the stalk and any withered outside leaves.

2. We put it in a basin of cold water, with a *dessertspoonful of salt*, and let it stand for *two or three minutes*.

3. We take a large saucepan full of water, and put it on the fire to boil.

4. When the water is quite boiling we put in a *tablespoonful of salt*.

5. We take the *cauliflower* out of the salt and water, and place it in the saucepan with the flower downwards, and let it boil till it is quite tender for from *fifteen or twenty minutes*.

6. We must take it carefully out with a slice, and feel the centre of the flower with our finger, to see that it is quite tender.

7. After that time we take it out of the saucepan, and put it on a sieve to drain.

8. For serving, we place it on a hot vegetable dish.

If *Cauliflower au Gratin* be required—

1. We take the cauliflower and wash it, and boil it in the same way as described above, from Note 1 to Note 6.

2. When the *cauliflower* is sufficiently boiled, we take it out of the saucepan with a slice and put it on a plate.

3. We take a knife and cut off all the outside green leaves.

4. We take a cloth and squeeze all the water out of the *cauliflower*.

5. We put *half an ounce of butter* and *one ounce of flour* in a stewpan, and mix them well together with a wooden spoon.

6. We pour in *one gill* (or quarter of a pint) *of cold water*.

7. We put the stewpan on the fire, and stir smoothly until it boils and thickens.

8. We now add *one tablespoonful of cream, cayenne pepper* (about as much as would very thinly cover *half the top of a threepenny piece*), and *salt*, according to taste.

9. We stand the stewpan by the side of the fire, until the *sauce* is required for use.

10. We take *two ounces of Parmesan cheese*, and grate it with a grater on to a piece of paper.

11. We now take the stewpan off the fire and stand it on a piece of paper on the table.

12. We stir rather more than half the grated *cheese* into the *sauce*.

13. We place the *cauliflower* on a tin dish.

14. We pour the *sauce* all over the *cauliflower*.

15. We take the remainder of the grated *cheese* and sprinkle it over the *cauliflower*, and brown the top of it with a hot salamander.

16. The *cauliflower* should become a pale brown, and be served hot.

Now it is finished.

VEGETABLES.

Lesson No. 8.

SPINACH.

Average cost of dressing "*Spinach.*"

INGREDIENTS.

	s.	d.
2 lbs. of spinach	0	6
Salt		
3 ounces of butter	0	3¾
Half a gill of cream	0	3
Pepper		
A slice of bread	0	0¼
	1	1

Time required, about half an hour.

Now we will show you how to dress *Spinach.*

1. We take *two pounds of spinach* and place it on a board.

2. We must pick off all the stalks from the leaves.

3. We put the leaves in plenty of cold water, and wash them two or three times.

4. We turn the *spinach* on to a cullender to drain.

5. We take a large saucepan and put the *spinach* into it, sprinkle a *saltspoonful of salt* over it, and put it on the fire to boil. The drops of water on the leaves and their own juice are sufficient without adding any water.

6. We let it boil quickly for *ten minutes*, with the cover off.

7. We then pour the *spinach* into the cullender to drain.

8. We must now press all the water out of the *spinach*, squeezing it quite dry.

9. We put it on a board and chop it up as finely as possible.

N.B.—If preferred, the spinach might be rubbed through a wire **sieve** instead of chopped up.

10. We take a stewpan and put in it *one ounce of butter.*

11. We put the *spinach* in the stewpan, and add about *half a saltspoonful of pepper* and a *saltspoonful of salt* or more, according to taste, and *half a gill of cream*, and mix all together with a wooden spoon.

12. We put the stewpan on the fire and stir the *spinach* until it is quite hot.

13. We cut a slice of *crumb of bread*, about a *quarter of an inch* in thickness, put it on a board, and cut it up into triangular pieces.

14. We take a frying-pan, and put into it *two ounces of butter or clarified dripping*.

15. We put the frying-pan on the fire to heat the *fat*.

16. When the *fat* is quite hot, we throw in the pieces of *bread*, and let them fry a pale brown.

17. We take the pieces of fried *bread* and arrange them round a hot vegetable dish to form a wall.

18. We serve the dressed *spinach* in the centre.

Now it is finished.

VEGETABLES.

Lesson No. 9.

PEAS.

Average cost of dressing "*Peas.*"

INGREDIENTS.

	s.	d.
½ a peck of Peas	1	0
Salt		
¼ of a saltspoonful of carbonate of soda	0	0¾
½ an ounce of butter		
Castor sugar	0	0¼
	1	1

Time required, about half an hour.

Now we will show you how to dress *Peas.*

1. We take the *peas* and shell them.

2. We take a saucepan full of warm water and put it on the fire to boil.

3. When the water is quite boiling, we put in the shelled *peas*, a *teaspoonful of salt*, and a *quarter of a saltspoonful of carbonate of soda.*

N.B.—The soda will keep the peas a good colour.

4. We let them boil for from *fifteen to twenty minutes*, according to the age of the *peas.* (The cover should be off the saucepan.)

5. After that time we should feel the *peas*, that they are quite soft, we then take them out of the saucepan and drain off all the water in a cullender.

6. We now turn the *peas* into a sauté-pan with *half an ounce of butter.*

7. We sprinkle about *half a teaspoonful* of *salt*, and about a *teaspoonful of castor sugar* over the *peas*, and toss them over the fire for a few minutes, but they must not fry.

8. For serving, we arrange them on a hot vegetable dish.

Now it is finished.

VEGETABLES.

Lesson No. 10.

HARICOT BEANS.

Average cost of *"Haricot Beans"* with *"Parsley and Butter."*

INGREDIENTS.

	d.
1 pint of beans	3
1 oz. of butter	1
A sprig of parsley	
Pepper and salt	0½
¼ oz. of clarified dripping	
	4½

Time required, after the beans are soaked, about two hours and ten minutes.

Now we will show you how to boil *Haricot Beans*, and serve them with *parsley and butter.*

1. We soak *one pint of haricot beans* in cold water all night.

2. We put them into a saucepan with *three pints of cold water*, and a *quarter of an ounce of clarified dripping.*

3. We put the saucepan on the fire, and when it boils we move it rather to the side of the fire and let it boil very gently for *two hours.*

4. After that time we turn the *beans* on to a cullender, drain off the water, and put the *beans* back into the dry saucepan with *one ounce of butter.*

5. We take a *sprig of parsley*, wash it, and dry it in a cloth, put it on a board and chop it up as finely as possible.

6. We sprinkle the *parsley* over the *beans* and season them with *pepper and salt.*

7. We put the saucepan on the fire and stir the contents carefully for about *five minutes.*

8. For serving, we turn the *beans* on to a hot dish.

Now it is finished.

VEGETABLES.

LESSON No. 11.

TURNIPS.

Average cost of a dish of "*Turnips*" boiled and mashed.

INGREDIENTS.

	d.
4 large turnips	4
1 oz. of butter	} 1
Pepper and salt	
	5

Time required, about three-quarters of an hour.

Now we will show you how to boil *Turnips* and mash them.

1. We put *two quarts of warm water* and a *tablespoonful of salt* into a saucepan, and put it on the fire to boil.

2. We take some *turnips*, wash them in cold water, and peel them thickly with a sharp knife.

3. If the *turnips* are very large, we should cut them in quarters.

4. When the *water* in the saucepan is quite boiling we put in the *turnips* and let them boil gently until they are quite tender.

5. We should feel them with a fork to see if they are tender all through.

6. We then turn them into a cullender and drain them very dry.

7. For serving, we put them on to a hot dish. If *mashed turnips* are required,

8. We boil them as above.

9. We squeeze them as dry as possible in the cullender, pressing them with a plate.

10. When the *turnips* are quite free from *water*, we hold the cullender over a saucepan and rub the *turnips* through with a wooden spoon.

11. We put *one ounce of butter* into the saucepan with the *turnips* and *pepper and salt* to taste.

12. We put the saucepan on the fire, and stir the contents until the *butter* is well mixed with the *turnips* and they are thoroughly warmed through.

13. For serving, we turn the *turnips* on to a hot dish.

Now it is finished.

VEGETABLES.

Lesson No. 12.

CARROTS.

Average cost of a dish of "*Carrots.*"

INGREDIENTS.

	d.
Carrots, 6 young 3*d.*, or 4 old	
1 tablespoonful of salt	4
A small piece of soda the size of a nut	
	4

Now we will show you how to boil *Carrots*.

1. We put *two quarts of warm water* into a saucepan with *one good tablespoonful* of *salt*, and a small piece of *soda* the size of a nut, and put it on the fire to boil.

2. We take the *carrots* and cut off the *green tops* and wash the *carrots* well in *cold water*.

3. We scrape the *carrots* clean with a sharp knife, and carefully remove any black specks.

4. If the *carrots* are very large we cut them in halves and quarters.

5. When the *water* in the saucepan is quite boiling, we put in the *carrots* and let them boil until they are tender.

> N.B.—*Young carrots* need not be cut up, nor do they take so long to boil as old ones.

6. For serving we turn the *carrots* into a cullender to drain, and then put them on a hot dish.

Now it is finished.

SAUCES.

Lesson No. 1.

WHITE SAUCE.

Average cost of "*White Sauce*" (*about one pint and a half*).

INGREDIENTS.

	s.	d.
1 pint of white stock	0	7¼
2 oz. of butter	0	2¼
1 and ½ oz. of flour	0	0¼
6 Mushrooms	0	3
Half a pint of cream	1	0
	2	0¾

Time required (*if the Stock is made*), *about half an hour.*

Now we will show you how to make *White Sauce*.

1. We put *two ounces of butter* into a stewpan.

2. We put the stewpan on the fire, and when the *butter* is melted we stir in *one ounce and a half of flour* with a wooden spoon.

3. We add *one pint of white stock* (see Lesson on "Stock"), and stir it until it boils.

4. We take *half a dozen mushrooms,* wash them and peel them.

5. We add them to the *sauce*.

6. We let it come to the boil again, then move the stewpan to the side of the fire, with the lid half on, to simmer for twenty minutes, to throw up the *butter*.

7. As the *butter* rises we skim it off with an iron spoon.

8. We pour the *sauce* through a tammy cloth into another saucepan.

9. We put this saucepan on the fire, and stir till it boils, then add *half a pint of cream*.

10. We pour it into a basin and stir while it cools, it is then ready for use.

Now it is finished.

Lessons on Making Sauces.—Brown Sauce.

SAUCES.

LESSON No. 2.

BROWN SAUCE.

Average cost of "*Brown Sauce*" (*about one pint*).

INGREDIENTS.

	s.	d.
1 pint of brown stock	0	8
1 and ½ oz. of flour } Salt and pepper }	0	0½
2 oz. butter	0	2
4 mushrooms	0	2
	1	0½

Time required, about 15 minutes.

Now we will show you how to make *Brown Sauce.*

1. We put *two ounces of butter* into a stewpan, and put it on the fire to melt.

2. We take *four mushrooms* (if large, or *six small*), wash them well in cold water, cut off the end of the stalks, and peel them.

3. When the *butter* in the stewpan is melted, we stir in *two ounces of flour*, and mix them into a smooth paste with a wooden spoon.

4. We now add *one pint of brown stock* and the *mushrooms*, and stir the sauce smoothly over the fire, until it boils and thickens.

N.B.—The *mushrooms* might be omitted if liked, and the *sauce* flavoured according to the dish with which it is to be served.

5. We then move the stewpan to the side of the fire, and let it simmer gently for ten minutes.

6. We must watch it carefully, and skim off all the *butter* as it rises to the top of the *sauce*.

7. We season the *sauce* with *pepper* and *salt* according to taste.

N.B.—If the *sauce* is not brown enough in colour, *a teaspoonful of caramel* (*burnt sugar*) might be stirred into it.

8. We now strain the *sauce* through a tammy sieve into a basin, and it is then ready for use.

Now it is finished.

SAUCES.

LESSON No. 3.

MAYONNAISE SAUCE.

Average cost of "*Mayonnaise Sauce*" (*about half a pint*).

INGREDIENTS.

	d.
2 eggs	2
Salt and pepper	
1 teaspoonful of French vinegar	1
1 teaspoonful of mustard	
1 teaspoonful of Tarragon vinegar	1½
1 gill of salad oil	6
	10½

Time required, about 10 minutes.

Now we will show you how to make *Mayonnaise Sauce.*

1. We take *two eggs* and put the *yolks* in one basin and the *whites* (which will not be wanted) into another basin.

2. We take a wooden spoon and just stir the *yolks* enough to break them.

3. We add to them *a saltspoonful of salt* and *half a saltspoonful of pepper*, and *a tablespoonful of French vinegar.*

4. We take a bottle of *salad oil,* and, putting our thumb half over the top, pour in, drop by drop, the *oil,* stirring well with a whisk the whole time; *a gill of oil* will be sufficient.

N.B.—We might add *a teaspoonful of ready-made mustard or tarragon vinegar* if liked, stirring it in smoothly.

5. The *sauce* is now ready for use.

Now it is finished.

SAUCES.

Lesson No. 4.

SAUCE PIQUANTE.

Average cost of *Sauce Piquante* or sharp sauce (*about half a pint*).

INGREDIENTS.

	d.
1 shalot, half a carrot, 3 mushrooms	3
1 oz. of butter	1¼
1 oz. of flour	0¼
Half a pint of good brown stock	3½
1 sprig of thyme	
1 bay leaf	
Salt and Cayenne pepper	1
2 tablespoonsful of vinegar	
	9

Time required, about twenty-five minutes.

Now we will show you how to make *Sauce Piquante* or sharp sauce.

1. We take *a shalot* and *three mushrooms*, and peel them, we scrape *half a carrot*, and then chop them up together very finely on a board.

2. We put the chopped *shalot, carrot,* and *mushroom* into a stewpan with *one ounce of butter*.

3. We put the stewpan on the fire and fry them brown.

4. We then stir in *one ounce of flour* and *half a pint of good brown stock* (see Lesson on "Stock").

5. We also add *one sprig of thyme, a bay-leaf,* and *one tablespoonful of Harvey Sauce,* and stir the *sauce* well until it boils.

6. We then move the stewpan to the side of the fire, and let it simmer for twenty minutes.

7. We season the *sauce* with *salt* according to taste, *Cayenne pepper* (enough to cover very thinly *half the top of a threepenny piece*), and *two tablespoonsful of vinegar*.

8. We strain the *sauce* and it is then ready for use.

Now it is finished.

SAUCES.

Lesson No. 5.

DUTCH SAUCE.

Average cost of " *Dutch Sauce.*"

INGREDIENTS.

	d.
Half a pint of melted butter	3
5 yolks of eggs	5
Salt and Cayenne pepper	
2 teaspoonsful of lemon juice	1
	9

Time required, about ten minutes.

Now we will show you how to make *Dutch Sauce*.

1. We take *half a pint of melted butter* and put it into a stewpan.

2. We add the *yolks of five eggs*.

3. We stand the stewpan in a saucepan of *hot water* over the fire, and *stir* well with a wooden spoon.

4. We season it with *salt* according to taste, and *Cayenne pepper* (enough to cover very thinly *half the top of a threepenny piece*).

5. We must *stir* continually until it *thickens*, and we must *not* let the *sauce boil* or it will *curdle*.

6. Just before the *sauce* is finished we stir in *two teaspoonsful of lemon juice*.

Now it is finished.

PASTRY.

Lesson No. 1.

PUFF PASTE.

Average cost of "*Puff Paste.*"

INGREDIENTS.

	d.
¼ lb. of flour	¾
¼ lb. of fresh butter	5½
Yolk of 1 egg	
Salt	1
A few drops of lemon juice	
	7¼

Time required, one hour and a quarter.

Now we will show you how to make *Puff Paste.*

1. We take *a quarter of a pound of flour* and put it in a heap, on a clean board, and make a well in the centre of the *flour.*

2. We take *half* the *yolk* of an *egg* and put it in the well.

3. We add *six drops of lemon juice.*

4. We take *a quarter of a pound of butter* and lay it on a clean cloth.

5. We fold the cloth over the *butter* and squeeze it to get all the water out of the *butter.*

6. We mix all these ingredients well together (with our hands), adding *water* to make the paste of the same consistency as the *squeezed butter.*

7. We take a *rolling pin* and *flour* it, and also sprinkle *flour* on the board to prevent the *paste* from sticking.

8. We roll out the *paste* rather thin, to about a quarter of an inch in thickness.

9. We place the pat of *squeezed butter* on one half of the *paste* and fold the other half over the *butter*, so as to cover it entirely, pressing the edges together with our thumb.

10. We let it stand on a plate in a cool place for a quarter of an hour.

>   N.B.—It is not necessary to do this in cold weather, it might be rolled at once.

11. We bring the *paste* back and place it on the board, we roll it out with the rolling pin and fold it over in three.

12. We turn it round with the rough edges towards us.

13. We roll it again and fold it in three.

14. We put it aside again for a quarter of an hour.

15. We bring it back on the board and roll it with a rolling pin and fold it in three, twice as before.

16. We put it aside again for a quarter of an hour.

17. We bring it back to the board and roll it and fold it in three as before.

18. We put it aside for another quarter of an hour.

19. We bring it back to the board, and roll it out ready, either to cover an *apple tart*, to make *tartlets*, or *patty cases*.

20. If the *paste* is used for an *apple tart*, we put it over the *apples* in the same way as the *short crust* over the *fruit tart* (see "Pastry," Lesson No. 2).

21. If the *paste* is used for *tartlets*, the *paste* should be one-eighth of an inch thick.

22. We take the *tartlet tins* and wet them with the *paste brush*.

23. We cut the *paste* out with a *cutter*, a size larger than the tins. The *cutter* must be *floured* or the *paste* will stick to it.

24. We fix the *paste* into the tins, and put a *dummy* to prevent the *paste* rising straight.

25. We put the tins on a baking sheet.

26. We put the baking sheet in a hot oven for *six minutes*, the *heat* of the *oven* should rise to 300° *Fahrenheit*, according to the *thermometer* fixed in the oven.

27. When the *tartlets* are baked sufficiently, we take them out of the oven.

Lessons on Making Pastry.—Puff Paste. 245

28. We take out the *dummies*, and turn the *paste* out of the tin.

29. We fill in the *tartlets* with *jam*.

N.B.—If *Patty Cases* are required,

1. We take the *puff paste*, it should be half an inch thick, and stamp it out with a round *cutter*, the usual size of an oyster patty.

2. We take these cut rounds, and place them on a baking sheet.

3. We take a *round cutter*, three sizes smaller, and dip it in hot water, and stamp the cut rounds of *paste* in the centre, but not right through.

4. We put the baking sheet in a *hot* oven for *six minutes*.

N.B.—The *heat* of the *oven* should be the same as for *tartlets*.

5. When the *patties* are sufficiently baked, we take the baking sheet out of the oven.

6. The cut centre of each *patty case* will have risen so that we can take it off.

7. We take a small knife, and with the point cut out all the *moist paste* from the centre of the *patty case*.

8. Now the *cases* are ready to be filled in with either *prepared oysters, minced veal, chicken,* or *pheasant,* &c., according to taste.

Now it is finished.

PASTRY.

LESSON No. 2.

SHORT CRUST.

Average cost of "*Short Crust.*"

INGREDIENTS.

	d.
6 oz. of flour	1
4 oz. of butter	4½
1 oz. of castor sugar	
Yolk of 1 egg	
Salt	1½
A teaspoonful of lemon juice	
	7

Time required for making, about a quarter of an hour.

Now we will show you how to make *Short Crust.*

1. We take *six ounces of flour* and *four ounces of butter.*

2. We put these on a clean board, and mix them well together, rubbing them lightly with our hands until there are no lumps of *butter* left, and the *flour* and *butter* resemble sifted bread crumbs.

3. We take a *large tablespoonful of castor sugar.*

4. We mix the *sugar* well into the *buttered flour.*

5. We heap it on the board, making a well in the centre.

6. We take the *yolk of one egg* and place it in the well.

7. We sprinkle a *quarter of a saltspoonful of salt* over the *egg.*

8. We add a *teaspoonful of lemon juice.*

9. We add a *large tablespoonful of cold water.*

10. We slowly and lightly mix all these ingredients with our fingers until they are formed into a stiff paste.

11. We must keep our hands and the board well floured that the *paste* may not stick.

12. We fold the *paste* over and knead it lightly with our knuckles.

13. We take a rolling pin and *flour* it, and roll out the *paste* to the size and thickness required.

14. If the *paste* is for a *fruit tart* we roll it out to the shape of the pie dish, only a little larger, and to the thickness of about a *quarter of an inch*.

15. We arrange the *fruit* in the pie dish, heaped up in the centre.

16. We sprinkle a *tablespoonful of moist sugar* over the *fruit*, or more or less according to the *fruit* used.

17. We take a paste brush and wet the edge of the dish with *water*, or a little *white of egg*.

18. We cut a strip of the *paste* the width of the edge of the pie dish and place it round the edge of the dish.

19. We take the paste brush again, and wet the edge of the *paste* with *water* or *white of egg*.

20. We take the remaining *paste* and lay it over the pie dish, pressing it down with our thumb all round the edge.

21. We must be very careful not to break the *paste*.

22. We take a knife and trim off all the rough edges of the *paste* round the edge of the dish.

23. We take a knife and with the back of the blade we make little notches in the edge of the *paste*, thus, pressing the *paste* firmly with our thumb to keep it in its proper place.

24. We take a skewer and make a little hole through the *paste* on either side of the tart, to let out the steam.

25. We take the paste brush, and wet the tart all over with *water*.

26. We sprinkle some *castor sugar* over the tart. This is to glaze it.

27. We now put the *tart* into a hot oven (the *heat* of the *oven* should rise to 240° *Fahrenheit*) for *half an hour*, or *three quarters of an hour*, according to the size of the tart. We must watch it occasionally and turn it, to prevent its burning. It should become a pale brown.

Now it is finished.

PASTRY.

Lesson No. 3.

GENOESE PASTRY.

Average cost of "*Genoese Pastry.*"

INGREDIENTS.

	s.	d.
6 ozs. of flour	0	1
6 ozs. of butter	0	6¾
8 ozs. of castor sugar	0	3
7 eggs	0	7
	1	5¾

Time required, about one hour.

Now we will show you how to make *Genoese Pastry.*

1. We take a small stewpan and put in it *six ounces of butter.*

2. We put the stewpan on the fire to melt the butter. We must be careful that it does not *burn* or *boil.*

3. We take a round tin two inches deep and fit into it a sheet of paper, cut round so that it will allow one inch of paper to be above the edge of the tin.

4. We must butter the paper with a paste brush dipped in the melted *butter.*

5. We stand a wire sieve over a plate, and rub through it *six ounces of flour.*

6. We take a large basin and break into it *seven eggs.*

7. We add *half a pound of castor sugar.*

8. We take a large saucepan of *boiling* water and put it on the fire.

9. We stand the basin containing the *eggs* and *sugar* in the saucepan of boiling water, and whip the *eggs* and *sugar* for twenty minutes. They must not get very hot.

10. We take the basin out of the saucepan, and stand it on the table.

Lessons on Making Pastry.—Genoese Pastry.

11. We now add the *butter* and then sprinkle in the sifted *flour*, stirring lightly with a wooden spoon all the time.

12. We pour this mixture into the prepared tin.

13. We put the tin into a quick oven to bake (the *heat* of the *oven* should rise to 220°) for *half an hour*. The mixture should become a pale brown.

> N.B.—When the paste is sufficiently baked no mark should remain on it if pressed with the finger.

14. When it is quite baked, we take the tin out of the oven, and turn the cake upside down on a hair sieve to cool.

15. When it is cold we cut it into little shapes with a cutter. Sandwiches of jam can be made with it if required.

Now it is finished.

PASTRY.

LESSON No. 4.

ROUGH PUFF PASTE.

Average cost of "*Rough Puff Paste.*"

INGREDIENTS.

	d.
8 ozs. of flour	1½
6 ozs. of butter	6¾
The yolk of 1 egg	⎫
Salt	⎬ 1
½ a teaspoonful of lemon juice	⎭
	9

Time required, about a quarter of an hour to make.

Now we will show you how to make *Rough Puff Paste*.

1. We take *eight ounces of flour* and *six ounces of butter* and put them on a clean board.

2. We take a knife and chop up the *butter* in the *flour*.

3. We heap it on the board, making a well in the centre.

4. We take the *yolk of one egg*, and place it in the well.

5. We sprinkle a *quarter of a saltspoonful of salt* over the *egg*, and squeeze *half a teaspoonful of lemon juice*.

6. We add a *large tablespoonful of cold water*, and beat it up slightly with a knife.

7. We now slowly, and lightly, mix it all with our fingers, adding more water if necessary, until it be formed into a stiff paste.

8. We must keep our hands and the board well floured, that the paste may not stick.

9. We take a rolling pin, flour it, and roll out the paste, and fold it over in half.

10. We turn it round with the rough edges towards us.

11. We roll it again and fold it in half.

12. We must roll out the paste, and fold it twice more as before.

> N.B.—The paste is now ready to be used for a meat pie, apple tart, tartlets, &c. The *heat* of the *oven* should rise to 280°, but it must be reduced down to 220° after the first *quarter of an hour.*

Now it is finished.

PASTRY

LESSON No. 5.

SUET CRUST FOR BEEF-STEAK PUDDING.

Average cost of *"One Quart Beef-Steak Pudding with Oysters."*

INGREDIENTS.

	s.	d.
½ lb. of flour	0	1½
5 ozs. of beef suet	0	2¼
2 lbs. of rump or beef-steak } Pepper and salt }	2	8
1 doz. of oysters	2	0
1 gill of stock	0	1¾
	5	1¾

Time required, about three hours and a half.

Now we will show you how to make *Suet Crust*, to be used for either a *Beef-Steak Pudding*, or *Roly-Poly*, &c.

1. We take *five ounces of beef suet*, and put it on a board.

2. We take a knife, and cut away all the skin, and chop up the *suet* as finely as possible.

3. We put *half a pound of flour* into a basin, and add to it the *chopped suet* and *a teaspoonful of salt*.

4. We rub the *suet* well into the *flour* with our hands.

5. We then add, by degrees, enough *cold water* to make it into a smooth paste. We should mix it well.

6. We take the paste out of the basin, and put it on a board.

7. We take a rolling-pin and flour it. We also sprinkle *flour* on the board, to prevent the paste from sticking.

8. We roll out the paste once, to the thickness of rather more than one-eighth of an inch.

> N.B.—Now the paste is ready for use, and if it is required for beef-steak pudding—

9. We take a quart pudding basin, and butter it well inside.

10. We line the basin smoothly inside with paste.

11. We take a knife, flour it, and cut away the paste that is above the edge of the basin.

12. We fold this paste together, and roll it out to a round, the size of the top of the basin, one-eighth of an inch in thickness.

13. We take *two pounds of rump or beef-steak*, put it on a board, and cut it into thin slices.

14. We flour the slices well (using about *a tablespoonful of flour*), and season them with plenty of *pepper* and *salt*.

15. We take *one dozen oysters*, and the liquor that is with them, and put them into a saucepan.

16. We put the saucepan on the fire, and just bring them to the boil.

> N.B.—This is to blanch the oysters.

17. We take the saucepan off the fire, and strain the *oyster liquor* into a basin.

18. We take the *oysters* and lay them on a plate.

19. We cut off the beards and all the hard parts of the *oysters*, leaving only the soft part.

20. We roll up the slices of *beef-steak*, and fill the basin with the *meat* and the *oysters*.

> N.B.—If oysters be disliked, kidneys might be used instead, or the pudding might be flavoured with shallot, parsley, and mushrooms, according to taste.

21. We now pour into the basin the *liquor* from the *oysters*, and *one gill of stock* (see Lesson on "Stock").

22. We wet the paste round the edge of the basin with *cold water*, and cover over the top of the basin with the round of paste.

23. We must join the paste together at the edge of the basin, pressing it down with our thumb.

24. We take a pudding cloth, flour it, and lay it over the top of the basin, tying it on tightly with a piece of twine.

25. We take a large saucepan of *warm water*, and put it on the fire to boil.

26. When the water is quite boiling, we put in the *pudding*, and let it boil for *three hours*.

27. For serving, we take off the cloth and turn the *pudding* carefully out of the basin on to a hot dish.

Now it is finished.

PASTRY.

Lesson No. 6.

SHORT CRUST FOR APPLE TURNOVERS AND APPLE DUMPLINGS, &c.

Average cost of "*Apple Turnovers*" (about three).

INGREDIENTS.

	d.
¾ lb. of flour	2
¼ lb. of clarified dripping or butter	2
½ a teaspoonful of baking powder	2
3 apples	
3 teaspoonsful of moist sugar	1
	7

Time required, about half an hour.

Now we will show you how to make *Apple Turnovers*.

1. We take *three apples*, peel and quarter them, cut out the core, and cut them into thin slices.

    N.B.—One apple is required for each turnover.

    N.B.—If a *fruit pie* or *apple dumplings* are required, see below.

2. We put *three quarters of a pound of flour* into a basin, and mix into it *half a teaspoonful of baking powder*.

3. We take a *quarter of a pound of clarified dripping* or *butter*, and rub it well into the *flour* with our hands.

4. We add enough *cold water* to moisten it, and mix it into a stiff *paste*.

5. We take a board, flour it, and turn the *paste* out on to it.

6. We flour a rolling pin, and roll out the *paste* to about *a quarter of an inch* in thickness.

7. We cut the *paste* into *rounds;* each *round* should be about the size of a small plate.

8. We lay the *apple* on one half of the *round of paste*, and sprinkle over it *one teaspoonful of moist sugar*.

9. We wet the edges of the *paste*, fold the *paste* over the *apple*, pressing the edges together with our thumb.

> N.B.—We must be careful to join the *paste* together on all sides, or the *juice* of the *apple* will run out whilst it is cooking.

10. We grease a tin with a little *dripping*, and place the *turnovers* on it.

11. We put the tin into the oven (the *heat* of it should rise to 220°) to bake for *a quarter of an hour*.

12. For serving we place the *turnovers* on a hot dish.

For *Baked Apple Dumplings*.

1. We divide the *paste* into *three portions*.

2. We take *three apples*, peel them, and cut out the *core* from the centre.

> N.B.—We must not cut the *apples* in pieces.

3. We fill the centre of the *apples* with *moist sugar*.

4. We press each *apple* into the centre of each *portion of paste*, and gradually work the *paste* over the *apple*, until the *apple* is entirely covered in.

> N.B.—We must be very careful to join the *paste* together as neatly as possible, so as not to show the join; and there must be no cracks in the *paste*.

5. We grease a *tin*, as described above, place the *dumplings* on it, and put it in the oven (the *heat* should rise to 220°) to bake for *a quarter of an hour*.

6. For serving we take the *dumplings* off the tin, and put them on a hot dish.

1. If the *paste* is for a *Fruit Pie*, we roll it out to the shape of the *pie dish*, only a little larger, and to the thickness of about *a quarter of an inch*.

2. We arrange the *fruit* in the *pie dish*, heaped up in the centre.

3. We sprinkle *a tablespoonful of moist sugar* over the fruit, or more or less according to the *fruit* used.

4. We take a *paste brush* and wet the edge of the *dish* with *water*, or a little *white of egg*.

5. We cut a *strip of the paste* the *width of the edge of the pie dish*, and place it round the *edge of the dish*.

6. We take the *paste brush* again and *wet* the edge of the *paste* with *water* or *white of egg*.

7. We take the remaining *paste* and lay it over the *pie dish*, pressing it down with our thumb all round the edge.

8. We must be very careful not to break the *paste*.

9. We take a *knife* and trim off all the *rough edges* of the *paste* round the edge of the *dish*.

10. We take a *knife*, and with the *back of the blade* we make little *notches* in the *edge of the paste*, pressing the *paste* firmly with our thumb to keep it in its proper place.

11. We take a *skewer* and make a little *hole* through the *paste* on either side of the *tart*, to let out the steam.

12. We take the *paste brush* and wet the *tart* all over with *water*.

13. We sprinkle some *pounded loaf sugar* over the *tart*, this is to glaze it.

14. We now put the *tart* into a hot oven (the *heat* of it should rise to 240°) for *half an hour*, or *three quarters of an hour*, according to the size of the *tart*. We must watch it occasionally and turn it, to prevent its burning; it should become a pale brown.

N.B.—If a better *crust* is required for *apple turnovers*, &c., see "Pastry," Lesson No. 2.

Now it is finished.

PASTRY.

LESSON No. 7.

FLAKY CRUST FOR PIES AND TARTS.

Average cost of "*Flaky Crust*" (to cover a four pint pie or tart).

INGREDIENTS.

	d.
1 lb. of flour	2½
½ lb. of butter	8
2 eggs	2
1 teaspoonful of baking powder	0¼
	1 0½

Time required (for making the pastry), about a quarter of an hour.

Now we will show you how to make *Flaky Crust* for *pies* or *tarts*.

1. We put *one pound of flour* into a basin, and mix into it a *teaspoonful of baking powder*.

2. We break *two eggs*, put the *whites* on a plate (the yolks we put aside in a cup), and whip them to a stiff froth with a knife.

3. We add the *whipped whites of the eggs* to the *flour*, and mix it into a stiff *paste* with *water* (about one gill).

4. We *flour* a board, and turn the *paste* out on it.

5. We take a *rolling pin*, *flour* it, and roll out the *paste* to a thin sheet.

6. We divide the *half-pound of butter* into *three portions*.

7. We take one portion of the *butter* and spread it all over the *paste* with a knife.

8. We sprinkle a little *flour* over the *butter* and fold the *paste* into three.

9. We *flour* the *rolling pin* and roll out the *paste*, and spread another portion of the *butter* over it.

10. We fold the *paste* as before, roll it out, and add the remainder of the *butter*.

11. We then fold the *paste* again, and roll it out to the size and thickness required either for a *fruit pie* or an *open tart*.

> N.B.—This *crust* should be baked in a quick oven (the *heat* should rise to 240°).
>
> N.B.—The top of a *fruit pie* should be brushed over with *water*, and then sprinkled with *pounded white sugar*.
>
> N.B.—For an *open tart* we take a tin (the size required) and grease it with *clarified dripping* or *butter*. We should roll out the *paste* to a thin sheet about *a quarter of an inch* in thickness, and rather larger than the size of the tin. We place the *paste* in the greased tin, pressing it into the shape of the tin with our thumb. We should place a *dummy* or a piece of *crust of bread* in the centre of the *paste* to prevent the *paste* from rising while baking. We put the tin in the oven to bake for twenty minutes. The *jam* should be put into the *tart* after it is baked.

Now it is finished.

PUDDINGS.

Lesson No. 1.

CABINET PUDDING.

Average cost of "*Cabinet Pudding*" (about *one pint and a half*).

INGREDIENTS.

	s.	d.
1 doz. cherries or raisins and two or three pieces of angelica..................	0	1½
1 doz. finger biscuits and ½ a doz. ratafias ..	0	7
1 oz. of loaf sugar and 15 drops of essence of Vanilla	0	0½
4 eggs.....................................	0	4
1 pint of milk	0	2½
	1	3½

Time required, about one hour.

Now we will show you how to make a *Cabinet Pudding*.

1. We take *a pint and a half mould*, and *butter* it inside with our fingers.

2. We take a *dozen raisins*, or *dried cherries*, and two or three pieces of *angelica*, and ornament the bottom of the mould with them.

3. We take *one dozen* stale sponge *finger biscuits* and break them in pieces.

4. We partly fill the mould with *pieces of cake* and *half a dozen ratafias*.

5. We take 4 *yolks* and 2 *whites of eggs*, and put them in a basin.

6. We add to the *eggs one ounce* of white *sugar*, and whip them together lightly.

7. We stir in by degrees *one pint of milk*.

8. We flavour it by adding *fifteen drops of essence of Vanilla*.

9. We pour this mixture over the *cakes* in the mould.

10. We place a piece of *buttered paper* over the top of the mould.

11. We take a saucepan half full of *boiling water*, and stand it on the side of the fire.

12. We stand the mould in the saucepan to steam for from *three quarters of an hour* to *an hour*.

> N.B.—The *water* should only reach *half-way* up the *mould*, or it would boil over and spoil the *pudding*.

13. For serving, we turn the *pudding* carefully out of the mould on to a hot dish.

> N.B.—For a *cold* "*Cabinet Pudding*," see "Puddings," Lesson No. 27.

Now it is finished.

PUDDINGS.

LESSON NO. 2.

LEMON PUDDING.

Average cost of "*Lemon Pudding.*"

INGREDIENTS.

	s.	d.
3 lemons	0	6
6 ozs. of sugar	0	1½
6 eggs	0	6
1 gill of cream	0	6
1 gill of milk	0	0½
3 ozs. of cake crumbs }	0	4
1 inch of cinnamon stick }		
	2	0

Time required, about one hour.

Now we will show you how to make a *Lemon Pudding*.

1. We take *three lemons*, wipe them clean in a cloth, and grate the rind of them on *six lumps of sugar*.

2. We take *an inch of the stick of cinnamon*, and put it in a mortar.

3. We pound the *cinnamon* well in the mortar with the *sugar*.

4. We put this into a basin.

5. We take *three ounces of cake crumbs*, and add to the above in the basin, and mix all well together.

6. We take the *three lemons*, cut them in *halves*, and squeeze the *juice* of them into the basin through a strainer.

7. We add the *yolks of six eggs*, and beat them in with the above. (*Two* of the *whites of eggs* we put on a plate, the others we put aside.)

8. We stir in well and smoothly *one gill (quarter pint) of cream* and *one gill of milk* with a wooden spoon.

9. We whip the *whites of the two eggs* to a stiff froth with a knife, and add them at the last moment to the above mixture, stirring it lightly.

10. We take a *pie dish*, and line the edge of it with *puff paste* (see "Pastry," Lesson No. 1).

11. We pour the mixture into the *pie dish*.

12. We put the *pie dish* in the oven (the *heat* of it should rise to $220°$) to bake till the mixture is set, and of a light brown colour; it is then ready for serving.

Now it is finished.

PUDDINGS.

LESSON No. 3.

APPLE CHARLOTTE.

Average cost of "*Apple Charlotte.*"

INGREDIENTS.

	s.	d.
2 lbs. of apples	0	6
½ lb. of loaf sugar	0	2
The rind of one lemon	0	1
Bread and clarified butter	0	6½
	1	3½

Time required, about two hours and a half.

Now we will show you how to make an *Apple Charlotte.*

1. We take *two pounds of good cooking apples*, and peel them thinly with a sharp knife.

2. We take a knife and cut them in *slices*, and take out the *core*.

3. We put these *sliced apples* into a stewpan, with sufficient *sugar* to sweeten them, and *one gill of water.*

4. We take a *lemon*, wipe it clean in a cloth, and peel it very thinly.

5. We take the *rind* of the *lemon*, and tie it together with a piece of twine, and put it in the stewpan with the *apples.*

6. We put the stewpan on the fire, and stir well with a wooden spoon until it boils, and the *apples* are reduced to about half the quantity. It will take from *one hour* to *one hour and a half.*

7. We take the stewpan off the fire, and stand it on a piece of paper on the table, and we must take out the *lemon peel.*

8. We take a plain round tin mould (about *one pint and a half*).

9. We cut a *slice of the crumb of bread, one-eighth of an inch in thickness,* and round to the size of the mould.

10. We put a *quarter of a pound of butter* in a stewpan to *melt* and *clarify*.

11. We must cut the *round of bread* into *quarters*, dip them in the *clarified butter*, and place them at the bottom of the mould.

12. We now cut *slices of the crumb of bread, one-eighth of an inch in thickness*, and the depth of the mould in length.

13. We cut these *slices* into strips *an inch wide*.

14. We dip these strips into the *clarified butter*, and place them round inside the mould, allowing them to lie half over each other.

15. We must now pour the *apples* into the middle of the mould.

16. We cover the *apples* with a *round of bread* dipped in the *clarified butter*.

17. We put the mould into a good oven (the *heat* of the oven should be about 220°) to bake for *three-quarters of an hour*.

N.B.—The bread should be quite brown and crisp.

18. For serving, we turn it carefully out of the mould on to a hot dish.

Now it is finished.

PUDDINGS

Lesson No. 4.

PANCAKES.

Average cost of "*Pancakes*" (about *eight*).

INGREDIENTS.

	d.
3 ozs. of flour	1
2 eggs	2
½ a pint of milk	1
½ a saltspoon of salt	
3 ozs. of lard	2½
The juice of a ¼ of a lemon	1
2 ozs. of moist sugar	1
	8½

Time required, about twenty minutes.

Now we will show you how we make *Pancakes*.

1. We take *three ounces of flour*, and put it in a basin.

2. We add *half a saltspoonful of salt*, and mix it well into the *flour*.

3. We break *two eggs* into the *flour*, and add a *dessertspoonful of milk*, and mix all well together with a wooden spoon.

4. We stir in gradually *half a pint of milk*, making the mixture very smooth.

N.B.—If possible it is better to let this mixture stand before frying it into pancakes.

5. We put a fryingpan on the fire, and put into it a piece of *lard* the size of a nut, and let it get quite hot, but it must not burn.

6. We then pour into the fryingpan *two large tablespoonsful of the batter*, and let it run thinly all over the pan.

7. When the *pancake* has become a light brown on one side, we should shake the pan, and toss the *pancake* over, to brown the other side the same.

Lessons on Making Puddings.—Pancakes.

8. We should stand a plate on the hot-plate, or in the front of the fire to heat.

9. When the *pancake* is fried, we turn it on to this heated plate.

10. We should squeeze about *fifteen drops of lemon juice*, and sprinkle a *teaspoonful of moist sugar* over it.

11. We now roll up the *pancake*, and place it on the edge of the plate, so as to leave room for the remainder of the *pancakes*.

> N.B.—We should fry all the pancakes in this manner, adding each time a piece of lard the size of a nut.

12. For serving we arrange the *pancakes* on a hot dish, placing one on the top of the other.

Now it is finished.

PUDDINGS.

Lesson No. 5.

RICE PUDDING.

Average cost of "*Rice Pudding*" (about *one pint*).

INGREDIENTS.

	d.
1½ oz. of Carolina rice	0½
Butter	0½
1 tablespoonful of moist sugar	0½
1 pint of milk	2½
	3½

Time required, about two hours.

Now we will show you how to make a plain *Rice Pudding*.

1. We take a *pint dish* and *butter* it well inside.

2. We take *one ounce and a half of Caroline rice*, and *wash* it well in *two* or *three waters*.

3. We put the *rice* into the *buttered* dish, and sprinkle over it a *tablespoonful of moist sugar*.

4. We fill up the dish with *new milk*.

> N.B.—*Nutmeg* may be grated, or *pounded cinnamon* be sifted, over the top of the *pudding* before it is put in the oven.

5. We put the dish into a moderate oven (the *heat* should be about 220°) to bake for *two hours*.

6. We must watch it occasionally, and as the *rice* soaks up the *milk*, more *milk* should be added (carefully lifting up the skin and pouring the *milk* in at the side), so as to keep the dish always full.

Now it is finished.

PUDDINGS.

Lesson No. 6.

CUSTARD PUDDING.

Average cost of "*Custard Pudding*" (about *one pint and a half*).

INGREDIENTS.

	d.
4 eggs	4
1 pint of milk	2
Grated nutmeg 1 tablespoonful of castor sugar	0½
Butter and flour for paste	2
	8½

Time required, about thirty-five minutes.

Now we will show you how to make a *Custard Pudding*.

1. We take a *pint and a half dish*, *butter* it well inside, and line the edge with *paste* (see "Pastry," Lesson No. 2).

2. We break *four eggs*, and put the *yolks* into a basin. (*Two whites of eggs* we put on a plate, the others we put aside.)

3. We stir *one pint of milk* in with the *eggs*.

4. We add a *tablespoonful of castor sugar*.

5. We whip the *whites* of the *two eggs* with a knife to a stiff froth, and add it to the basin, mixing it all lightly.

6. We pour this *custard* into the *buttered* dish lined with *paste*.

7. We grate *half a teaspoonful of nutmeg* over the top.

8. We put the dish into a moderate oven (the *heat* should rise to 220°) to bake for *half an hour*. It is then ready for serving.

Now it is finished.

PUDDINGS.

Lesson No. 7.

PLUM PUDDING.

Average cost of "*Plum Pudding.*"

INGREDIENTS.

INGREDIENTS.	s.	d.
½ lb. of beef suet	0	5
½ lb. of currants	0	3
½ lb. of sultanas or raisins	0	3
¼ lb. of mixed candied peel, viz., citron, lemon & orange	0	3
¼ lb. of bread crumbs ⎱ ¼ lb. of flour ⎰	0	2½
½ lb. of moist sugar	0	2
1 lemon	0	2
4 eggs	0	4
1 gill (¼ pint) of milk	0	0½
1 wineglassful of brandy	0	6
2 ozs. of almonds	0	1½
½ of a teaspoonful of salt ⎱ ½ a nutmeg ⎰	0	1
	2	9½

INGREDIENTS for *Brandy* or *Wine Sauce.*	s.	d.
3 eggs	0	3
1 gill of cream (or milk ½)	0	6
1 wineglassful of brandy or sherry	0	6
1 dessertspoonful of sugar	0	0½
	1	3½

Time required, about five hours and a half.

Now we will show you how to make a *Plum Pudding*.

1. We put a saucepan of *warm water* on the fire to boil.

2. We take *half a pound of beef suet*, put it on a board, cut away all the *skin*, and chop up the *suet* as finely as possible with a sharp knife.

3. We take *half a pound of currants*, wash them clean in water, and rub them dry in a cloth.

4. We take up the *currants* in handfuls, and drop them a few at a time, on to a plate, so as to find out if there are any stones with them.

5. We take *half a pound of sultana raisins*, and pick them over.

¹ B.—If large *raisins* are used, they should be stoned.

6. We place a wire sieve over a piece of paper.

7. We take some *crumb of bread* and rub it through the sieve. (There should be a *quarter of a pound of bread crumbs.*)

8. We take a *quarter of a pound of mixed peel, citron, lemon, and orange,* and cut it up into small pieces.

9. We put a *quarter of a pound of flour* into a kitchen basin, and add to it the *chopped suet,* and *half a teaspoonful of salt.*

10. We rub the *suet* well into the *flour* with our hands.

N.B.—We should be careful not to leave any lumps.

11. We now add the *bread crumbs,* the *currants* and *raisins, half a pound of moist sugar,* and the pieces of *candied peel,* and mix all well together.

12. We take a *lemon,* wipe it clean in a cloth, and grate the *rind* of it into the basin.

13. We also grate *half a nutmeg* into the basin, and add *two ounces of almonds* (previously blanched and chopped up finely).

14. We break *four eggs* into a basin, and add to them *one gill* (quarter of a pint) of *milk* and a *wineglassful of brandy.*

15. We stir this into the ingredients in the basin, mixing them all together.

16. We take a strong pudding-cloth, sprinkle about *a teaspoonful of flour* over it, and lay it in a basin.

17. We turn the mixture from the basin into the centre of the floured cloth.

18. We tie up the *pudding* tightly in the cloth with a piece of string.

N.B.—If preferred, the *pudding* might be put into a buttered mould and a cloth tied over the top.

19. When the water in the saucepan is quite boiling, we put in the *pudding,* and let it boil for *five hours.*

20. For serving, we take the *pudding* out of the cloth and turn it on to a hot dish.

> N.B.—*Brandy or wine* sauce (see below) can be served with the pudding if liked, either poured over it or served separately in a sauce boat.

For *Brandy or Wine Sauce.*

1. We put *three yolks of eggs* into a small stewpan.

2. We add a *dessertspoonful of castor sugar, one gill* (a quarter of a pint) of *cream* or *milk*, and a *wineglassful of brandy* or *sherry*, and whisk all well together with a whisk.

3. We take a saucepan, fill it half full of hot water, and put it on the fire.

4. We stand the stewpan in the saucepan of *hot water*, and whisk the *sauce* well for about *six or eight minutes*.

> N.B.—We must be careful that the sauce does not boil, or it will curdle.

5. After that time we take the stewpan out of the saucepan.

6. We pour the *sauce* over the *plum pudding* (see above) or into a sauce-boat.

Now it is finished.

PUDDINGS.

Lesson No. 8.

VENNOISE PUDDING.

Average cost of a "*Vennoise Pudding*" (*one pint and a half mould*).

INGREDIENTS.

	s.	d.
5 oz. of crumb of bread	0	2
2 ozs. of candied peel	0	2
3 ozs. of castor sugar 1 oz. of lump sugar	0	1½
1 lemon	0	2
4 eggs	0	4
½ a pint of milk	0	1½
1 gill (¼ pint) of cream	0	6
3 ozs. of Sultana raisins	0	1½
1 wineglassful of sherry	0	6
	2	2¼

Time required, about two hours.

Now we will show you how to make a *Vennoise Pudding*.

1. We take a piece of stale *crumb of bread* (about five ounces), put it upon a board, and cut it up in the shape of dice.

2. We put the *bread* into a basin with *three ounces of castor sugar* and *three ounces of sultana raisins*.

3. We take a *lemon*, wipe it clean with a cloth, and grate the *rind* of it into the basin.

4. We chop up *two ounces of candied peel* and put it into the basin.

5. We pour in a *wineglassful of sherry*.

6. We put a saucepan of *warm water* on the fire to boil.

7. We put *one ounce of lump sugar* into a stewpan, and put it on the fire to brown.

8. When it has become a dark brown liquid we add to

it *half a pint of milk*, and stir it until the *milk* is sufficiently coloured.

> N.B.—We must be careful that the *sugar* is quite dissolved, that there be no lumps left.

9. We then stand the stewpan on a piece of paper on the table.

10. We put the *yolks of four eggs* into a basin (the *whites* we should put aside, as they are not required for present use).

11. We pour the *coloured milk* into the *eggs*, stirring well all the time.

12. We stir the *milk* and *eggs* into the *ingredients* in the basin.

13. We also add *one gill* (a quarter of a pint) of *cream*.

14. We take a *pint and a half mould* and butter it inside.

15. We pour the *pudding* into the *mould*.

16. We butter a piece of *kitchen paper* and lay it over the top of the *mould*.

17. When the water in the saucepan is quite boiling, we place in the *mould* to steam (the water should only reach half way up the mould, or it will boil over and get into the pudding).

18. We let the *pudding* steam for *one hour and a half*.

19. For serving, we take the buttered paper off from the top of the mould, and turn the *pudding* out carefully on to a hot dish.

> N.B.—*German Sauce* (see "Puddings," Lesson No. 10) can be served with the *pudding* if liked, either poured round it, or served separately in a sauceboat.

Now it is finished.

PUDDINGS.

Lesson No. 9.
AMBER PUDDING.

Average cost of an *"Amber Pudding"* (*one pint dish*).

INGREDIENTS.

	s.	d.
6 apples	0	4
3 ozs. of moist sugar	0	1
1 lemon	0	2
2 ozs. of butter	0	3
3 eggs	0	3
Puff paste	0	4
	1	5

Time required, about one hour and a quarter.

Now we will show you how to make an *Amber Pudding.*

1. We take *six large apples, peel them,* cut out the *core*, and cut them up into *slices.*

2. We put the *apples* into a stewpan with *three ounces of moist sugar,* and *two ounces of butter.*

3. We take a *lemon,* wipe it clean with a cloth, and peel it as thinly as possible with a sharp knife.

4. We cut the *lemon* in half and squeeze the *juice* through a strainer into the stewpan.

5. We also add the *lemon peel.*

6. We put the stewpan on the fire and let it stew till the *apples* are quite tender (it will take about *three-quarters of an hour*).

7. We place a hair sieve over a large basin.

8. When the *apples* are sufficiently stewed, we pour them on to the sieve and rub them through into the basin with a wooden spoon.

9. We stir the *yolks of three eggs* into the basin.

10. We take a pie-dish (about *one pint*), and line the edge with *puff paste* (see " Pastry," Lesson No. 1).

<small>N.B.—If we have no puff paste, short paste (see "Pastry," Lesson No. 2) will do.</small>

11. We pour the *mixture* into the pie-dish, and put it in the oven (the *heat* should be 240°) for *twenty minutes*.

12. We whip the *whites of the eggs* to a stiff froth.

13. When the *pudding* is a light brown, we take it out spread the whipped *whites of the eggs* over the top, and sift about a *dessertspoonful of castor sugar* over it.

14. We put the dish back in the oven till the *icing* is a light brown; the *pudding* is then ready for serving.

Now it is finished.

PUDDINGS.

LESSON NO. 10.

BROWN BREAD PUDDING.

Average cost of a "*Brown Bread Pudding and German Sauce*" (*one pint mould*).

INGREDIENTS.

	s.	d.
A loaf of brown bread	0	2
1 lemon	0	2
Half a teaspoonful of essence of Vanilla.. 3 ozs. of castor sugar	0	1½
1 gill (¼ pint) of milk	0	0¾
1 gill (¼ pint) of cream	0	6
4 eggs	0	4
	1	4¼

German *Sauce.*

	s.	d.
2 eggs	0	2
1 wineglassful of sherry	0	6
1 dessertspoonful of castor sugar	0	0¼
	0	8¼

Time required, about one hour and a half.

Now we will show you how to make a *Brown Bread Pudding.*

1. We take a *stale brown loaf* and cut off all the crust.

2. We put a wire sieve over a plate and rub the *crumb of bread* through it.

3. We put *one gill* (quarter of a pint) of *milk* into a stewpan, and put it on the fire to boil.

4. We put *five ounces of the bread crumb* into a basin, with *three ounces of castor sugar.*

5. We take a *lemon*, wipe it clean in a cloth, and grate the *rind* over the *bread crumbs.*

6. We also add *half a teaspoonful of essence of Vanilla.*

7. We put a stewpan full of *warm water* on the fire to boil.

8. When the *milk* boils we pour it over the *crumbs*.

9. We put *one gill* (quarter of a pint) of *cream* into a basin, and whip it to a stiff froth with a whisk.

10. We add the *cream* to the other *ingredients*, and also stir in one at a time the *yolks of four eggs* (the *whites of two of the eggs* we put on a plate, the others we put aside).

11. We whip the *whites of the two eggs* to a stiff froth with a knife, and then stir them lightly into the basin, mixing all the *ingredients* together.

12. We take a *pint mould* and butter it well inside.

13. We pour the *mixture* into the *mould*, butter a piece of kitchen paper, and place it over the top.

14. When the *water* in the stewpan is quite boiling, we stand the *mould* in it to steam the *pudding* (the *water* should only reach half-way up the mould, or it will boil over and spoil the *pudding*).

15. We let it steam for *one hour and a quarter*.

16. For serving we take off the buttered paper, and turn the *pudding* on to a hot dish.

GERMAN SAUCE.

1. We put the *yolks of two eggs* into a stewpan with a *wineglassful of sherry* and a *dessertspoonful of castor sugar*.

2. We put the stewpan on the fire and mill it with a whisk till it comes to a thick froth.

N.B.—We must be careful that the sauce does not boil, or it will curdle.

3. We pour the *sauce* round the *pudding*.

Now it is finished.

PUDDINGS.

Lesson No. 11.
CARROT PUDDING.

Average cost of a "*Carrot Pudding*" (*one pint*).

INGREDIENTS.

	s.	d.
3 or 4 carrots..............................	0	1½
3 ozs. of bread crumbs	0	1
2 ozs. of butter.............................	0	2
⅛ a gill of cream	0	3
2 eggs.......................................	0	2
½ a gill of sherry	0	3
1 oz. of castor sugar	0	1
1 tablespoonful of orange flower water	0	1½
Puff paste	0	4
	1	7

Time required, about three quarters of an hour.

Now we will show you how to make a *Carrot Pudding*.

1. We take *three or four carrots* (according to their size), wash them and scrape them clean with a knife.

2. We take a grater and grate all the *red part* of the *carrots* into a basin (there should be about a *quarter of a pound*).

3. We stand a wire sieve over a plate.

4. We take some *crumb of bread* and rub it through the sieve (there should be about *three ounces of bread crumbs*).

5. We put the *bread crumbs* into the basin with the *carrot*, we also add *one ounce of castor sugar*.

6. We put *two ounces of butter* into a stewpan, and put it on the fire to melt.

7. When the *butter* is melted, we take the stewpan off the fire and stand it on a piece of paper on the table.

8. We then stir into it *half a gill* (one gill is a quarter of a pint) *of sherry, half a gill of cream*, and a *tablespoonful of orange flower water*.

9. We also add the *yolks of two eggs* (the *whites* we put on a plate).

10. We whip the *whites of the two eggs* to a stiff froth with a knife, and then stir them lightly into the stewpan, mixing all the *ingredients* together.

11. We then pour the contents of the stewpan into the basin with the *carrot and bread crumbs*, and mix them well together.

12. We take a pie-dish (about *one pint*) and line the edge of it with *puff paste* (see "Pastry," Lesson No 1).

13. We pour the *pudding* into the pie-dish, and put it into the oven (the *heat* should be 240°) to bake for *half an hour;* it is then ready for serving.

Now it is finished.

PUDDINGS.

Lesson No. 12.

ALEXANDRA PUDDING.

Average cost of an "*Alexandra Pudding*" (*one pint*).

INGREDIENTS.

	s.	d.
10 eggs	0	10
2 ozs. of castor sugar	0	1
1 gill (¼ pint) of milk	0	0¾
½ a pint of good cream	1	0
1 teaspoonful of essence of Vanilla	0	1
	2	0¾

Time required, about one hour and twenty minutes.

Now we will show you how to make an *Alexandra Pudding*.

1. We put a saucepan of warm water on the fire to boil.

2. We put the *yolks of ten eggs* into a basin (the *whites of five of the eggs* we put in another basin, the others we put aside).

3. We stir into the *yolks* of the *eggs two ounces of castor sugar*.

4. We also add *one gill* (quarter of a pint) of *milk* and *half a pint of good cream*.

5. We whip the *whites* of the *five eggs* slightly with a whisk or knife.

6. We take a plain tin *mould* (about *one pint*) and butter it inside, we cover the bottom with three rounds of buttered paper.

7. We add the *whipped whites of the eggs*, and a *teaspoonful of essence of Vanilla* to the *mixture* in the basin, and stir all lightly together.

8. We pour the *mixture* through a strainer, into the *mould*, and tie over it a piece of stiff paper with a string.

9. When the water in the saucepan boils we stand in the *mould*. (The water should only reach half way up the mould, or it will boil over and spoil the *pudding*.)

10. We let it simmer gently until the *pudding* is quite firm. (It will take about *one hour and a quarter*.)

<small>N.B.—It must on no account boil fast.</small>

11. After that time we take the *pudding* out of the saucepan and stand it in *ice*.

12. For serving, we take off the buttered paper and turn the *pudding* carefully out on to a dish, and ornament it with *red currant jelly* according to taste.

Now it is finished.

PUDDINGS.

LESSON NO. 13.

BLANC-MANGE.

Average cost of "*Blanc-mange*" (about *one quart*).

INGREDIENTS.

4 tablespoonsful of cornflour	2
1 quart of milk	4
3 ozs. of loaf sugar	} 1
1 inch of the stick of cinnamon or lemon peel	
	7

Time required, about a quarter of an hour to make, and about three quarters of an hour to get cold.

Now we will show you how to make a *Blanc-mange.*

1. We put *one quart of milk* into a saucepan with *three ounces of loaf sugar,* and *one inch of the stick of cinnamon* or the *peel of a quarter of a lemon* for flavouring.

2. We put the saucepan on the fire to boil.

3. We put *four tablespoonsful of cornflour* into a basin and mix it smoothly with a *tablespoonful of cold milk.*

4. When the *milk* in the saucepan is quite boiling, we stir in the *cornflour* quickly and let it boil for *two minutes,* stirring continually.

N.B.—We must be very careful not to let it get lumpy.

5. We take a quart basin or a mould and rinse it out in *cold water.*

6. We now take the piece of cinnamon or lemon peel out of the cornflour, and pour the *cornflour* into the basin, and stand it aside to cool.

7. When the *blanc-mange* is quite cold, we turn it out of the basin on to a dish, and it is ready for serving.

Now it is finished.

PUDDINGS.

Lesson No. 14.

BOILED BATTER PUDDING.

Average cost of a "*Boiled Batter Pudding*" (about a pint).

INGREDIENTS.

	d.
½ lb. of flour }	1¼
Salt }	
2 eggs	2
1 pint of milk	2½
	5¾

Time required, about two hours and fifteen minutes.

Now we will show you how to make a *Boiled Batter Pudding*.

1. We put a saucepan of warm water on the fire to boil.

2. We put *half a pound of flour* into a basin and mix *half a saltspoonful of salt* with it.

3. We break *two eggs* into the *flour*, and beat them well together.

4. We now add by degrees *one pint of milk*, stirring smoothly all the time, until the *batter* is well mixed.

5. We let the batter stand for one hour.

6. We take a pudding basin and grease it inside with *butter*.

7. We stir the *batter*, and then pour it into the basin.

8. We dip a pudding cloth in boiling water, wring it out and flour it well.

9. We place the *cloth* over the *batter* and tie it on securely with a piece of string, just below the rim of the basin. We pin or tie the four corners of the cloth over the top.

10. When the *water* in the saucepan is quite boiling we put in the *pudding*, and let it boil for *one hour*.

11. For serving, we take the basin out of the saucepan, take off the cloth, and turn the *pudding* carefully out on a hot dish.

Now it is finished.

PUDDINGS.

LESSON No. 15.

CORNFLOUR PUDDING.

Average cost of a "*Cornflour Pudding*"(in a cup).

INGREDIENTS.

2 dessertspoonsful of cornflour	1
½ pint of milk	1
6 lumps of sugar	½
1 egg	1
	3½

Time required, about an hour.

Now we will show you how to make a *Cornflour Pudding* (in a cup, for infants or invalids).

1. We put a saucepan half full of warm water on the fire to boil.

2. We put *two dessertspoonsful of cornflour* into a saucepan.

3. We pour in by degrees *half a pint of milk*, mixing it very smoothly.

  N.B.—We must be careful that it does not get *lumpy*.

4. We now add to it *six lumps of sugar*, put the saucepan on the fire and stir smoothly until it boils; it will take about *ten minutes*.

5. We then move the saucepan to the side of the fire.

6. We break *one egg* into the saucepan, and beat it up until it is all well mixed.

7. We take a cup (just large enough to hold the *pudding*), and grease it inside with a piece of *butter*.

8. We pour the *mixture* out of the saucepan into the cup.

9. We take a small cloth, wring it out in boiling water,

flour it well, and tie it over the top of the cup with a piece of string.

N.B.—We should tie the four corners of the cloth over the top of the cup.

10. When the *water* in the saucepan is quite boiling, we put in the cup and let it boil for *twenty-five minutes*.

11. For serving, we take the cloth off the cup, and the *pudding* may be turned out or not, according to taste.

Now it is finished.

PUDDINGS.

Lesson No. 16.

BATTER PUDDING.

Average cost of a "*Batter Pudding*" (in a cup).

INGREDIENTS.

	d.
1 egg	1
1 tablespoonful of flour	¼
1 teacupful of milk	½
Salt	
	1¾

Time required, about thirty-five minutes to make and thirty minutes to stand.

Now we will show you how to make *Batter Pudding* (in a cup for infants or invalids).

1. We put a saucepan half full of warm water on the fire to boil.

2. We put a *tablespoonful of flour* into a basin with a *few grains of salt*.

3. We break *one egg* into the basin and mix it well into the *flour*.

4. We now add by degrees a *teacupful of milk*, stirring vigorously with a wooden spoon.

5. We let the batter stand for *half an hour*.

6. After that time we take a cup (just large enough to hold the *batter*) and grease it well inside with a piece of *butter*.

7. We stir the *batter*, and then pour it into the cup.

8. We take a small cloth, wring it out in boiling water, *flour* it well, and tie it over the top of the cup, with a piece of string.

N.B.—We tie the four corners of the cloth together over the top of the cup.

9. When the *water* in the saucepan is quite boiling, we put in the cup, and let it boil for *half an hour*.

10. For serving, we take the cloth off the cup, and the *pudding* may be turned out or not, according to taste.

Now it is finished.

PUDDINGS.

Lesson No. 17.

CORNFLOUR PUDDING.

Average cost of a "*Cornflour Pudding*" (about one quart).

INGREDIENTS.

	d.
4 tablespoonsful of cornflour	1
1 quart of milk	5
3 tablespoonsful of pounded sugar	1
2 eggs	2
1 inch of the stick of cinnamon or a bay leaf Grated nutmeg	0¼
	9¼

Time required, about half an hour.

Now we will show you how to make a *Cornflour Pudding*.

1. We put *four tablespoonsful of cornflour* into a basin, and mix it quite smooth with a *tablespoonful of cold milk*.

2. We put the remainder of the *quart of milk* into a saucepan with *three tablespoonful of pounded sugar* and *one inch of the stick of cinnamon* or a *bay-leaf*.

3. We put the saucepan on the fire to boil.

4. When the *milk* boils we pour it on to the *mixture*, stirring it smoothly all the time.

5. We break *two eggs* into the *cornflour*, and beat it up lightly.

6. We take a *quart* pie-dish and grease it inside with *butter*.

7. We pour the *mixture* into the pie-dish, and grate *half a teaspoonful of nutmeg* over the top.

8. We put the dish into the oven (the *heat* should be 220°) to bake for *half an hour*.

9. It will then be ready for serving.

Now it is finished.

PUDDINGS.

LESSON NO. 18.

RICE PUDDING.

Average cost of "*Rice Pudding*" (about *one quart*).

INGREDIENTS.

	d.
½ lb. of rice	1½
1 quart of milk	5
2 eggs	2
2 oz. of moist sugar	0½
2 oz. of suet	1
Grated nutmeg	0¼
	10¼

Time required, from forty minutes to an hour.

Now we will show you how to make a *Rice Pudding*.

1. We wash *half a pound of rice* in two or three waters, and then put it into a saucepan of *cold water*, and put it on the fire till it boils and swells.

2. We break *two eggs* into a basin.

3. We add to them *two ounces of moist sugar* and *one quart of milk*, and stir them together.

4. We put *two ounces of suet* on a board, cut away all the skin, and shred it as finely as possible.

5. We take a *quart dish*, and grease it inside with *clarified dripping* or *butter*.

6. We drain off the *rice* on a cullender as dry as possible, and lay it in the greased dish.

7. We pour the mixture of *milk* and *eggs* over the *rice*, and sprinkle the *shredded suet* over the top.

8. We take a grater, and grate *half a teaspoonful of nutmeg* over the top.

9. We put the dish into an oven (the *heat* should be 220°) to bake for from *forty minutes to an hour*.

10. After that time it is ready for serving.

Now it is finished.

PUDDINGS.

LESSON No. 19.

CURATE'S PUDDING.

Average cost of "*Curate's Pudding*" (about *one quart*).

INGREDIENTS.

	d.
1 lb. of potatoes	1
3 eggs	3
1 pint of milk	2½
Sugar	0½
	7

Time required, about one hour.

Now we will show you how to make a *Curate's* or *Sweet Potato Pudding*.

1. We take *one pound of potatoes*, wash them, and boil them as described (see "Vegetables," Lesson No. 1).

N.B.—Any remains of *cold boiled potatoes* could be used instead of fresh ones.

2. We rub these *boiled potatoes* through a cullender into a basin with a wooden spoon.

3. We break *three eggs* into another basin, and stir into them *one pint of milk*.

4. We stir the *milk* and *eggs* smoothly into the *potatoes*, and sweeten it with *sugar* according to taste.

5. We take a *quart pie dish*, grease it inside, and pour the mixture into it.

6. We put the pie dish in the oven (the *heat* should be 220°) to bake for *half an hour;* it will then be ready for serving.

Now it is finished.

PUDDINGS.

Lesson No. 20.

BREAD PUDDING.

Average cost of "*Bread Pudding*" (*one quart*).

INGREDIENTS.

	d.
1 lb. of scraps of bread	1½
1 quart of milk	5
2 eggs	2
2 tablespoonsful of moist sugar	0½
4 oz. of raisins or currants	1
	10

Time required, three-quarters of an hour.

Now we will show you how to make a *Bread Pudding*.

1. We put *one pound of scraps of bread* into a basin, with plenty of *cold water* to soak.

> N.B.—Any scraps of bread, either crumb or crust, however stale, so long as they are not mouldy or burnt, can be used for this pudding.

2. We put *one quart of milk* into a saucepan, and put it on the fire to boil.

3. We put into the *milk* a piece of *butter* the size of a nut, to prevent it from burning.

4. We take the *bread* out of the basin and squeeze out all the *water*.

5. We empty the *water* out of the basin, and put back the *bread*.

6. When the *milk* boils we pour it over the *bread*, and let the *bread* soak until it is soft.

7. We break *two eggs* into a small basin, add to them *two tablespoonsful of moist sugar*, and beat them lightly together.

8. We take *four ounces of large raisins* and stone them, or, if *currants* are preferred, we should wash them, dry them in a cloth, and pick them over to see there are no stones with them.

Lessons on Making Puddings.—Bread Pudding.

9. We now beat the *bread* up with a fork as smooth as possible.

10. We put in the *raisins* or *currants*, and the *eggs* and *sugar*, and mix them all well together.

11. We take a *pie dish* or *tin*, holding *two pints and a half*, grease it well inside, and pour in the mixture.

12. We put it in the oven (the *heat* should be 220°) to bake for *half an hour;* it will then be ready for serving.

Now it is finished.

PUDDINGS.

LESSON No. 21.

TREACLE PUDDING.

Average cost of "*Treacle Pudding*" (*one quart*).

INGREDIENTS.

	d.
1 lb. of flour..................................	2¼
¼ lb. of suet...................................	2
1 teaspoonful of baking powder .... }	
Salt .... }	0¼
1 teaspoonful of ground ginger .... }	
About a ¼ lb. of treacle......................	1
About ¼ of a pint of milk	0¼
1 egg...	1
	7

Time required, *two hours and a half*.

Now we will show you how to make a *Treacle Pudding*.

1. We put a large saucepan of *warm water* on the fire to boil.

2. We take a *quarter of a pound of suet*, put it on a board, cut away the *skin*, and chop up the *suet* as finely as possible.

3. We put *one pound of flour* into a basin with a little *salt*, and *one teaspoonful of baking powder*.

4. We add the *chopped suet* and *one teaspoonful of ground ginger*, and mix all well together with a spoon.

5. We put a *quarter of a pound of treacle* into a basin with a *quarter of a pint of milk* and *one egg*, and mix them together.

N.B.—If liked, rather more *treacle* can be added.

6. We stir this into the mixture in the basin, and add more *milk* if required to make the *pudding* moist.

N.B.—When the pudding is mixed it should be rather stiff.

7. We take a *quart basin*, grease it well inside, and pour the *mixture* into it.

N.B.—We should be careful that the basin is full, for if not quite full the water will get into it and spoil the pudding.

8. We sprinkle some *flour* over the top of the *pudding*, put a cloth over it, and tie it tightly down with a piece of string, just below the rim of the basin, and tie or pin the corners of the cloth together.

9. When the water in the saucepan is quite boiling, we put in the *pudding*, and let it boil for *two hours*.

10. For serving, we take the *pudding* out of the saucepan, take off the cloth, place a hot dish over the *pudding*, and turn it carefully out of the basin.

Now it is finished.

PUDDINGS.

Lesson No. 22.

PLUM PUDDING.

Average cost of "*Plum Pudding*" (*three-quarters of a pound*).

INGREDIENTS.

	d.
5 oz. of bread crumbs	1½
7 oz. of flour	0½
¼ lb. of suet	2
¼ lb. of raisins	1½
¼ lb. of currants	1½
2 oz. of moist sugar	0½
2 oz. of candied peel	1
1 teaspoonful of baking powder	0¼
2 eggs	2
1 gill (¼ pint) of milk	0½
	11

Time required, two and a half hours.

Now we will show you how to make a *Plum Pudding*.

1. We put a large saucepan of *warm water* on the fire to boil.

2. We stand a grater on a piece of paper, and grate some *bread crumbs*; there should be *five ounces*.

3. We take a *quarter of a pound of suet* and put it on a board.

4. We take a knife, cut away all the *skin*, and chop up the *suet* as finely as possible.

5. We should sprinkle *flour* over the *suet* to prevent it sticking to the board or knife.

6. We take a *quarter of a pound of currants*, wash them well in cold water, and rub them dry in a cloth.

7. We take up the *currants* in handsful and drop them, a few at a time, on to a plate, so as to find out if there are any *stones* mixed with the *currants*.

8. We take a *quarter of a pound of large raisins* and stone them.

9. We take *two ounces of mixed candied peel, i.e., citron lemon,* and *orange,* and cut them up into small pieces.

    N.B.—If disliked, the candied peel may be omitted.

10. We put *seven ounces of flour* into a basin, and add to it the *chopped suet, quarter of a saltspoonful of salt,* and a *teaspoonful of baking powder.*

11. We rub the *suet* well into the *flour* with our hands.

    N.B.—We should be careful not to leave any lumps.

12. We now add the *bread crumbs,* the *currants* and *raisins, two ounces of moist sugar,* the pieces of *candied peel,* and mix all well with a wooden spoon.

    N.B.—If preferred, treacle may be used instead of sugar.

13. We break *two eggs* into a basin, add to them *one gill* (a quarter of a pint) of *milk* and beat them up.

14. We now stir the *milk* and *eggs* into the *pudding* and mix all well together.

15. We take a cloth, wring it out of hot water, flour it, and lay it over a quart basin.

    N.B.—We should be careful that the cloth is strong and that there are no holes in it.

16. We turn the mixture from the basin into the centre of the floured cloth.

17. We hold up the four corners of the cloth and tie up the *pudding* tightly with a piece of string.

18. When the water in the saucepan is quite boiling, we put in the *pudding,* and let it boil for *two hours.*

    N.B.—The lid should be on the saucepan.

19. For serving, we take the *pudding* out of the cloth and turn it on to a hot dish.

Now it is finished.

PUDDINGS.

Lesson No. 23.

TAPIOCA AND APPLES.

Average cost of "*Stewed Tapioca and Apples.*"

INGREDIENTS.

	d.
2 tablespoonsful of Tapioca.................	0½
6 apples	2
4 cloves and the peel of half a lemon..........	1
2 tablespoonsful of sugar	0½
	4

Time required (*after the tapioca has soaked twelve hours*), *about three-quarters of an hour.*

Now we will show you how to make a stew of *Tapioca and Apples.*

1. We put *two tablespoonsful of tapioca* into a basin with *one pint of water*, and let it soak for *twelve hours.*

N.B.—This should be done over-night.

2. We take *six apples*, peel, quarter, and core them.

3. We put in *four cloves* (for flavouring).

4. We take *one lemon*, wipe it clean with a cloth, and peel half of it very thinly with a sharp knife.

N.B.—We must be careful not to cut any of the white, as it is very bitter.

5. We put the soaked *tapioca* into a large saucepan, with the *lemon peel*, and *two tablespoonsful of pounded white sugar.*

6. We put the saucepan on the fire and stir it well until it boils.

N.B.—We should be careful not to let any stick to the bottom.

7. We let it boil for *ten minutes*, until the *tapioca* has become clear.

8. After that time we put the *apples* into the saucepan arranging them at the bottom, so that they are covered with the *tapioca.*

9. We move the saucepan to the side of the fire and let the *apples* stew gently for from *fifteen to thirty minutes*, according to their size.

10. We must not let them boil, or they will break.

11. When they are stewed quite tender, we take them out of the saucepan and put them on a dish.

12. We pour the *tapioca* over the *apples*.

N.B.—If liked, the *tapioca sauce* can be coloured by stirring in about *half a teaspoonful of cochineal*.

Now it is finished.

PUDDINGS.

Lesson No. 24.

INVALID PUDDING.

Average cost of "*Invalid Pudding*" (*half a pint*).

INGREDIENTS.

		d.
3 tablespoonsful of chopped suet		2½
3 do. bread crumbs		1
3 do. flour		0½
3 do. moist sugar		0½
3 do. milk		0½
2 eggs		2
		6¾

Time required, about one hour and three-quarters.

Now we will show you how to make an *Invalid Pudding*.

1. We take about a *quarter of a pound of mutton suet*, put it upon a board, and chop it up as finely as possible.

2. When it is chopped there should be about *three tablespoonsful*.

N.B.—Mutton suet is much lighter of digestion than beef suet.

3. We put a saucepan half full of warm water on the fire to boil.

4. We take a piece of *bread* and a grater, and grate some *bread crumbs* on to a piece of paper. There should be about *three tablespoonsful of bread crumbs*.

5. We put the *bread crumbs* and the *chopped suet* into a basin with *three tablespoonsful of flour* and *three tablespoonsful of moist sugar*.

6. We mix all these well together.

7. We now break in *two eggs*, and add *three tablespoonsful of milk*, and stir all well together with a spoon.

8. We take a *half-pint pudding basin* and grease it well inside.

9. We pour the *mixture* into the basin.

10. We take a cloth, dip it in hot water, and flour it.

11. We put this cloth over the top of the basin, and tie it on with a piece of string, just under the rim of the basin.

12. We tie the four corners of the cloth together loosely over the top of the basin.

13. We put this basin into the saucepan of boiling water, but we must be very careful that the water only reaches half way up the basin, or it will boil over and get into the *pudding*.

14. We let the *pudding* steam for *one hour and a half*.

<small>N.B.—We keep a kettle of water boiling to add to the water in the saucepan as it boils away.</small>

15. After that time we take the basin out of the saucepan, take off the cloth, and carefully turn the *pudding* out on to a warm dish.

Now it is finished.

PUDDINGS.

LESSON No. 25.

SEMOLINA PUDDING.

Average cost of "*Semolina Pudding.*"

INGREDIENTS.

	d.
½ pint milk	1½
1 tablespoonful crushed semolina	0¾
1 egg	1
1 dessertspoonful moist sugar } Butter and nutmeg }	0½
	3¼

Time required, about twenty-five minutes.

Now we will show you how to make a *Semolina Pudding.*

1. We put *half a pint of milk* and *one tablespoonful of semolina* into a saucepan.

2. We put the saucepan on the fire and stir occasionally until it boils and swells, then we set it by the side of the fire.

3. We break *one egg* into a basin and add to it *a dessertspoonful of moist sugar* and beat them lightly together with a fork.

4. We take a three-quarters of a pint pie-dish and grease it inside with a piece of *butter*.

5. When the *semolina* is sufficiently cool, we stir in lightly the *sweetened egg*.

6. We pour this *mixture* into the pie-dish.

7. We take a grater and a *nutmeg* and grate a *quarter of a teaspoonful* over the *mixture*.

8. We put the dish into the oven (the *heat* should be 220°) to bake for a *quarter of an hour*.

N.B.—Puddings can be made in the same way with sago, tapioca, or rice.

Now it is finished.

PUDDINGS.

Lesson No. 26.

BATTER AND FRUIT.

Average cost of "*Batter and Fruit Pudding*" (*one pint and a half*).

INGREDIENTS.

	d.
¼ lb. of flour	0¾
Salt	} 1¼
½ pint milk	
2 eggs	2
¼ lb. fruit	0¾
½ oz. butter	0¼
Sugar	0¼
	5¾

Time required, about forty minutes.

Now we will show you how to make a *Batter Pudding* with *fruit* in it.

1. We take a *quarter of a pound of flour* and put it in a basin.

2. We add a *quarter of a teaspoonful of salt.*

3. We stir in gradually *half a pint of milk.*

4. When it has become sufficiently liquid, we should beat it with a spoon instead of stirring it, as that will make it lighter.

5. We break an *egg* into a cup, and then add it to the *batter*, beating it up lightly all the time, until it is thoroughly mixed.

6. We then break a *second egg* into the cup and add it to the *batter*, mixing it thoroughly as before.

> N.B.—Eggs should always be broken separately into a cup to see if they are good before cooking.
>
> The more the batter is beaten the lighter it becomes.

7. We take a *pint and a half pie-dish* and grease it well inside with *butter*.

8. We pour the *batter* into the pie-dish.

9. We take *a quarter of a pound of damsons* (or any other fruit), and wipe them with a cloth to be sure that they are quite clean.

10. We sprinkle the *fruit* into the *batter*, and put *two or three* bits of *butter* on the top to prevent its being dry.

11. We put the pie-dish into the oven (the *heat* should be 220°) to bake for *half an hour*.

12. After that time we take the pie-dish out of the oven and sprinkle some *sugar* over the top.

    N.B.—Sugar should, of course, be eaten with the batter pudding.

    N.B.—If sugar was added to the batter before it was baked it would make t heavy.

Now it is finished.

PUDDINGS.

Lesson No. 27.

COLD CABINET PUDDING.

Average cost of a "*Cold Cabinet Pudding*" (*one pint mould*).

INGREDIENTS.

	s.	d.
6 sponge finger biscuits	0	3
2 oz. ratafias	0	2
½ pint of milk	0	1¼
½ oz. of best gelatine	0	1½
The yolks of 4 eggs	0	4
2 oz. of dried cherries ⎱	0	1½
Two or three pieces of angelica ⎰		
½ a gill of cream	0	3
1 teaspoonful of essence of vanilla ⎱	0	2
1 tablespoonful of castor sugar ⎰		
	1	6¼

Time required to make, about half an hour.

Now we will show you how to make a *Cold Cabinet Pudding*.

1. We take a *pint mould* and ornament the bottom of it (according to taste) with the *dried cherries*, and *pieces of angelica*.

2. We split the *sponge-biscuits* in half and line the inside of the tin with them and the *ratafias* in the *mould*.

N.B.—We must place the *biscuits* only round the sides of the tin (not over the bottom), arranging them alternately back and front next the tin.

3. We break *four eggs*, put the *yolks* in a basin (the *whites* we put aside, as they are not required for present use), and beat them well with a wooden spoon.

4. We stir *half a pint of milk* into the *eggs*, and pour the *mixture* into a jug.

5. We take a saucepan, fill it half full of *hot water*, and put it on the fire to boil, when the *water* boils we move the saucepan to the side of the fire.

6. We stand the jug in the saucepan, and stir the *custard* very smoothly until it thickens and becomes the substance of *cream*, but it must not boil or it will curdle.

7. We put *half an ounce of gelatine* in a small stewpan or gallipot, with a *tablespoonful of water*, and stand it near the fire to melt.

8. When the *custard* is sufficiently thick, we take the jug out of the saucepan and stand it aside to cool.

> N.B.—We should place a piece of paper over the mouth of the jug to prevent the dust getting in.

9. We stir the *gelatine* until it is quite melted.

10. We pour the *melted gelatine* through a strainer into the *custard*.

11. We also add *half a gill* (one gill is a quarter of a pint) of *cream*, a *teaspoonful of essence of vanilla*, and a *tablespoonful of castor sugar*.

12. We pour it all on the *cakes* in the mould.

13. We stand the mould in a cold place to set; in summer time it should be placed on *ice*.

14. When the *pudding* is quite cold and set, we turn it out carefully on to a dish, and it is ready for serving.

Now it is finished.

PUDDINGS.

Lesson No. 28.

SUET PUDDING.

Average cost of a "*Suet Pudding*" (about *two pounds*).

INGREDIENTS.

	d.
½ lb. of suet	4
1 lb. of flour	2¼
1 teaspoonful of baking powder	0¼
	6½

Time required, about one hour and three-quarters.

Now we will show you how to make a *Suet Pudding*.

1. We put a saucepan of *warm water* on the fire to boil.

2. We take *half a pound of suet*, put it on a board, cut away all the *skin*, and chop the *suet* up as finely as possible with a sharp knife.

3. We put *one pound of flour* into a basin, with *one teaspoonful of baking powder*.

4. We add the *chopped suet* and rub it well into the *flour* with our hands.

N.B.—We must be careful not to have any *lumps*.

5. We now add enough *cold water* to mix it into a stiff *paste*.

6. We take a strong pudding cloth, wring it out in boiling water, and sprinkle *flour* over it.

7. We turn the *paste* out on to the cloth, hold up the ends of the cloth, and tie it tightly round the *pudding* with a piece of string, leaving room for the *pudding* to swell.

8. When the *water* in the saucepan is quite boiling, we put in the *pudding*, and let it boil gently for *one hour and a half*.

N.B.—We should keep a kettle of boiling water and fill up the saucepan as the water in it boils away.

9. For serving, we take the *pudding* out of the saucepan, take off the cloth, and turn it on to a hot dish.

N.B.—This *pudding* can be eaten with *meat*, or it can be eaten with *sugar*, *jam*, or *treacle*.

Now it is finished.

PUDDINGS.

Lesson No. 29.

YORKSHIRE PUDDING.

Average cost of a "*Yorkshire Pudding*" (about *one pint*).

INGREDIENTS.

	d.
8 oz. of flour	1½
1 pint of milk	2
½ of a teaspoonful of baking powder	0¼
Salt	
2 eggs	2
	5¾

Time required, one hour.

Now we will show you how to make a *Yorkshire Pudding*.

1. We put *eight ounces of flour* into a basin and mix into it *half of a teaspoonful of baking powder* and half a *saltspoonful of salt*.

2. We break *two eggs* into the *flour* and stir it well.

3. We now add by degrees *a pint of milk*, beating all the time with a wooden spoon to make the *batter* as smooth and as light as possible.

4. We take a pudding tin (about a *pint*), place it under the *meat* that is roasting in front of the fire, to catch some *dripping* to grease the tin.

5. We then pour the *batter* into the tin and let it cook under the *meat* for *half an hour*, or put it in the *oven* to *bake* for *twenty minutes*.

6. We must watch it, and turn the tin, so that the *pudding* does not get burnt.

> N.B.—It is better to make *batter* some time before it is required to be used, so that it may rise.
>
> N.B.—A commoner and more substantial Yorkshire pudding can be made in the same way as above, only with 6 oz. *of flour*, 1 *egg*, 1 *pint of milk*, and 1 *tablespoonful of chopped suet* sprinkled over the *batter* when it is poured into the tin.

7. When the *pudding* is sufficiently cooked, we turn it carefully out of the tin on to a hot dish, and it is then ready for serving with the *roast meat*.

Now it is finished.

DUMPLINGS.

LESSON No. 1.

HARD DUMPLINGS.

Average cost of "*Hard Dumplings.*" (about *five.*)

INGREDIENTS.

	d.
½ lb. of flour	1¼
Salt	
	1¼

Time required, about twenty-five minutes.

Now we will show you how to make *Hard Dumplings.*

1. We put a saucepan of warm water on the fire to boil.

2. We put *half a pound of flour* into a basin, and mix in it *half a saltspoonful of salt.*

3. We now add enough *cold water* to make it into a firm *dough.*

4. We flour our hands and divide the *dough* into pieces about the size of an egg, and roll each piece into a smooth ball, without a crack in it.

5. When the water in the saucepan is quite boiling, we drop in the *dumplings* and let them boil for *twenty minutes.*

N.B.—They are best boiled with *meat,* either *salt beef* or *pork.*

6. After that time we take them out of the saucepan, put them on a hot dish, and they are ready for serving.

Now it is finished.

DUMPLINGS.

LESSON No. 2.

NORFOLK DUMPLINGS.

Average cost of "*Norfolk Dumplings*" (about *ten*).

INGREDIENTS.

	d.
1 lb. of patent flour .... }	3
Water .... }	
	3

Time required, about half-an-hour.

Now we will show you how to make *Norfolk Dumplings*.

1. We put a saucepan of warm water on the fire to boil.

2. We put *one pound of patent flour* into a basin.

3. We add to it enough *cold water* to make it into a smooth *dough* ;—it must not be too stiff.

4. We form this *dough* into round balls about the size of a large egg.

N.B.—This quantity will make about *ten dumplings*.

5. When the water in the saucepan is quite boiling, we put in the *dumplings*, and let them boil for *twenty minutes*.

6. After that time we take them out of the saucepan, and they are then ready for serving.

Now it is finished.

JELLIES.

Lesson No. 1.

WINE JELLY.

Average cost of "*Wine Jelly* from *Calves' Feet*" (about one quart).

INGREDIENTS.

	s.	d.
2 calves' feet	1	8
2 lemons	0	3
2 eggs	0	2
2 oz. of loaf sugar }		
1 inch of the stick of cinnamon }	0	0½
4 cloves }		
1 wine-glass of sherry	0	6
Half a wine-glass of brandy	0	3
	2	10½

Time required: the jelly stock should be made the day before required for use; to finish making it, about an hour.

Now we will show you how to make about *one quart of Wine Jelly* from *Calves' Feet*.

1. We take *two calves' feet* and put them on a board.

2. We chop each *foot* in *four pieces* with a chopper.

3. We put these pieces in a basin of clean *cold* water and wash them well.

4. We take them out of the basin and put them in a stew-pan with sufficient *cold* water to cover them.

N.B.—This is to blanch them.

5. We put the stew-pan on the fire to boil.

6. When the water boils we take the stew-pan and stand it on a piece of *paper* on the table.

7. We take the pieces of the *feet* out of the stew-pan with a fork and put them in a basin of *cold* water and wash them well.

8. We empty the water out of the stew-pan.

9. We wash the stew-pan well.

10. We take the pieces of the *feet* out of the basin and put them in the stew-pan with *five pints of cold water.*

> N.B.—This stock will be reduced to about *one pint and a half,* when it is sufficiently boiled.

11. We put the stew-pan on the fire to boil.

12. We must watch it and skim it often with a skimming spoon.

13. We must let it boil very gently for *five hours.*

14. After that time we strain off the liquor through a hair sieve into a basin.

15. We must put this basin in a cool place for some hours, until the *stock* is perfectly cold and is in a jelly.

16. We now take this basin of *jelly stock* and skim off all the *fat* carefully with a spoon.

17. We take a clean cloth and put it in *hot* water.

18. We take this damp cloth and dab it over the *jelly stock,* so as to remove every particle of *grease.*

19. We take a clean dry cloth and rub lightly over the *jelly stock* to dry it.

20. We take *two lemons,* wipe them clean in a cloth, and peel them very thinly with a sharp knife.

> N.B.—We must be careful, in peeling the *lemons,* not to cut any of the *white skin,* as it would make the *jelly* bitter.

21. We put the *lemon peel* into a stew-pan.

22. We squeeze the juice of the *two lemons* through a strainer into the stew-pan.

23. We take *two eggs* and put the *yolks* in one basin, and the whites in another.

24. We whip the *whites* of the *eggs* slightly, but not very stiff.

25. We put the *whipped white* of the *egg* into the stew-pan and the *crushed egg shell.*

26. We put in also *two ounces of loaf sugar, one inch of the stick of cinnamon,* and *four cloves.*

27. We whip all these together with a whisk.

28. We now add the *jelly stock*.

29. We put the stew-pan on the fire, and whisk well till it boils.

30. We now put the lid on the stew-pan, and stand it by the side of the fire for *twenty minutes* to form a crust.

31. We place the *jelly bag stand* in front of the fire, and hang the *jelly bag* in it, we must put a basin on the stand underneath the *jelly bag*.

>   N.B.—We must be sure that the *jelly bag* is quite clean.

32. We take a jug of *boiling* water, and pour it through the *jelly bag*.

33. We must do this *four* or *five times*, always using *boiling* water until the bag is quite warm.

34. We must look at the *jelly* in the stew-pan, and when the crust is formed, it is ready to be strained.

>   N.B.—We must be sure that there is no *water* left in the bag, before passing the *jelly* through, and the basin in the stand should be quite dry.
>
>   N.B.—The pouring of the *jelly* into the bag forces the water (the few drops that remain) first out into the basin; these first few drops should be thrown away and a clean basin put in its place immediately.

35. We now take the stew-pan off the fire, and pour the *jelly* carefully into the bag to pass into the basin.

36. We repeat this two or three times, until the *jelly* runs through quite clear.

>   N.B.—We must be careful in pouring the *jelly* through the bag, that we do not disturb the sediment at the bottom of the bag, which will serve as a filter.

37. We add a *wineglassful of sherry*, and *half a wineglassful of brandy*, or any other *wine* or *liqueur* according to taste.

38. We take a *quart mould*, scald it with *boiling* water, and then rinse it in *cold water*.

39. We place the *mould* in *ice*.

>   N.B.—We must be careful that the *mould* stands quite straight and firm.

40. We pour in enough of the *jelly* just to cover the bottom of the mould.

41. When this *jelly* has set slightly, we can garnish the mould with *grapes, strawberries, &c.*, according to taste.

42. We then pour the remainder of the *jelly* into the mould, and let it stand in the *ice*, until it is firmly set.

43. When the *jelly* is required for use, we dip the mould into a basin of *hot* water for about a second.

44. We shake the mould to loosen the *jelly*, place a dish over the top of the mould, and turn the jelly carefully out, so as not to break it.

Now it is finished.

JELLIES.

LESSON No. 2.

ASPIC JELLY.

Average cost of "*Savoury* or *Aspic Jelly*" (about *one quart*).

INGREDIENTS.

	s.	d.
2 calves' feet	1	8
2 lbs. of knuckle of veal	1	4
Salt		
30 peppercorns		
2 blades of mace		
1 clove of garlic	0	1
2 shallots		
1 sprig of thyme		
Two or three sprigs of parsley		
1 onion, stuck with four cloves		
1 leek	0	3
½ a head of celery	0	1½
2 carrots	0	1
1 turnip		
1 sprig of tarragon		
1 sprig of chervil		
2 bay leaves	0	6
The rind of 1 lemon		
The juice of 3 lemons		
The whites of 2 eggs	0	2
1 lb. of lean veal	0	10
1 gill of chablis or sherry	0	6
2 tablespoonsful of French vinegar	0	2
	5	8½

Time required (the jelly stock should be made the day before) to finish making it, if not decorated, about an hour.

Now we will show you how to make one quart of *Savoury* or *Aspic Jelly*.

1. We take *two calves' feet* and put them on a board.

2. We chop the *feet* in *eight pieces* with a chopper.

3. We put these pieces in a basin of clean *cold* water and wash them well.

4. We take them out of the basin and put them in a stew-pan, with sufficient *cold* water to cover them.

5. We put the stew-pan on the fire to boil.

N.B.—This is to blanch them.

6. When the water boils, we take the stew-pan off, and stand it on a piece of paper, on the table.

7. We take the pieces of *feet* out of the stew-pan with a fork, put them in a basin of *cold* water, and wash them well.

8. We empty the water out of the stew-pan.

9. We wash the stew-pan well.

10. We take the pieces of *feet* out of the basin, and put them back into the stew-pan.

11. We take *two pounds of knuckle of veal*, and put it on a board.

12. We take a sharp knife, and cut off the *meat* from the bone.

13. We put the *meat* and the *bone* into the stew-pan, with the *feet*.

14. We pour in *five pints of water*, put the stew-pan on the fire, and just bring it to the boil.

15. We must watch it, and skim it with a spoon.

16. We now add *half a teaspoonful of salt, thirty peppercorns, two blades of mace, one clove of garlic, two shallots, one sprig of thyme,* and *two or three sprigs of parsley.*

17. We take an *onion*, peel it, and stick *four cloves* in it.

18. We take *one leek*, and *half a head of celery*, and wash them in *cold* water.

19. We take *two carrots*, wash them, and scrape them clean.

20. We take a *turnip*, wash it and peel it.

21. We put all these vegetables into the stew-pan.

22. We also add *one sprig of tarragon, one sprig of chervil,* and *two bay leaves.*

23. We let all these boil gently for *five hours.*

24. After that time, we strain off the liquor, through a hair sieve into a basin.

25. We must put this basin into a cool place, for some hours until the stock is perfectly cold, and in a jelly.

Lessons on Making Jellies.—Aspic Jelly.

26. We now take the basin of *jelly*, and skim off all the *fat* carefully with a spoon.

27. We take a clean cloth and put it in *hot* water.

28. We take this damp cloth, and dab it over the *jelly stock*, so as to remove every particle of *grease*.

29. We take a clean dry cloth, and rub lightly over the *jelly stock*, to dry it.

30. We take *one lemon*, wipe it clean in a cloth, and peel it very thinly, with a sharp knife.

> N.B.—We must be careful in peeling the *lemon* not to cut any of the pith, as it would make the *jelly* bitter.

31. We put the *lemon peel* into a stew-pan.

32. We squeeze the *juice of three lemons*, through a strainer, into the stew-pan.

33. We whip the *whites of two eggs* slightly, but not very stiff.

34. We put the *whipped whites of the eggs* into the stew-pan also the *egg shells*.

35. We take *one pound of lean veal*, put it on a board, and chop it up finely.

36. We put this chopped veal in the stew-pan.

37. We pour in *one gill of chablis* or *sherry*, and *two tablespoonsful of French vinegar*.

38. We add *salt* and *pepper* to taste, and whip altogether with a whisk.

39. We put in the *jelly stock*.

40. We put the stew-pan on the fire, and whisk well until it boils.

41. We now take a large spoon and skim it carefully if necessary.

42. We put the stew-pan by the side of the fire, and let it stand for *half an hour* to form a crust.

43. We take a clean soup cloth, or a jelly bag, and fix it on the stand.

44. We take a large basin, and place it below the cloth.

45. We take the stew-pan off the fire, and pour the contents into the cloth, and let it all pass into the basin.

>N.B.—The chopped veal acts as a filter to the jelly.

46. After the *jelly* has all passed through, we remove the basin, and put a clean one in its place.

47. We take a soup ladle, and pour a *ladle-ful* of the *jelly*, at a time, over the meat in the cloth, and let it pass for the second time, very slowly, into the basin.

>N.B.—We must be careful not to disturb the deposit of chopped veal, which settles at the bottom of the cloth.

48. If a border mould of *Aspic jelly* be required, we take the mould, scald it with *boiling* water, and then rinse it in *cold* water.

>N.B.—If the Aspic jelly is only required for garnishing cold meats, &c., we stand the basin of jelly on ice, or in a cool place, until it be firmly set; we can then cut the jelly into fancy shapes, or chop it up finely with a knife.

49. We place the mould in *ice*.

>N.B.—We must be careful that the mould stands quite straight and firm.

50. We pour in enough of the *jelly* just to cover the bottom of the mould.

51. When this *jelly* has slightly set, we can garnish the mould with *fish or vegetables*, &c., according to taste, or with what it is to be served.

52. We then pour the remainder of the *jelly* into the mould, and let it stand in the *ice* until it is firmly set.

53. When the *jelly* is required for use, we dip the mould into a basin of *hot* water for about a second.

54. We shake the mould to loosen the *jelly*, and place a dish over the top of the mould, and turn the *jelly* carefully out, so as not to break it.

>N.B.—The centre of the mould can be filled with a salad of *mixed vegetables*. (See No. 13 in *Entrées*, Lesson No. 5.)

Now it is finished.

JELLIES.

Lesson No. 3.

ICELAND MOSS.

Average cost of "*Water Jelly* or *Milk Jelly* made with *Iceland Moss*" (about *one quart*).

INGREDIENTS.

For Water Jelly.	d.	*For Milk Jelly.*	d.
1 oz. of Iceland Moss		1 oz. of Iceland Moss	1
1 quart of water	1	1 quart of milk	4
2 tablespoonsful of pounded loaf sugar	½	2 tablespoonsful of pounded loaf sugar	1
	1½		6

(To be eaten with *wine* or *milk*.)

Time required (*after the Iceland Moss has soaked all night*), for "*Water Jelly*," about one hour; for "*Milk Jelly*," about two hours.

Now we will show you how to make *Jelly* with *Iceland Moss*.

1. We wash *one oz. of Iceland Moss* well in cold water.

2. We then put it in a basin of cold water, and let it soak all night.

3. After that time we take it out of the water and squeeze it dry in a cloth.

4. We then put it in a saucepan with *one quart of cold water*.

5. We put the saucepan on the fire and let it boil for *one hour*; we must stir it frequently.

6. We then strain it through a sieve into a basin, and sweeten it with *loaf sugar*.

7. It can be taken with either *wine or milk* according to taste.

For Milk Jelly :—

1. We boil the *moss* in the same quantity of *milk* instead of *water* (after it has been soaked) as above, only for *two hours* instead of *one hour*.

2. We then strain it into a basin and sweeten with *loaf sugar* according to taste.

3. When it is cold we turn the *jelly* out of the basin on to a dish and it is ready for use.

Now it is finished.

JELLIES.

Lesson No. 4.

MILK JELLY FROM COW-HEEL,
AND THE MEAT SERVED WITH ONION SAUCE.

Average cost of about one quart of "*Milk Jelly,*" and the *meat served with the onion sauce*—

INGREDIENTS.

Milk Jelly.	*d.*	*Onion Sauce.*	*d.*
1 cow-heel	6	3 or 4 onions	1½
1 quart of milk	4	½ pint of milk	1
2 inches of the stick of cinnamon	0½	¼ an oz. of flour ½ an oz. of butter	0¾
Sugar			
	10½		3¼

Time required, about four hours.

Now we will show you how to make a *Milk Jelly from Cow-heel.*

1. We buy a dressed *cow-heel* from a tripe shop.

2. We put the *cow-heel* on a board, and cut it up into small pieces.

3. We put these pieces into an earthen jar or a saucepan with *one quart of milk* and *two inches of the stick of cinnamon.*

4. We put the lid on the top of the jar, put a piece of paper over the lid, and tie it tightly down.

5. We put the jar into a very slow oven to stew for at least *three hours.*

6. If there is no oven to the stove, we can stand the jar by the side of the fire to stew.

N.B.—It reduces less if stewed in the oven.

7. When the *stew* is finished we take the jar out of the oven, take off the lid, and strain the *milk* into a basin, and sweeten it according to taste.

x

8. We put the basin aside till the *jelly* is set; it may be eaten hot or cold according to taste.

For serving the *Cow-Heel* with *Onion Sauce* :—

1. We take *three or four onions*, peel them, and cut them in quarters.

2. We put them into a saucepan with *half a pint of milk*.

3. We put the saucepan on the fire to boil till the *onions* are quite tender; it will take about *one hour*.

4. After that time we strain off the *milk* into a basin, put the *onions* on a board, and chop them up small.

5. We put *half an ounce of butter* into the saucepan and put it on the fire to melt.

6. When the *butter* is melted we add *half an ounce of flour*, and mix them smoothly together with a wooden spoon.

7. We pour the *milk* in gradually, stirring it till it boils and thickens.

8. We then add the *onions*, season with *pepper and salt* according to taste; and move the saucepan to the side of the fire.

9. We put the pieces of *cow-heel* into the *sauce*, and let them warm through.

10. For serving we put the pieces of *cow-heel* on a hot dish, and pour over them the *onion sauce*.

> N.B.—The meat from the cow-heel might be served as a curry. The curry should be made in the same way as described in "Cooked Meat," Lesson No. 4.
>
> N.B.—The bones of the cow-heel should be put into the stock-pot.

Now it is finished.

JELLIES.

Lesson No. 5.

JELLY AND STEW FROM OX FOOT.

Average cost of about one quart of "*Jelly and a stew*" made from *Ox Foot.*—

INGREDIENTS.

For *Jelly*.	s.	d.	For *Stew*.	d.
1 ox foot	1	0	1 carrot, 1 turnip, 1 onion ..	1½
¼ lb. of lump sugar	0	1	½ oz. of dripping	0½
1 egg	0	1	½ oz. of butter	0½
2 lemons	0	2	Flour and seasoning	0½
Spices	0	0½		
	1	4½		2½

Jelly flavoured with porter would be 1s. 2½d.

Time required:—

1st day to stew the foot	7 hours.
2nd day to finish jelly	1½ ,,
To make stew	1½ ,,
Total	10 hours.

Now we will show you how to make a jelly from *Ox Foot*.

1. We take a scalded *ox foot*, put it in *cold water*, and wash it well.

2. We take it out of the *water*, dry it in a cloth, and put it on a board.

3. We cut the *foot* with a sharp knife across the *first joint* and down between the *hoofs*, and chop the long piece in half.

4. We put these pieces into a saucepan with enough *cold water* to cover them.

5. We put the saucepan on the fire and just bring it to the boil.

6. We then take the pieces out, and wash them thoroughly in a basin of *cold water*.

7. We empty the water out of the saucepan, and wash it out well.

8. We put the pieces of *foot* back in the saucepan, covering them well with cold water (about *two quarts* will be enough for a moderate sized foot).

9. We put the saucepan on the fire, and when it boils we should move it to the side of the fire and let it stew gently for *six hours*.

10. We must watch it and skim it carefully with a spoon from time to time.

11. After that time we strain off the *stock* into a basin, and put it aside to cool.

<small>N.B.—The foot we should put aside until required for use.</small>

12. When the *stock* is quite cold we take an iron spoon, dip it in *hot water*, and carefully skim off the *fat*.

13. We take a clean cloth, dip it in hot water, and wipe over the top of the *jelly*, so as to remove every particle of *fat*.

<small>N.B.—For *Porter Jelly*, see below.</small>

14. We take *two lemons*, wipe them with a cloth to be sure that they are quite clean, and peel them very thinly with a sharp knife.

<small>N.B.—We must be careful in peeling the lemons not to cut any of the white skin, as it would make the jelly bitter.</small>

15. We put the *peel of one lemon* into the stewpan or saucepan.

16. We cut the *lemons* in halves, and squeeze the *juice* of the two into the saucepan.

<small>N.B.—We must be careful to remove all the pips.</small>

17. We take *one egg*, put the *yolk* in one basin and the *white* in another.

18. We whip up the *white of the egg* slightly.

19. We put the whipped *white of the egg* and the *egg shell* into the saucepan.

20. We put in *a quarter of a pound of lump sugar, half an inch of the stick of cinnamon, four cloves*, and about a quarter of an inch of saffron.

21. We now add the *jelly stock*.

22. We put the saucepan on the fire and stir the contents well with a whisk or iron spoon until it boils.

23. We now put the lid on the saucepan, and stand it by the side of the fire for *twenty minutes or half an hour*.

24. If there is no *jelly bag* we should take a clean cloth folded over cornerways, and sew it up one side, making it in the shape of a *jelly bag*.

25. We place two chairs back to back in front of the fire.

26. We take the sewn up cloth, hang it between the two chairs, by pinning it open to the top bar of each chair.

27. We must place a basin underneath the bag.

28. We must look at the *jelly* in the saucepan, and when there is a good crust formed over it is ready to be strained.

29. We then take the saucepan off the fire and pour the *jelly* carefully into the bag to pass into the basin.

30. We repeat this two or three times until the *jelly* runs through quite clear.

> N.B.—A glass of wine may be added now if desired.

31. We take a *quart basin* or a mould, scald it with *hot water*, and then rinse it out with *cold*.

32. We pour the *jelly* into the basin and stand it aside to cool and set until it is required for use.

> N.B.—If *porter jelly* is required we put the *jelly-stock* into a saucepan with a quarter of a pound of lump sugar, half a teaspoonful of mixed spice, and half a pint of porter; we put it on the fire and let it boil *for an hour and a half*, stirring occasionally; we then strain it in the same way as for the *lemon jelly*.

Now it is finished.

Now we will show you how to make a *stew of the meat of the foot*.

1. We take *one carrot*, wash it, scrape it clean, and cut it in slices with a sharp knife.

2. We take a *small turnip* and an *onion*, peel them, and cut them in slices.

3. We put these *vegetables* into a saucepan with *half an ounce of clarified dripping*.

4. We put the saucepan on the fire and let the *vegetables* fry a light brown; we must be careful they do not burn.

5. We cut the *meat* off the bones of the *foot*, cut it up into nice pieces, and season them with *pepper and salt* according to taste.

6. We put these pieces of *meat* into the saucepan with the *vegetables*.

7. We then pour in *one pint of cold water*, just bring it to the boil, and remove the saucepan to the side of the fire to stew gently *one hour* or till the *vegetables* are tender.

8. We then strain off the *liquor* and put the *vegetables* and *meat* on a dish.

9. We put the dish near the fire to keep warm.

10. We put *half an ounce of butter* into the saucepan and put it on the fire to melt.

11. When the *butter* is melted we add *half an ounce of flour*, and mix them well together with a wooden spoon.

12. We stir in gradually the *liquor*, and stir it till it boils and thickens.

13. We then remove the saucepan to the side of the fire.

N.B.—The sauce can be coloured with burnt sugar or a browned onion.

14. We now place in the *meat* and the *vegetables*, and let them just warm through.

15. We serve this *stew* on a hot dish with *boiled potatoes* (see *Vegetables*, Lesson No. 1), or *rice* (see *Rice*, Lesson No. 1).

N.B.—The bones of the foot should be put in the stock-pot.

Now it is finished.

JELLIES.

Lesson No. 6.

APPLE JELLY.

Average cost of "*Apple Jelly*" (*about one and a half pint*).

INGREDIENTS.

	d.
1 pound of apples	4
1 lemon	2
3 oz. of lump sugar	1
1 oz. of gelatine	3
½ a teaspoonful of cochineal	1
	11

Time required, about one hour.

Now we will should you how to make *Apple Jelly*.

1. We take *one pound of apples*, peel them with a sharp knife, cut them in half, take out the *core*, and then cut the *apples* in small pieces.

2. We put the *apples* in a stewpan with *three ounces* of *lump sugar* and *half a pint of water*.

3. We take a *lemon*, wipe it clean with a cloth.

4. We take a grater and grate the *rind of the lemon* over the *apples*.

> N.B.—We should be very careful only to grate the *yellow peel* of the *lemon*, as the white rind is very bitter.

5. We cut the *lemon* in half, and squeeze the *juice* through a strainer on the *apples*.

6. We put the stewpan on the fire to boil, and cook the *apples* quite tender.

7. We must stir the *apples* occasionally to prevent it sticking to the bottom of the pan and burning.

8. We put *one ounce of gelatine* in a gallipot or small saucepan with *half a gill* (*one gill is a quarter of a pint*) of *cold water*, and stand it by the side of the fire to dissolve.

9. When the *apples* are cooked to a pulp, we place a hair sieve over a basin and rub the *apples* through with a wooden spoon.

10. We now stir the *melted gelatine* into the *apple*.

> N.B.—We must be very careful that the *gelatine* is quite smoothly dissolved, there should be no lumps.
>
> N.B.—If liked, part of the *apple* might be coloured by stirring in half a teaspoonful of cochineal.

11. We take a pint and a half *mould*, rinse it out in boiling water and then in cold water.

12. We can ornament the bottom of the mould with *pistachio nuts* cut in small pieces, or *preserved cherries*, according to taste.

13. We now pour the *apple* in the mould, and if part of the *apple* is coloured we should fill the mould with alternate layers of coloured and plain *apple*.

14. We stand the mould aside in a cool place to set the *apple*.

15. For serving we dip the mould in boiling water for a second and then turn out the *apple jelly* carefully on to a dish.

> N.B.—*Half a pint of double cream* whipped to a stiff froth should be served with the *apple jelly*, either put round the edge of the dish or in the centre of the *mould*.

Now it is finished.

CREAMS.

Lesson No. 1.

VANILLA CREAM.

Average cost of "*Vanilla Cream*" (*about a pint and a half*).

INGREDIENTS.

	s.	d.
3 eggs	0	3
½ pint of milk	0	1
½ an ounce of best gelatine	0	1½
½ pint of double cream	1	3
1 tablespoonful of castor sugar	0	0¼
½ teaspoonful of essence of Vanilla	0	0½
	1	9¼

Time required for making, about three-quarters of an hour.

Now we will show you how to make a *Vanilla Cream*.

1. We take the *yolks of three eggs* and *one white*, put them into a basin, and beat them well with a wooden spoon.

2. We stir in *half a pint of milk*.

3. We pour this *mixture* into a jug.

4. We take a saucepan half full of *hot water*, and put it on the fire to boil.

5. When the water is quite boiling, we move the saucepan to the side of the fire.

6. We stand the jug of *custard* in the saucepan of *boiling water*, and stir the *mixture* very smoothly until it thickens and becomes the substance of *cream*.

> N.B.—We must stir it very carefully and watch it continually that it does not curdle.

7. When the *custard* is sufficiently thick, we take **the jug** out of the water and stand it aside to cool.

8. We put *half an ounce of the best gelatine* in a small stew-pan, with *half a gill* (one gill is a quarter of a pint) *of cold water* to soak and swell.

9. We then put the stewpan on the fire, and stir the *gelatine* until it is quite melted.

10. We pour this *melted gelatine* through a strainer and stir it into the *custard*.

11. We pour *half a pint of double cream* into a basin, and whisk it to a stiff froth with the whisk.

12. We add to it *a tablespoonful of castor sugar* and *half a teaspoonful of essence of Vanilla.*

> N.B.—If any other flavouring be preferred, it should be now added, instead of the essence of Vanilla.

13. When the *custard* is sufficiently cooled, we stir it lightly into the *whipped cream.*

14. We take a *pint and a half mould*, scald it with *hot water*, and then rinse it out with cold.

15. We pour the *cream* into the mould, and stand it in *ice*, until required for use.

16. For serving, we should dip the mould into *boiling water* for a second, shake it to loosen the *cream*, and then turn it out carefully on to a dish.

> N.B.—This is an economical recipe for making cream, but if made entirely of cream, instead of cream and custard, it would of course be richer.

Now it is finished.

CREAMS.

Lesson No. 2.

STRAWBERRY CREAM.

Average cost of "*Strawberry Cream*" (*about one pint*).

INGREDIENTS.

	s.	d.
1 pint of fresh strawberries	0	6
2½ ozs. of castor sugar	0	0¾
½ an oz. of the best gelatine	0	1½
The juice of one lemon	0	1
½ pint of good cream	1	3
	2	0¼

Time required, about half an hour.

Now we will show you how to make a *Strawberry Cream*.

1. We take *a pint of fresh strawberries,* and put them on a board.

2. We must pick them over, and put aside any that are not quite good.

3. We must stalk them, and put them in a basin.

4. We sprinkle over them *half an ounce of white castor sugar*, which will help to draw out the juice.

5. We take a silk sieve and place it over a basin.
  N.B.—A *hair sieve* could be used instead.

6. We pass the *fruit* through the sieve with a wooden spoon.

7. We put *half an ounce of the best gelatine* into a small stewpan, with *half a gill* (one gill is a quarter of a pint) *of cold water*, to soak and to swell.

8. We then put the stewpan on the fire, and stir the *gelatine* until it is quite melted.

9. We add *two ounces of castor sugar,* and squeeze the *juice of one lemon* through a strainer into the stewpan.

10. We pour this *mixture* through a strainer, and stir it into the *strawberries* in the basin, and mix them well together.

11. We pour *half a pint of good cream* into a basin, and whip it to a stiff froth with a whisk.

12. We now add this *cream* to the *strawberries* in the basin, and stir them lightly together.

13. We take *a pint mould*, scald it with *hot water*, and then rinse it out with cold.

14. We pour the *strawberry cream* into the mould, and stand it in *ice*, until required for use.

15. For serving, we should dip the mould into *boiling water* for a second, shake it to loosen the *cream*, and then turn it out carefully on to a dish.

Now it is finished.

CREAMS.

Lesson No. 3.
CHARLOTTE RUSSE.

Average cost of "*Charlotte Russe*" (*about one pint*).

INGREDIENTS.

	s.	d.
12 sponge finger biscuits..................	0	6
½ oz. of the best gelatine..................	0	1½
1 gill of milk	0	0½
½ pint of double cream	1	3
1 dessertspoonful of sifted sugar	0	0½
30 drops of essence of Vanilla	0	1
	2	0½

Time required for making, about half an hour.

Now we will show you how to make a *Charlotte Russe*.

1. We take a *pint tin*, and line it inside with *sponge finger biscuits*.

   N.B.—We must be careful to fit the biscuits close to each other, so that they form a wall of themselves.

2. We take a knife and cut off the tops of the *finger biscuits* that stand above the tin.

3. We put *half an ounce of the best gelatine* in a small stewpan, with *one gill* (a quarter of a pint) *of cold milk*, to soak and swell.

4. We pour *half a pint of double cream* into a basin, and whip it to a stiff froth with a whisk.

5. We add to it *a dessertspoonful of sifted castor sugar*, and *thirty drops of essence of vanilla*.

6. We put the stewpan on the fire, and stir the *gelatine* until it is quite melted.

7. We stir the *melted gelatine* into the *cream*, pouring it through a strainer.

8. We pour this *cream* into the tin.

   N.B.—We must be careful, in pouring in the cream, not to disarrange the finger biscuits.

9. We stand this tin in *ice*, until it is required for use.

10. For serving, we dip the tin into *hot water* for a second, shake the tin to loosen the *cream*, and turn it carefully on to a dish.

    N.B.—A more economical Charlotte Russe might be made by using a quarter of a pint of custard to a quarter of a pint of cream (as in "Creams," Lesson No. 1).

Now it is finished.

SOUFFLÉS.

Lesson No. 1.

VANILLA SOUFFLÉ.

Average cost of " *Vanilla Soufflé* (*about one and a half pint*) and the *sauce* to be served with it.

INGREDIENTS.

	d.
4 eggs	4
1¼ oz. of butter at 1s. 6d. lb.	1½
A dessertspoonful of sugar	⎫
1 oz. of flour	⎬ 1
½ a teaspoonful of essence of Vanilla	⎪
Salt	⎭
1 gill of milk	0¾
	7¼

Time required, about three-quarters of an hour.

For Wine Sauce.	d.
1 oz. of sugar	0½
1 tablespoonful of jam	2
Wine glass of sherry	6
½ a teaspoonful of lemon-juice	1
	9½

Time required, about ten minutes.

For Custard Sauce.	d.
1 egg	1
Sugar and 6 drops of Vanilla	0½
1 gill of milk	0¾
	2¼

Time required, about ten minutes.

Now we will show you how to make a *Steamed Vanilla Soufflé Pudding*.

1. We must prepare the tin for the *soufflé pudding*.

2. We take a *pint and a half tin* and *butter* it well inside, using our fingers for that purpose.

3. We take a piece of paper and fold it so as to make a band round the tin, allowing about *two inches* of paper to stand up above the tin.

4. We *butter* the part of the paper above the tin with a knife.

5. We put the paper round the outside of the tin and tie it on with string.

Lessons on Making Souffles.—Vanilla Soufflé.

6. We take a stewpan and just melt *one ounce of butter* in it over the fire.

7. We take the stewpan off the fire and stand it on a piece of paper on the table.

8. We add *one ounce of flour* to the *melted butter*, and mix them both well together.

9. We then add rather more than *a dessertspoonful of pounded sugar*.

10. We add *one gill of milk* (a gill is a quarter of a pint).

11. We put the stewpan on the fire, and stir smoothly with a wooden spoon until it thickens.

12. We then take the stewpan off the fire again.

13. We add to the *mixture* the *yolks of three eggs*, one at a time, and beat all well together.

14. We take the *three whites* and put them in a basin with *one* more *white* to make *four*, adding *half a saltspoonful of salt*, and then whip the *whites* quite stiff.

15. We add the *whites* to the above *mixture* and stir it lightly.

16. We now add the flavouring—*half a teaspoonful of Vanilla essence*.

> N.B.—If the essence is very strong, or the bottle newly opened, so much is not required.

17. We mix all together and pour it into the *buttered* tin.

18. We have ready a saucepan half filled with *hot water*, and put it on the fire to boil.

19. When the water boils we stand the tin in it, but we must be careful that the water does not reach the paper round the tin, for it is only the steam which cooks the *pudding*.

20. We move the saucepan to the side of the fire, and let the *pudding* steam from *twenty to thirty minutes*.

21. We must watch it, not letting the water boil too fast, or the saucepan will get dry and the *pudding* will burn.

22. When it is sufficiently steamed, we take the tin out of the saucepan of water.

> N.B.—To test if the pudding is done, we should touch the centre of the pudding with our finger; it should feel firm.

23. We shake the tin and turn the *Soufflé Pudding* out on a hot dish, and pour the *sauce* round it, which we must prepare while the *soufflé* is being steamed.

> N.B.—If a baked Vanilla Soufflé Pudding is required, we put the tin in a quick oven (the heat should be 240°) to bake for half an hour, instead of putting it in the boiling water. No sauce is then wanted.

Now we will make the *sauce* for the *Steamed Vanilla Soufflé Pudding*.

For *Wine Sauce*.

1. We take a small saucepan and put in it *one ounce of loaf sugar* and *one gill* (or quarter pint) *of cold water*.

2. We put the saucepan on the fire, and stir the *sugar* and *water* with a spoon until the *sugar* has quite melted, and it has become a smooth syrup reduced in quantity.

3. We put into it *a tablespoonful of apricot jam*.

4. We stir it all together over the fire to melt the *jam*.

5. We add *a wineglassful of sherry* and *half a teaspoonful of lemon juice*. We stir it all again.

6. We take the stewpan off the fire and pour the *sauce* round the *soufflé pudding*.

> N.B. We must pour the sauce round the pudding very carefully, so as not to drop any of it on the side of it.

We can make a *Custard Sauce* if preferred:

1. We break a *whole egg* in a basin and whip it well.

2. We add *half a teaspoonful of pounded sugar*.

3. We add *one gill* (quarter pint) *of milk*, and *six drops of Vanilla essence*.

4. We pour all the *mixture* into a jug or gallipot.

5. We get a large saucepan *of hot water* and put it on the fire.

Lessons on Making Soufflés.—Vanilla Soufflé.

6. We stand the gallipot in a saucepan.

N.B.—The water must only come halfway up the gallipot.

7. We stir the *mixture* in the gallipot with a wooden spoon.

8. As soon as the *mixture* has thickened we take the gallipot out of the saucepan.

9. We pour the *custard* round the *Soufflé Pudding*.

Now it is finished.

SOUFFLÉS.

LESSON No. 2.

CHEESE SOUFFLÉ.

Average cost of "*Cheese Soufflé.*"

INGREDIENTS.

	d.
1 oz. of butter and 1 oz. of flour...............	1½
1 teaspoonful of mignonette pepper	0¼
Salt and pepper, and cayenne pepper	0¼
1 gill of milk	0½
3 eggs	3
3 oz. of parmesan cheese	4½
	10¼

Time required, about forty minutes.

Now we will show you how to make a *Cheese Soufflé.*

1. We take a stewpan, and put into it *one ounce of butter.*

2. We add *one teaspoonful of mignonette pepper.*

3. We put the stewpan on the fire, and let the *pepper* fry in the *butter* (to extract the flavour of the *pepper*) for *two* or *three minutes.*

4. We take the stewpan off the fire, and strain the *butter* into a basin ; as the *pepper* is only for flavouring, the grains must not be left in the *butter.*

5. We wash out the stewpan to prevent any of the grains remaining.

6. We pour the flavoured *butter* back in the stewpan.

7. We add *one ounce of flour, a teaspoonful of salt,* and *half a teaspoonful of pepper,* and *cayenne pepper* (about as much as would thinly cover *half the top of a threepenny piece*) according to taste ; and stir well together with a wooden spoon.

8. We add *one gill (or quarter of a pint) of milk.*

9. We put the stewpan on the fire, and stir the mixture smooth until it thickens.

10. We take the stewpan off the fire, and stand it on a piece of paper on the table.

11. We add *one* by *one* the *yolks* of *two eggs*, and beat them well together.

12. We take *three ounces of Parmesan cheese.*

13. We grate the *cheese* with a grater on to a plate or piece of paper.

14. We add the *three ounces of grated cheese* to the above mixture in the stewpan, and mix it all well together.

15. We whip the *whites of three eggs* with a little *salt* in a basin quite stiff.

16. We add the *whites* to the above mixture, and stir it lightly.

17. We take a plain *tin pint mould*, and prepare it in the same way as we did for the *Vanilla Soufflé Pudding*. (See *Soufflés*, Lesson No. 1.)

18. We pour the mixture into the buttered tin mould.

<small>N.B.—This same mixture, if poured into *Ramaquin* papers and baked, will make cheese *Ramaquins*.</small>

19. We put the tin in the oven (the heat should rise to 240°) to bake from *twenty minutes* to *half an hour*. We must look at it once or twice to see it does not burn, but the door of the oven should not be opened too often while the *soufflé* is inside, lest it should check the *soufflé* from rising properly.

<small>N.B.—To serve a baked soufflé it should be kept in its tin, the buttered paper taken off, and a clean napkin folded round the tin. It can also be baked in a mould which slips inside a plated or silver dish sold for the purpose. This is the more elegant way of serving a soufflé or fondu.</small>

Now it is finished.

SOUFFLÉS.

Lesson No. 3.

POTATO SOUFFLÉ.

Average cost of "*Potato Soufflé.*"

INGREDIENTS.

	d.
4 potatoes	1½
1 oz. of butter	1¼
½ a gill of milk	0¾
4 eggs	4
Seasoning	0½
	8

Time required, about an hour.

Now we will show you how to make *Potato Soufflé*.

1. We take *four good sized potatoes*, wash and scrub them with a scrubbing brush in a basin of *cold water*.

2. We take them out of the water, and dry them with a cloth.

3. We put them in the oven (the heat should rise to 230°) to bake; they will take from *half an hour* to *three quarters of an hour*, according to the heat of the oven, and the size of the *potatoes*.

4. We take a steel fork or skewer, and stick it into the *potatoes* to see if they are done. They must be soft inside.

N.B.—This should be carefully done so as not to spoil the *potato skins*.

5. When they are done we take them out and cut them (with a sharp knife) in half—so that each half of the *potato* will stand—because we shall want to use the skins to put the *potato* into them again.

6. We take a small spoon and scoup out carefully all the inside of the *potatoes*. We must take care not to make holes or spoil the skins in any way.

7. We take a wire sieve and put it over a plate, and take the inside of the *potatoes* and rub it through with a wooden spoon.

8. We put *one ounce of butter* and *half a gill of milk* in a stewpan, and put it on the fire to boil.

9. We add *salt* and *pepper* according to taste.

10. We then add *three ounces of the sifted potatoes*, and stir it smoothly.

11. We must now take the stewpan off the fire, and stand it on a piece of paper or wooden trivet, on the table.

12. We take *three eggs*, and add, *one* by *one*, only the *yolks*, beating all well together with a wooden spoon.

13. We take the *three whites*, and add another *white* to make *four*, and put them in a basin; we add a *quarter of a saltspoonful of salt* to them, and whip them to a stiff froth.

14. We add the *whites* to the above mixture, and stir the whole lightly.

15. We now stand the *eight half-potato skins* on a baking sheet.

16. We pour the mixture carefully into each *potato skin* (they should be only half full).

17. We put the sheet into the oven (the heat should rise to 240°) for *ten minutes*, until they have risen well, and become a pale brown colour.

18. We should fold a table napkin, and arrange them on it for serving.

Now it is finished.

OMELET SOUFFLÉ.

Average cost of "*Omelet Soufflé.*"

INGREDIENTS.

	d.
2 eggs	2
½ oz. of butter at 1s. 6d. a lb.	0¾
Jam	1
Sugar and salt	0½
1 teaspoonful of orange flower water	1
	5¼

Time required, about ten minutes.

Now we will show you how to make an *Omelet Soufflé* of *two eggs*.

1. We break *two eggs;* we put the *whites* in one basin and the *yolks* in another.

2. We put *one teaspoonful of orange flower water,* and *one tablespoonful of castor sugar* into a stewpan.

3. We put the stewpan on the fire, and let it boil quickly for *three minutes,* stirring occasionally.

4. We then pour it into a cup to cool; add to it the *yolks of eggs,* and beat them to a *cream.*

5. We add *a quarter of a saltspoonful of salt* to the *whites of egg,* and whip them to a stiff froth.

6. We add the *whites* to the mixture in the basin, and mix them together very lightly.

7. We put *half an ounce of butter* into a frying pan.

8. We put the pan on the fire, and let the *butter* get quite hot, but not burn.

9. When the *butter* is quite hot we must pour in the mixture.

10. We may let it stay on a slow fire for *two,* but not more than *three minutes.*

11. We must then take the pan off the fire and put it in the oven (the heat should rise to 240°).

12. We let it stay for about *three* or *four minutes* in the oven.

13. We take rather more than a *dessertspoonful of jam.*

14. We put the *jam* into a stewpan on the fire, and stir it until it has melted.

15. We take the pan out of the oven.

16. We take a knife and pass it round the edge of the *omelet soufflé*, to ease it from the pan.

17. We give the pan a shake to loosen the *omelet soufflé*.

18. We turn the *omelet soufflé* on to a hot dish.

19. We spread the *jam* on the *omelet soufflé*, and fold it over like a sandwich.

20. We sprinkle *about a teaspoonful of white castor sugar* over it.

Now it is finished.

SAVOURY OMELET.

Average cost of "*Savoury Omelet.*"

INGREDIENTS.

	d.
2 eggs at 1*d.* each	2
Salt, pepper, and parsley	0¾
1 oz. butter	1¼
	4

Time required, about four minutes.

Now we will show you how to make a *Savoury Omelet* of *two eggs*.

1. We break *two eggs* into a basin.

2. We add a *quarter of a teaspoonful of salt* and *pepper* to taste.

3. We take a *sprig of parsley*, wash it, dry it, and chop it up finely on a board (there should be about a *teaspoonful*).

4. We add the chopped *parsley* to the *eggs*.

5. We beat the *eggs* lightly for *two seconds* with a fork.

N.B.—The omelet could be flavoured with *chopped herbs* or *mushrooms*, with *bacon* or *kidney* cut in small pieces, or with *grated cheese*, according to taste.

6. We take *one ounce of butter*, and put it in an omelet or frying pan.

7. We put the pan on the fire to melt the *butter*.

N.B.—The fire should be bright and clear.

8. We wait till the *butter* is quite hot, taking care that it does not burn.

9. We pour the mixture of the *egg* into the pan.

10. We stir the mixture quickly with a wooden spoon.

11. We must not let it burn or stick to the pan. We must shake the pan to prevent the *omelet* sticking or burning.

12. We spread it over the bottom of the pan, and let it cook through.

13. We must watch it very carefully.

14. We take a knife and put it under the *omelet*, and fold the *omelet* over.

15. When the *omelet* has become a pale brown, we turn it out of the pan on to a hot dish.

Now it is finished.

MACCARONI.

Lesson No. 1.

Average cost of "*Maccaroni with Milk*" and "*Maccaroni with Cheese.*"

INGREDIENTS

	d.
½ lb. of Maccaroni	⎫ 2½
Salt	⎭
1 quart of skimmed milk	2
2 oz. of cheese.............................	2
1 oz. of butter.............................	1
Salt and pepper, and cayenne pepper	0¼
	7¾

Time required, about one hour and three-quarters.

Now we will show you how to cook *Maccaroni*.

1. We take *half a pound of maccaroni*, wash it, and put it in a saucepan of *cold water*, with *one tablespoonful of salt*.

2. We put the saucepan on the fire, bring it to the boil, and let it boil gently for *half an hour*.

3. After that time we pour the *water* out of the saucepan.

4. We put *one quart of skimmed milk* into the saucepan.

5. We put the saucepan on the fire, just bring it to the boil, and then move it to the side of the fire and let it simmer gently for *one hour*.

6. When the *maccaroni* is sufficiently cooked and quite tender, we turn it out on a hot dish, and it can be eaten with *sugar* or *treacle*.

N.B.—If liked, *maccaroni* and *cheese* can be made of it.

7. For *maccaroni and cheese*, we take *two ounces of cheese*, and grate it with a grater on to a piece of paper.

8. We take a dish or a tin and grease it well inside with a piece of *dripping* or *butter*.

9. When the *maccaroni* is sufficiently cooked (as above) we turn it out of the saucepan on to the greased dish.

10. We sprinkle over it *pepper and salt* and two or three grains of *cayenne pepper*, according to taste; or, *about half a teaspoonful of mustard* might be mixed with it.

11. We stir part of the *grated cheese* into the *maccaroni* and the remainder we sprinkle over the top.

12. We take *one ounce of butter*, cut it in small pieces, and put these pieces of *butter* about on the top of the *maccaroni*.

13. We put the dish in the oven (the heat should rise to 240°), or in a Dutch oven before the fire for *ten minutes;* it should become a pale brown.

14. It will then be ready for serving.

Now it is finished.

STEWED MACCARONI.

Lesson No. 2.

Average cost of "*Maccaroni Stewed in Stock.*"

INGREDIENTS.

	d.
½ lb. of maccaroni	2½
Salt and pepper	} 4
1 pint of stock	
	6½

Time required, about forty minutes.

Now we will show you how to stew *Maccaroni*.

1. We take *half a pound of maccaroni*, wash it, and put it in a saucepan with plenty of *cold water* and a *dessertspoonful of salt*.

2. We put the saucepan on the fire, bring it to the boil, and let it boil gently for *ten minutes*.

3. After that time we put the *maccaroni* into a cullender take it to the tap, and turn some *cold water* on it.

4. We now let the *maccaroni* drain in the cullender.

5. We then turn it on a board, and cut it up in pieces.

6. We put *one pint of stock* into a saucepan.

7. We put the *maccaroni* into the *stock*, and season it with *pepper and salt*, according to taste.

8. We put the saucepan on the fire, just bring it to the boil, and then move the saucepan to the side of the fire, and let it simmer gently for *twenty minutes*.

N.B.—The lid should be on the saucepan.

9. For serving, we turn the *maccaroni* out on a hot dish.

Now it is finished.

CHEESE STRAWS.

Average cost of "*Ingredients*" for "*Cheese Straws*" (about *three dozen*).

INGREDIENTS.

	d.
2 oz. of butter	2¼
2 oz. of flour	0½
2 oz. of grated Parmesan cheese	3
1 oz. of Cheddar cheese	1¼
1 egg	1
Salt and cayenne pepper	0¼
	8¼

Time required, about twenty minutes.

Now we will show you how to make *Cheese Straws.*

1. We put *two ounces of flour* on a board, and mix into it *half a saltspoonful of salt*, and a *quarter of a saltspoonful of cayenne pepper.*

2. We take *two ounces of Parmesan cheese* and *one ounce of Cheddar* or some strong *cheese*, and grate them on a grater.

3. We rub the *cheese* and *two ounces of butter* into the *flour.*

4. We now mix all the *ingredients* together with the *yolk of an egg* into a smooth *stiff paste.*

5. We *flour* the board and the rolling pin, and roll out the *paste* into a strip *one-eighth of an inch* in thickness, and *five inches* wide (the length the *cheese straws* are to be).

6. We now take a sharp knife, dip it in *flour*, and cut the *paste* into strips *one-eighth of an inch* wide, so that they will be *five inches* long and *one-eighth of an inch* in thickness.

7. We take *two* round cutters, dip them in *flour*, and cut little rings of *paste.*

8. We take a baking sheet, and grease it with *butter.*

9. We put the *cheese straws* and the *rings* on the baking sheet, and put it into a hot oven (the heat should rise to 240°) for *ten minutes.*

10. We must look at the *cheese straws* occasionally, and see that they do not burn ; they should be of a pale brown colour when done.

11. For serving, we take the *cheese straws* off the baking sheet, and put them through the *rings of paste* like a bundle of sticks.

Now it is finished.

PICKLED CABBAGE.

Average cost of "*Pickled Cabbage.*"

INGREDIENTS.

	s.	d.
A red cabbage	0	3
A gallon of vinegar	1	4
Mace, cloves, allspice, whole pepper	0	1½
Salt and ginger........................	0	0½
	1	9

Time required, about three days.

Now we will show you how to *Pickle a Cabbage*.

1. We take a *red cabbage*, cut it in half, and cut out the *stalk*, and wash it well in *salt* and *cold water*.

N.B.—A *white-heart cabbage* will do to pickle, but *green cabbages* cannot be used.

2. We put it on a board, and cut it in thin slices.

3. We lay the *slices* in a large pan, sprinkle a *handful of salt* over each layer of *slices*, cover the top well with *salt*, and leave them for *two days*.

N.B.—We must turn the slices every morning and evening, and sprinkle a handful of salt over the layers each time we turn them.

4. We then drain the *slices* on a hair sieve for *one day*.

5. We put a *gallon of vinegar*, *two blades of mace, twenty-four cloves, twenty-four allspice berries*, and *twenty-four peppercorns* into a saucepan, with *three pieces of ginger an inch* long.

6. We put the saucepan on the fire and let it boil up.

7. We then turn the *vinegar and spices* out of the saucepan into a broad pan to cool.

N.B.—They must on no account be allowed to cool in the saucepan.

8. We put the *cabbage* into a stone jar, and pour the *vinegar and spices* over it.

9. The *cabbage* must be quite covered with *vinegar*, and as it soaks it up more *vinegar* must be poured over it.

N.B.—This quantity of *vinegar* is sufficient for a large *cabbage;* a smaller one will take less.

10. We tie the jar over with wash leather, brown paper, or a bladder.

Now it is finished.

PICKLE FOR MEAT.

Average cost of "*Pickle for Meat*" (about *one gallon*).

INGREDIENTS.

	d.
1 and ½ lb. of salt	0¾
6 oz. brown sugar	1
1 oz. saltpetre	0½
1 gallon water	
	2¼

Time required, about half an hour to make.

Now we will show you how to make *Pickle for Meat*.

1. We put *one pound and a half of salt, six ounces of brown sugar, one ounce of saltpetre,* and *one gallon of water* into a large saucepan.

2. We put the saucepan on the fire to bring it to the boil, and then let it boil for *five minutes*. We must keep it well skimmed.

3. We then strain it into a tub or large basin.

4. When the *pickle* is quite cold, *meat* can be put into it.

N.B.—The *meat* should be kept well covered with the *pickle* 9 *days*.

N.B.—This *pickle* will keep for 3 *weeks* in *summer* and 3 *months* in *winter*.

N.B.—When the *pickle* is required again after it has once been used, it should be boiled up again, skimmed, strained, and allowed to get cold before the fresh *meat* is put into it.

N.B.—If used for pig's head the pickle should be thrown away and not used again.

Now it is finished.

CAKES.

Lesson No. 1.

SULTANA CAKE.

Average cost of a "*Sultana Cake.*"

INGREDIENTS.

	s.	d.
½ lb. of flour	0	1½
¼ lb. of butter	0	4
¼ lb. of sugar	0	1
¼ lb. of sultana raisins	0	1½
1 oz. of candied peel	0	1
2 eggs	0	2
1 teaspoonful of baking powder	0	0¼
½ a gill of milk	0	0½
1 lemon	0	2
	1	1½

Time required, about one hour and a half.

Now we will show you how to make a *Sultana Cake*.

1. We put *half a pound of flour* into a basin.

2. We rub a *quarter of a pound of butter* into the *flour* with our hands.

3. We now add a *quarter of a pound of castor sugar*, a *teaspoonful of baking powder*, and a *quarter of a pound of sultana raisins*.

4. We take a *lemon*, wipe it clean in a cloth, and grate the *rind* of it into the basin.

5. We cut up *one ounce of candied peel* into small pieces, and add it to the other ingredients.

6. We put *half a gill* (one gill is a quarter of a pint) *of milk* into a small basin, and add to it the *yolks of two eggs*. (The *whites* we put on a plate).

7. We stir the *milk* and the *eggs* together, and then pour it into the other ingredients, and mix all together.

8. We butter a cake tin.

9. We whip the *whites of the eggs* into a stiff froth with a knife, and stir it lightly into the *mixture*.

10. We now pour it into the tin, and put it into the oven (the heat should rise to 240°) to bake for [*one hour and a quarter*.

11. After that time we turn the *cake* out of the tin and stand it on its side, or on a sieve to cool.

N.B.—This will prevent its getting heavy.

Now it is finished.

CAKES.

Lesson No. 2.
GERMAN POUND CAKE.

Average cost of a "*German Pound Cake.*"

INGREDIENTS.

	s.	*d.*
10 oz. of flour	0	2
8 oz. of fresh butter	0	10
8 oz. of castor sugar	0	3
2 oz. of candied peel	0	1½
1 lemon	0	2
¼ lb. of sultana raisins	0	1½
4 eggs	0	4
	2	0

Time required, about two hours and a quarter.

Now we will show you how to make a *German Pound Cake.*

1. We stand a wire sieve over a plate and rub through it *ten ounces of flour.*

2. We put *eight ounces of fresh butter* into a basin, and work it to a *cream* with our hand.

3. We add a *tablespoonful of the sifted flour,* a *tablespoonful of castor sugar,* and *one egg,* and mix them well into the *butter.*

4. We continue to mix in by degrees the *flour, sugar,* and *eggs* until they are all used up.

5. We take a *lemon,* wipe it clean in a cloth, and grate the *rind* of it into the basin.

6. We also add a *quarter of a pound of sultana raisins,* and *two ounces of candied peel* (cut up in small pieces).

7. We stir all the ingredients together with a spoon.

8. We line a cake tin with buttered foolscap paper, and put three rounds of buttered paper at the bottom of the tin.

9. We pour the *mixture* into the tin, and put it into the oven (the heat should rise to 240°) to bake for *two hours*.

10. After that time we turn the *cake* out of the tin, and stand it on its side, or on a sieve to cool.

N.B.—This will prevent it getting heavy.

Now it is finished.

CAKES.

Lesson No. 3.

PLAIN CAKE.

Average cost of this "*Cake*" (*half a quartern*).

INGREDIENTS.

	d.
1 lb. of flour	2¼
4 oz. of dripping	2
Baking powder, allspice, and salt	0¾
½ lb. of currants	1½
½ pint of milk	1¼
¼ lb. of sugar	1
	8¾

Now we will show you how to make a *Plain Cake*.

1. We take *one pound of flour* and put it in a pan or large basin.

2. We mix into the *flour* a *teaspoonful of baking powder* and *half a saltspoonful of salt*.

3. We take *four ounces of clarified dripping*, rub it well into the *flour* with our fingers until there are no lumps remaining.

4. We take a *quarter of a pound of currants*, put them in a cloth, and rub them clean.

5. We add the *currants* to the *flour*, also *half a teaspoonful of ground allspice*, and a *quarter of a pound of brown sugar*.

6. We mix these ingredients together with a wooden spoon.

7. We now pour in *half a pint of milk*, and mix it all well together.

8. We take half a quartern tin and grease it inside with a piece of *dripping*.

9. We pour this *mixture* into the tin.

10. We put the tin into the oven (the heat should rise to 240°) to bake for *one hour*.

11. After that time we take the tin out of the oven.

12. We turn the *cake* out of the tin and stand it on its side to cool.

N.B.—This will prevent its getting heavy.

Now it is finished.

CAKES.

Lesson No. 4.
SEED CAKE.

Average cost of a " *Seed Cake.*"

INGREDIENTS.

	d.
10 oz. of flour	1½
2 oz. of sugar	0¼
1 teaspoonful of baking powder }	0½
1 teaspoonful of carraway seeds }	
2 oz. of clarified dripping	1
½ a gill of milk	0¼
1 egg }	1
Salt }	
	4¾

Time required, one hour and a half.

Now we will show you how to make a *Seed Cake.*

1. We take *ten ounces of flour* and put in a basin.

2. We mix into the *flour, one teaspoonful of baking powder,* and *half a saltspoonful of salt.*

3. We take *two ounces of clarified dripping* and rub it well into the *flour* with our hands, until there are no lumps remaining.

4. We add *two ounces of crushed loaf sugar* and *one teaspoonful of carraway seeds.*

5. We mix these well together with a wooden spoon.

6. We break *one egg* into a cup and beat it up with *half a gill* (one gill is a quarter of a pint) *of milk.*

7. We pour this into the basin and mix all quickly together into a stiff paste, stiff enough to allow a spoon to stand up in it.

8. We take a cake tin and grease it inside with a piece of *dripping.*

9. We pour the *mixture* into the tin and put it at once in the oven (the heat should rise to 240°) to bake for *one hour.*

10. To know when the *cake* is sufficiently baked, we run a clean knife into it, if it comes out perfectly bright and undimmed by steam, the *cake* is done.

11. We turn the *cake* out of the tin and stand it on its side to cool.

Now it is finished.

CAKES.

Lesson No. 5.

PLUM CAKE.

Average cost of a "*Plum Cake*" (about *three pounds*).

INGREDIENTS.

	d.
1 lb. of flour	2½
½ lb. of fruit (plums or currants)	2½
¼ lb. of dripping	2
¼ lb. of sugar	1
1 egg	1
½ a gill of milk	0¼
A teaspoonful of baking powder	} 0¼
Salt	
2 oz. of candied peel	1
	10¼

Time required, about one hour and a quarter.

Now we will show you how to make a *Plum Cake*.

1. We put *one pound of flour* into a basin, with a *teaspoonful of baking powder* and *half a saltspoonful of salt.*

2. We take a *quarter of a pound of clarified dripping* and rub it well into the *flour* with our hands until there are no lumps remaining.

3. We take *half a pound of plums or currants* or a *quarter of a pound* of each and add them to the *flour.*

> N.B.—If *currants* are used they should be well washed and dried in a cloth and picked over to see there are no stones in them. *Large plums* should be stoned before they are used.

4. We take *two ounces of candied peel,* cut it in small pieces and put it in the basin. We also add a *quarter of a pound of sugar.*

> N.B.—If *peel* is disliked it may be omitted.

5. We break *one egg* into a basin and add to it *half a gill* (one gill is a quarter of a pint) *of milk,* and beat them up.

6. We stir this into the ingredients in the basin, mixing them all well together.

7. We take a tin and grease it inside with *dripping*.

8. We pour the *mixture* into the tin and put it into the oven (the heat should rise to 240°) to bake for about an *hour*.

9. After that time we turn the *cake* out of the tin and stand it on its side slanting against a plate till it is cold.

N.B.—This will prevent it from getting heavy.

Now it is finished.

CAKES.

Lesson No. 6.
CORNFLOUR CAKE.

Average cost of a "*Cornflour Cake*" (about *three-quarters of a pound*).

INGREDIENTS.

		d.
¼ lb. of cornflour	....	2
¼ lb. of loaf sugar	....	1
2 oz. of butter	....	2
1 teaspoonful of baking powder	....	0¼
2 eggs	....	2
		7¼

Time required, about one hour.

Now we will show you how to make a *Cornflour Cake*.

1. We put *two ounces of butter* into a basin, and beat it to a *cream*.

2. We add to the *butter a quarter of a pound of pounded loaf sugar*, and mix it well.

3. We break in *two eggs* and beat all well together.

4. We now stir lightly into the *mixture* a *quarter of a pound of cornflour* and a *teaspoonful of baking powder*, and beat it well together for *five minutes*.

5. We grease a cake tin inside with *butter* or *dripping*.

6. We pour the *mixture* into the tin and put it immediately into the oven (the heat should rise to 240°) to bake for *half an hour*.

7. After that time we turn the *cake* out of the tin and slant it against a plate until it is cold. (This will prevent its getting heavy.)

N.B.—If preferred, the *mixture* could be baked in small tins instead of one large one, in which case it would only take *fifteen minutes* to bake.

Now it is finished.

CAKES.

[LESSON No. 7.

DOUGH CAKE.

Average cost of a "*Dough Cake*" (about *one quartern*).

INGREDIENTS.

	s.	d.
½ a quartern of dough	0	4
2 eggs	0	2
½ lb. of sugar	0	1½
1 lb. of currants	0	4½
	1	0

Time required, about an hour and a half.

Now we will show you how to make a *Dough Cake*.

1. We put *half a quartern of dough* (made as for *bread*, see "Bread," Lesson No. 1) into a basin.

2. We take *one pound of currants*, wash them, dry them in a cloth, and pick them over to see there are no stones mixed with them.

3. We add the *currants* and *half a pound of moist sugar* to the *dough*.

N.B.—If liked, *half a teaspoonful of mixed spice* might be added.

4. We now break *two eggs* into the basin, and beat all the ingredients well together.

5. We take a *quartern tin*, and grease it well inside with *dripping*.

6. We turn the *mixture* into the greased tin.

7. We put the tin into the oven (the heat should rise to 240°) until the *cake* is sufficiently baked; it will take about *forty minutes*.

N.B.—To test if the *cake* is done we should run a clean knife into it, and if it comes out clean the *cake* is sufficiently baked.

8. We then turn the *cake* out of the tin, and place it on its side, leaning against a plate until it is cold.

N.B.—This will prevent it getting heavy.

Now it is finished.

SHREWSBURY CAKES.

Average cost of " *Shrewsbury Cakes* " (about *one pound*).

INGREDIENTS.

	d.
¼ lb. of butter	4
¼ lb. of castor sugar	1½
6 oz. of flour	1
1 teaspoonful of pounded cinnamon and mace .	0¼
1 egg..	1
	7¾

Time required, about half an hour.

Now we will show you how to make *Shrewsbury Cakes*.

1. We put a *quarter of a pound of butter* and a *quarter of a pound of castor sugar* into a basin, and beat them together till the mixture is of the same consistency as cream.

N.B.—If the *butter* is very hard it might be beaten over hot water.

2. We add to the *mixture one egg* and about a *teaspoonful of pounded cinnamon and mace* (mixed together), and beat all well together.

3. We now stir in smoothly by degrees *six ounces of flour*.

N.B.—We must be careful not to let it get *lumpy*.

4. We *flour* a board and turn the *paste* out on it.

5. We take a rolling-pin, *flour* it, and roll out the *paste* as thin as possible.

6. We dip a cutter or wine-glass in *flour*, and cut the *paste* into *biscuits* or *cakes*.

7. We grease a baking tin with *dripping* or *butter*, and put the *cakes* on it.

8. We put the tin into the oven (the heat should rise to 240°) to bake for about *twenty minutes;* they should be a light brown when baked.

9. The *cakes* are then ready for use.

Now it is finished.

ROCK CAKES.

Average cost of "*Rock Cakes*" (about *one pound and a half*).

INGREDIENTS.

	d.
½ lb. of flour	1¼
¼ lb. of currants	1¼
¼ lb. of sugar	1
2 oz. of candied peel	1
2 teaspoonsful of baking powder	0¼
1 teaspoonful of grated nutmeg or ginger......	0¼
¼ lb. of clarified dripping	2
1 egg...	1
About ½ a gill of milk	0¼
	8¼

Time required, half an hour.

Now we will show you how to make *Rock Cakes*.

1. We put *half a pound of flour* into a basin.

2. We stir *two teaspoonsful of baking powder* into the *flour*.

3. We take a *quarter of a pound of clarified dripping*, and rub it well into the *flour* with our hands until there are no lumps remaining.

4. We take a *quarter of a pound of currants*, put them in a cloth, rub them clean, and pick them over to see that there are no stones with them.

5. We add the *currants* to the *flour*, also *one teaspoonful of ground ginger* or *grated nutmeg*, and a *quarter of a pound of crushed loaf sugar*.

6. We take *two ounces of candied peel*, cut it in pieces, and add it to the other ingredients.

7. We mix all these ingredients together with a wooden spoon.

8. We break *one egg* into a cup, and beat it up with about *half a gill* (one gill is a quarter of a pint) *of milk*.

9. We pour this into the basin, and mix all well together into a very stiff *paste*.

Lesson on Making Rock Cakes. 367

10. We take a tin, and grease it with *dripping*.

11. We divide the *paste* into small portions with two forks, and lay them in rough heaps on the tin.

12. We put them into the oven (the heat should rise to 240°) to bake for about *fifteen minutes*.

13. After that time we take them out of the oven, and the *cakes* are then ready for use.

Now it is finished.

BUNS.

Average cost of "*Buns*" (this quantity will make about *twenty-seven*).

INGREDIENTS.

	d.
½ oz. of German yeast	0½
1½ lb. of flour	3½
3 gills of milk	1½
1 oz. of butter	1
¼ lb. of moist sugar	1
¼ lb. of sultana raisins or currants	1¼
	9

Time required, about two hours and a half.

Now we will show you how to make *Buns*.

1. We put *one gill and a half* (one gill is a quarter of a pint) *of milk* into a saucepan and put it on the fire.

2. We put *half an ounce of German yeast* into a basin.

3. When the *milk* is just warm, we pour it by degrees on to the *yeast*, mixing them well together with a spoon.

4. We put *one pound of flour* into a large basin and stir into it the *milk and yeast*, mixing it into a *dough*.

5. We cover the basin with a cloth, and stand it on the fender, and let it rise for about *one hour*.

6. We put *one gill and a half of milk* into a saucepan, with *one ounce of butter*, and put it on the fire to warm.

7. We put *half a pound of flour* into a basin and stir into it the *milk and butter*.

8. When the *dough* is sufficiently risen, we turn it into this *mixture*, and work them well together.

9. We now add a *quarter of a pound of sultana raisins or currants* and a *quarter of a pound of moist sugar*, and mix all well together.

N.B.—If *currants* are used they should be well washed, dried in a cloth, and carefully picked over to see if there are any stones mixed with them.

10. We cover the basin with a cloth and stand it near the fire to rise again for *one hour*.

Lesson on Making Buns.

11. After that time we take a tin and grease it with *dripping* or *butter*.

> N.B.—If there is no tin, the shelf from the oven should be greased and used instead.

12. We flour a paste board and turn the *dough* out on it.

13. We take a knife, dip it in flour, and cut the *dough* into pieces.

14. We flour our hands, and form the *dough* into balls.

> N.B.—This quantity of *dough* will make about twenty-seven ordinary sized buns.

15. We put the *buns* on the tin.

16. We put the tin into the oven (the heat should rise to 240°) to bake the *buns* for about *half an hour*.

17. When they are half done we take the tin out of the oven, brush the *buns* over with *water*, and sprinkle *white sugar* over them.

18. We now put the tin back in the oven.

19. When the *buns* are sufficiently baked, we take them off the tin and slant them against a plate until they are cold.

> N.B.—This will prevent their getting heavy.

Now it is finished.

RICE BUNS.

Average cost of "*Rice Buns*" (about *eight* or *ten*).

INGREDIENTS.

	d.
¼ lb. of ground rice	1½
¼ lb. of sugar	1
2 oz. of butter	2
2 eggs	2
½ a teaspoonful of baking powder	0¼
	6¾

Time required, half an hour.

Now we will show you how to make *Rice Buns*.

1. We put a *quarter of a pound of ground rice* into a basin, with *half a teaspoonful of baking powder*.

2. We add a *quarter of a pound of pounded loaf sugar*, and *two ounces of butter*, and mix all together with a wooden spoon.

3. We break in *two eggs* and beat all lightly together.

N.B.—We should be careful to see that the *eggs* are *good* before adding them to the *mixture*.

4. We take some small tins or patty pans, and grease them well with a piece of *dripping* or *butter*.

5. We fill these tins *two-thirds* full with the *mixture*.

N.B.—This quantity will make about *eight or ten buns*.

N.B.—If there are no small tins the *mixture* could be put into a cake tin, which should be previously greased inside.

6. We put the tins into the oven (the heat should rise to 240°) to bake for *fifteen minutes*.

7. After that time, we turn the *buns* out of the tins, and lean them against a plate until they are cold.

N.B.—This will prevent their getting heavy.

Now it is finished.

GINGER-BREAD NUTS.

Average cost of *"Ginger-bread Nuts"* (about *twenty-four*).

INGREDIENTS.

	d.
1 lb. of flour	2½
½ lb. of treacle	2
4 oz. of butter	4
½ an oz. of ground ginger	0½
Allspice	
1 teaspoonful of carbonate of soda	0½
Salt	
	9

Time required, about twenty-five minutes.

Now we will show you how to make *Ginger-bread Nuts.*

1. We put *one pound of flour* into a basin with about *half a saltspoonful of salt.*

2. We also add *half an ounce of ground ginger, one teaspoonful of carbonate of soda,* and *allspice* (about as much as will cover a threepenny piece).

3. We put *half a pound of treacle* and *four ounces of butter* into a saucepan, and melt them together over the fire.

4. We mix the *ingredients* together and then add the melted *treacle* and the *four ounces of butter,* and mix all well together into a firm *paste.*

N.B.—We should be very careful that all the ingredients are well mixed and that there are no lumps left.

5. We flour a board and turn the *paste* out on to it.

6. We should flour our hands and knead the *paste.*

7. We now divide the *paste* into about *twenty-four* pieces.

8. We roll each piece into a ball, like a walnut, and put them *two inches* apart on a greased tin.

9. We put them in the oven (the heat should rise to 240°) for *fifteen minutes.*

10. After that time we turn the *ginger-bread nuts* off the tin and set them aside to cool.

Now it is finished.

MILK BISCUITS.

Average cost of "*Milk Biscuits*" (about *two dozen*).

INGREDIENTS.

	d.
1 gill (¼ pint) of milk	0¼
1 oz. of butter	1
½ lb. of flour	1¼
1 teaspoonful of baking powder	0¼
	3

Time required, about half an hour.

Now we will show you how to make *Milk Biscuits*.

1. We put *one gill* (a quarter of a pint) *of milk* into a saucepan; we add to it *one ounce of butter*, and put it on the fire to warm.

2. We put *half a pound of flour* into a basin with a *teaspoonful of baking powder*.

3. When the *milk* is hot, we pour it into the *flour* and stir it carefully into a smooth, stiff *paste*.

4. We flour a board and turn the *paste* out on it.

5. We take a rolling pin, flour it, and roll the *paste* out into as thin a sheet as possible.

6. We flour a docker or a tumbler and cut the *paste* out into rounds, about the size of the top of a teacup.

7. We grease a tin with *dripping* or *butter*, and place the *biscuits* on it.

8. We put the tin into the oven (the heat should rise to 240°) to bake for *twenty minutes*.

9. After that time we turn the *biscuits* off the tin and set them aside to cool.

Now it is finished.

OATMEAL BISCUITS.

Average cost of "*Oatmeal Biscuits*" (about *one pound*).

INGREDIENTS.

		d.
7 oz. of flour	....	1¼
3 oz. of oatmeal	....	0¾
3 oz. of castor sugar	....	0¾
3 oz. of lard or butter	....	3
¼ of a teaspoonful of carbonate of soda	....	0¼
1 egg	....	1
		6½

Time required, about half an hour.

Now we will show you how to make *Oatmeal Biscuits.*

1. We put *three ounces of lard or butter* into a saucepan, and put it on the fire to melt and warm.

2. We put *seven ounces of flour* into a basin with *three ounces of oatmeal, three ounces of castor sugar*, and a *quarter of a teaspoonful of carbonate of soda*, and mix all together with a spoon.

3. We now stir in the *melted lard.*

4. We put about *a tablespoonful of cold water* into a tea cup; we break *one egg* into the water and beat them slightly together.

5. We add this to the *mixture* in the basin, and mix all well and smoothly together with a spoon.

6. We flour a board and turn the *paste* out on it.

7. We take a rolling pin, flour it, and roll out the *paste* as thin as possible.

8. We flour a tumbler and cut the *paste* into *biscuits* according to taste.

9. We *grease* a baking tin with *dripping* or *butter*, and place the *biscuits* on it.

10. We put the tin into the oven (the heat should rise to 240°) to bake for *twenty minutes.*

Now it is finished.

SCONES.

Average cost of "*Scones*" (about *eight*).

INGREDIENTS.

	d.
1 lb. of flour	2¼
¼ pint of milk	0½
¼ lb. of butter	4
1 dessertspoonful of baking powder	0¼
	7

Time required, about forty minutes.

Now we will show you how to make *Scones*.

1. We put *one pound of flour* into a basin and mix into it a *dessertspoonful of baking powder*.

2. We take a *quarter of a pound of butter*, and rub it well into the *flour* with our hands.

3. We turn it out on to a floured board.

4. We *flour* a rolling pin and roll it out to make sure that the *butter* is well mixed in the *flour*.

5. We mix it into a smooth *paste* with rather less than a *quarter of a pint of milk*.

N.B.—The *paste* must not be too moist.

6. We *flour* the rolling pin and roll out the *paste* to a thin sheet, about *one-third of an inch* in thickness.

7. We take a knife, dip it in *flour*, and cut the *paste* into triangular pieces, each side about *four inches* long.

8. We *flour* a tin, put the *scones* on it, and bake them directly in the oven (the heat should rise to 240°) for *thirty to forty minutes*.

9. When the *scones* are half done, we should brush them over with *milk*.

Now it is finished.

SHORT-BREAD.

Average cost of "*Short-Bread.*"

INGREDIENTS.

	d.
¼ lb. of flour................................	0¾
2 oz. of butter................................	2
1 oz. of castor sugar	0¼
	3

Time required, about half an hour.

Now we will show you how to make *Short-Bread.*

1. We put *two ounces of butter* in a saucepan, and put it on the fire to melt and warm.

2. We put a *quarter of a pound of flour* into a basin with *one ounce of castor* (pounded lump) *sugar*, and the *melted butter.*

3. We mix these *ingredients* well together.

4. We flour a board and turn the *paste* out on it.

5. We flour our hands and knead the *paste* well.

6. We take a rolling pin, flour it, and roll out the *paste* to about *one-third of an inch* in thickness.

7. We flour a knife and cut the *paste* into oval shapes.

8. We grease a baking tin with *dripping* or *butter.*

9. We put the *short-bread* on the tin, and put it in the oven (the heat should rise to 240°) to bake till a pale brown.

Now it is finished.

MILK ROLLS.

Average cost of "*Milk Rolls*" (about *twelve*).

INGREDIENTS.

	d.
1 lb. of self-raising flour	3
2 oz. of butter	2
Milk	1
	6

Time required, about half an hour.

Now we will show you how to make *Milk Rolls.*

1. We put *one pound of self-raising flour* into a basin and rub *two ounces of butter* into it with our hands.

2. We add sufficient *milk* to make it into a lithe firm *dough.*

3. We sprinkle *flour* over a board, and turn the *dough* out on it.

4. We take a knife, dip it in *flour,* and cut the *dough* into *twelve pieces.*

> N.B.—We should keep our hands floured to prevent the *dough* from sticking to them.

5. We form each piece into a small roll.

6. We *flour* a baking tin.

7. We put these rolls on to the tin and put the tin in the oven (the heat should rise to 240°) to bake for *twenty minutes.*

8. The *milk rolls* will then be ready for use.

Now it is finished.

YORKSHIRE TEA CAKES.

Average cost of "*Yorkshire Tea Cakes*" (about *two*).

INGREDIENTS.

	d.
¾ of a lb. of flour	1¾
1½ gill of milk	0¾
1 oz. of butter	1
1 egg	1
½ an oz. of German yeast	0½
	5

Time required, about one hour and a half.

Now we will show you how to make *Yorkshire Tea Cakes*.

1. We put *one gill and a half* (one gill is a quarter of a pint) *of milk* into a small saucepan and put it on the fire.

2. We put *half an ounce of German yeast* into a basin, and when the *milk* is just warm we pour it on to the *yeast*.

3. We put *three-quarters of a pound of flour* into a large basin, and rub into it *one ounce of butter*.

4. We beat up *one egg* in a cup, and then add it to the *flour*.

5. We now pour the *yeast and milk* through a strainer into the basin, and mix all well together with a wooden spoon.

6. We flour a board and turn the *dough* out on it.

7. We flour our hands and knead the *dough* for a minute or two.

8. We take a knife, dip it in flour, and divide the *dough* into *cakes*.

9. We take some cake tins (as many as are required), and grease them inside with *dripping*.

10. We put the *cakes* into the tins.

N.B.—The *tins* should be only *three-quarters full*, so as to allow for the *cakes* to rise.

11. We stand the tins near the fire, and allow the *cakes* to rise for *one hour*.

12. After that time we put the tins into the oven (the heat should rise to 240°) to bake for a *quarter of an hour*.

13. We then turn the *cakes* out of the tins, and place them on a sieve, or on the seat of a cane chair to cool.

N.B.—This will prevent them from getting heavy,

Now it is finished.

BREAD.

LESSON No. 1.

Average cost of "*Bread*" (*about a quartern*).

INGREDIENTS.

	d.
3½ lbs. flour (2nds) at 2s. 4d. the peck	7
1 oz. German yeast	} 1
½ saltspoonful of salt	
	8

Time required, quarter of an hour for making, two or three hours for rising, and one hour and a half for baking.

Now we will show you how to make *Bread*.

1. We take *three pounds and a half of seconds flour*, put *three pounds* of it into a large pan, and make a hole or well in the centre of the flour.

N.B.—Half a pound is reserved to work the bread up with.

2. We put *one ounce of German yeast* into a basin.

3. We add about a gill of *tepid water*, and stir the *yeast* into a stiff *paste*.

4. We then fill the basin with *luke-warm water*, and stir the *yeast* smoothly, making in all about *one pint and three gills*.

5. We add to the *flour half a teaspoonful of salt*, and then pour in by degrees the *yeast*, mixing the *flour* lightly into a *dough* with our hands.

6. We should add more *lukewarm water* if the *dough* is too stiff.

N.B.—We must be sure to mix up all the flour into dough.

7. We sprinkle about *a tablespoonful of dry flour* over the *dough*, and cover the pan with a cloth.

8. We place the pan near the fire for at least *two hours* to let the *dough* rise.

9. When the *dough* has risen sufficiently, we take up the pan and work in more *flour*, if necessary, to make the *dough* stiff enough to turn out of the pan.

>N.B.—We must keep our hands well floured all through the process of bread making.

10. We turn the *dough* out on a well-floured board, and knead it well, using up a good deal more *flour*.

11. We divide the *dough* into *six* equal pieces, knead each piece separately, and make into a *loaf*.

>N.B.—If the bread is to be baked in tins we form each loaf into a dumpling or ball (with a smooth surface and no cracks in it), either long or round according to the shape of the tin.

12. We put the *bread* into the tins, which should be well floured.

13. We cut a slit in the top of the *dough*, or prick it with a fork.

>N.B.—If the bread is to be made into cottage loaves,—

14. We divide each piece into *two*, one rather larger than the other.

15. We make each into a ball, put the smaller one on the top of the other, and press our forefinger into the middle of the top.

>N.B.—Cottage loaves are baked on floured tins.

>N.B.—If there are no tins the oven shelf should be washed and floured, and a tin is not then necessary.

16. We let the *loaves* rise *half an hour* in a warm place before we put them in the oven.

17. We then put them in the oven (the heat should rise to 280°, and after *a quarter of an hour* be reduced to 220°) for about *one hour and a half*.

>N.B.—To test if the *bread* is sufficiently baked we should run a clean knife into the loaves, and if it comes out perfectly bright the bread is done.

18. When we take the *bread* out of the oven we stand each *loaf* up on its side to cool.

Now it is finished.

BREAD.

Lesson No. 2.

UNFERMENTED BREAD.

Average cost of "*Unfermented Bread*" (about *two loaves*).

INGREDIENTS.

	d.
1 lb. of flour	2¼
1 teaspoonful of baking powder	} 0¼
Salt	
	2½

Time required, about three-quarters of an hour.

Now we will show you how to make *Unfermented Bread*.

1. We put *one pound of flour* into a basin and mix into it *one teaspoonful of baking powder* and *half a saltspoonful of salt*.

2. We add sufficient *water* to make it into a light firm *dough* (not too stiff).

N.B.—It will take about *half a pint of water*.

3. We sprinkle *flour* over a board, and turn the *dough* out on it.

N.B.—We should keep our hands floured to prevent the dough from sticking to them.

4. We should knead it with our hands, and make it up quickly into small *loaves*.

N.B.—Small loaves do better than large ones for unfermented bread, and the quicker the bread is made and put into the oven the better.

5. We put the *loaves* on a floured baking sheet, and put them in the oven (the heat should rise to 240°) to bake for *half an hour*.

N.B.—To see if bread is sufficiently baked we run a clean knife into it, and if it comes out bright and untarnished, the bread is done.

6. We take the *bread* out of the oven, and stand each *loaf* on its side to cool.

Now it is finished.

SICK-ROOM COOKERY.

Lesson No. 1.

CHICKEN PANADA.

Average cost of "*Chicken Panada.*"

INGREDIENTS.

	s.	d.
½ a chicken	1	9
A tablespoonful of cream	0	1½
	1	10½

Time required, about four hours.

Now we will show you how to make *Chicken Panada*.

1. We take a *chicken* and clean it in the same way that we do for roasting a *fowl* (see "Trussing a Fowl for Roasting").

2. We cut the *chicken* in half, dividing it down the middle of the back with a sharp knife.

3. We take all the flesh off the bones of half the *chicken*, and cut it into small pieces with a sharp knife.

4. We put the pieces of *chicken* into a gallipot, and sprinkle over them *half a saltspoonful of salt*.

5. We take a piece of paper and tie it over the top of the gallipot.

6. We take a saucepan half full of *boiling water*, and put it on the fire.

7. We stand the gallipot in the saucepan, and let it simmer for *two hours*. The water must not cover the gallipot.

8. After that time we take the gallipot out of the saucepan.

9. We take the pieces of *chicken* out with a spoon. We must not lose any of the liquor.

10. We take the pieces of *chicken*, and put them into a mortar and pound them well to a pulp.

11. We take a tammy sieve and stand it over a basin.

12. We take the *pounded chicken* and pass it through the sieve, rubbing it with a wooden spoon.

13. We pour a little of the *chicken liquor* into the pulp on the sieve to make it pass through more easily.

14. When all the *chicken pulp* has been passed through into the basin, we stir in *one tablespoonful of cream*.

Now it is finished.

We use the bones for *Chicken Broth*.

1. We take the *chicken bones* and put them in a saucepan with *one pint of cold water*.

2. We put the saucepan on the fire and let it boil for *three hours*.

3. We must watch it, and skim it occasionally.

4. When required for use, we take a strainer and strain the *chicken broth* into a basin.

5. We flavour it with *pepper* and *salt* according to the taste of the patient.

Now it is finished.

SICK-ROOM COOKERY.

LESSON No. 2.
BEEF ESSENCE.

Average cost of "*Beef Essence.*"

INGREDIENT.

1 lb. of gravy beef .... 9*d*.

Time required, about two hours.

Now we will show you how to make *Beef Essence.*

1. We take *one pound of gravy beef,* and cut off all fat and gristle with a sharp knife.

2. We cut the *lean* up into small pieces, and put them into a jar.

3. We put the cover over the jar and tie a piece of paper over it.

4. We take a saucepan half full of *boiling water,* and stand it on the fire.

5. We stand the jar in the saucepan of boiling water to steam for two hours. The water must not cover the jar.

6. When it is done we take a strainer and put it over a basin.

7. We strain off the liquor into the basin, and flavour it with *pepper and salt* according to the patient's complaint.

N.B.—The *meat* can be put aside and used again for second stock.

Now it is finished.

SICK-ROOM COOKERY.

Lesson No. 3.

CREAM OF BARLEY.

Average cost of "*Cream of Barley.*"

INGREDIENTS.

	d.
½ lb. veal cutlet	7½
½ oz. of barley	0¼
½ gill of cream	3
	10¾

Time required, about four hours.

Now we will show you how to make *Cream of Barley*.

1. We take *half a pound of veal cutlet*, and cut off all the *fat* with a sharp knife.

2. We cut the *lean* into small pieces and put it in a saucepan with *one pint of cold water*.

3. We add *half an ounce of barley*, (previously well washed and soaked an *hour in cold water*), and *half a saltspoonful of salt*.

4. We put the saucepan on the fire, and let it boil gently for *two hours*.

5. We strain off the *liquor* into a basin, and put the *meat* and *barley* in a mortar and pound them together.

6. We take a hair sieve, and put it over a basin.

7. We turn the *pounded meat* and *barley* on to the sieve and rub them through with a wooden spoon.

8. We pour the *liquor* on to the sieve to help the *pulp* to pass through.

9. When it has all passed through the sieve into the basin, we stir in smoothly *two tablespoonsful of cream*.

Now it is finished.

SICK-ROOM COOKERY.

Lesson No. 4.

A CUP OF ARROWROOT AND ARROW-ROOT PUDDING.

Average cost of "*Cup of Arrowroot*" and "*Arrowroot Pudding.*"

INGREDIENTS.

	d.
A dessertspoonful of arrowroot	0¼
½ a pint of milk	1
Castor sugar	
	1½
2 eggs	2
	3¼

Time required, about a quarter of an hour.

Now we will show you how to make a *Cup of Arrowroot*.

1. We take *a dessertspoonful of Arrowroot*, and put it into a small basin.

2. We add *a dessertspoonful of cold milk*, and stir it smoothly into a *paste* with a spoon.

3. We add a *small teaspoonful of castor sugar*, according to taste.

4. We take a small saucepan, and put in it *half a pint of cold milk*.

5. We put the saucepan on the fire, and watch the *milk* carefully until it boils.

6. When it is quite boiling, we pour it on to the *arrowroot paste*, stirring all the time to get it quite smooth.

N.B.—If the patient prefers an *Arrowroot Pudding:*—

7. We add to the *mixture* described above, the *yolks of two eggs*, whipping it all well together.

N.B.—The *eggs* should not be added till the *mixture* has cooled a little, or they would curdle.

8. We put the *whites* of the same *eggs* into another basin, and whisk them to a stiff froth.

9. We add the *whites of the eggs* to the *arrowroot mixture*, stirring them lightly together.

10. We pour the *mixture* into a buttered dish, and put it into the oven (the heat should rise to 240°) to bake for *ten minutes*.

Now it is finished.

SICK-ROOM COOKERY.

Lesson No. 5.

RICE WATER.

Average cost of "*Rice Water.*"

INGREDIENTS.

	d.
3 oz. of Carolina rice...............	0¾
1 inch of the stick of cinnamon .... } Sugar .... }	0¼
	1

Time required, about one hour.

Now we will show you how to make *Rice Water*.

1. We take *three ounces of Carolina rice*, and wash it well in two or three waters.

2. We take a stewpan with *one quart of warm water*.

3. We put the stewpan on the fire to boil.

4. When the *water* is quite boiling, we put in the *rice*, and *one inch of the stick of cinnamon*, and let it boil for *one hour*, until the *rice* has become a pulp.

5. We then take the stewpan off the fire, and strain the *rice water* into a basin, and sweeten it according to taste.

N.B.—When cold it is ready for use.

Now it is finished.

SICK-ROOM COOKERY.

Lesson No. 6.

BARLEY WATER.

Average cost of "*Clear Barley Water*" (about *half a pint*).

INGREDIENTS.

	d.
2 oz. of pearl barley	0½
The rind of a quarter of a lemon	0¼
2 lumps of loaf sugar	0¼
	1

Time required, about one hour.

For *Making Thick Barley Water* (about *one pint*).

	d.
2 oz. of pearl barley	0½
The rind of half a lemon	0½
Sugar	0¼
	1¼

Time required, about two hours.

Now we will show you how to make two kinds of *Barley Water*—*Clear Barley Water* and *thick Barley Water*.

For *half a pint of clear barley water :—*

1. We take *two ounces of pearl barley*, and wash it well in two or three waters.

2. We put a kettle of water on the fire to boil.

3. We take a *quarter of a lemon*, wipe it clean in a cloth, and peel it very thinly.

N.B.—We must be careful, in peeling the lemon, not to cut any of the white skin, as it would make it bitter.

4. We put the *washed barley* into a jug.

5. We put in the *lemon peel*, and *two lumps of loaf sugar*.

6. When the *water* in the kettle is quite boiling, we pour *one pint* of it on to the *barley* in the jug.

7. We cover over the top of the jug, and let it stand on ice or in a cool place, until it is perfectly cold.

8. We then strain the *water* into a clean jug for use.

N.B.—The barley can be used again, with the addition of *one ounce* of fresh.

Now it is finished.

For *one pint of thick Barley Water* :—

1. We take *two ounces of pearl barley*, and wash it well in two or three waters.

2. We put the *barley* into a stewpan, with *one quart of cold water*.

3. We put the stewpan on the fire, and let it boil gently for *two hours*.

4. We take *half a lemon*, wipe it clean in a cloth, and peel it very thinly.

5. We put the *lemon peel* into a jug.

6. When the *barley water* is sufficiently boiled, we strain it into the jug over the *lemon*.

7. We put the jug into a cool place, and when it is perfectly cold, we take out the *lemon peel*, and sweeten the water, according to taste.

Now it is finished.

SICK-ROOM COOKERY.

Lesson No. 7.
APPLE WATER.

Average cost of "*Apple Water*" (*one quart*).

INGREDIENTS.

	d.
6 apples	2
The rind of half a lemon	½
Sugar	
	2½

Time required for making, about eight minutes.

Now we will show you how to make *Apple Water*.

1. We take *six apples*, peel them, and cut out the core.

    N.B.—When the apples are juicy, six will be sufficient, but more may be required according to the season of the year.

2. We put a kettle of water on the fire to boil.
3. We cut the *apples* up in slices.
4. We take *half a lemon*, wipe it clean in a cloth, and peel it very thinly.
5. We put the *slices of apple* and the *lemon rind* into a jug.
6. When the water is quite boiling, we pour *one quart* of it on to the *apples* in the jug.
7. We sweeten it according to taste.
8. We stand the jug of *apple water* aside to cool.
9. When the *water* is quite cold we strain it into another jug, and it is then ready for use.

Now it is finished.

SICK-ROOM COOKERY.

Lesson No. 8.

LEMONADE.

Average cost of "*Lemonade*" (*one pint and a half*).

INGREDIENTS.

	d.
2 lemons	3
Loaf sugar	0¼
	3¼

Time required, about one hour.

Now we will show you how to make *Lemonade*.

1. We put a kettle of water on the fire to boil.

2. We take *two lemons*, wipe them clean in a cloth, and peel them very thinly.

> N.B.—We should be careful, in peeling the lemons, not to cut any of the pith, or white skin, as it would make the lemonade bitter.

3. We now cut off all the pith.

4. We cut up the *lemons* into thin slices, take out all the pips, and put the slices and *half the rind of the lemons* into a jug.

5. We add *loaf sugar*, according to taste, about *one ounce*.

6. When the water is quite boiling, we pour *one pint and a half* on to the *lemons* in the jug.

7. We cover over the jug, and stand it aside to cool.

8. When the *lemonade* is quite cold, we strain it into another jug, and it is then ready for use.

Now it is finished.

SICK-ROOM COOKERY.

Lesson No. 9.

TOAST AND WATER.

Average cost of "*Toast and Water*" (*one quart*).

INGREDIENTS.

1 crust of bread............................ ¼d.
1 quart of cold water.

Time required, half an hour.

Now we will show you how to make *Toast and Water*.

1. We take a *crust of bread* and toast it quite brown on all sides in front of the fire.

N.B.—Crumb should not be used as it would turn sour.

2. We put the *toasted crust of bread* into a jug, and pour on it *one quart of cold water*.

3. We cover the jug over with a cloth, and stand it aside for *half an hour*.

N.B.—This is a pleasant drink, and considered more refreshing than when made with boiling water.

Now it is finished.

SICK-ROOM COOKERY.

Lesson No. 10.

GRUEL.

Average cost of "*Gruel*" (*one pint*).

INGREDIENTS.

	d.
2 dessertspoonsful of patent groats	0¼
Sugar	0¼
A nut of fresh butter	0¼
½ gill (2 tablespoonsful) of rum	3
	4

Time required, about fifteen minutes.

Now we will show you how to make *Gruel*.

1. We put a stew-pan with *one pint of water* on the fire to boil.

2. We take *two dessertspoonsful of patent groats*, and put them in a basin.

3. We add by degrees *two tablespoonsful of cold water* to the *groats*, and stir it into a smooth *paste*.

4. When the *water* in the stew-pan is quite boiling, we pour in the mixed *gruel*, and stir it well with a wooden spoon, until it has boiled for *ten minutes* (it must not be lumpy), we then pour it into a basin.

5. Now it is ready for use.

N.B.—If the gruel is required for a cold

6. We stir in a piece of *fresh butter* the size of a nut, and sweeten it according to taste.

7. We also add *two tablespoonsful of rum*.

N.B.—If the patient is feverish, spirits should not be added.

Now it is finished.

SICK-ROOM COOKERY.

LESSON NO. 11.

WHITE WINE WHEY, OR TREACLE POSSET.

Average cost of "*White Wine Whey*," or "*Treacle Posset*" (*half a pint*).

INGREDIENTS.

For *White Wine Whey*.			For *Treacle Posset*.	
	d.			d.
½ pint of milk	1		½ pint of milk.............. ...	1
4 lumps of sugar............	0½	or	½ a gill of treacle	1
1 wineglassful of wine	3			
	4½			2

Time required, about ten minutes.

Now we will show you how to make *White Wine Whey*.

1. We put *half a pint of milk* into a saucepan and *four lumps of sugar*.

2. We put the saucepan on the fire to boil.

3. When it boils we pour in a *wineglassful of wine* (*sherry* or *cowslip*) according to taste.

N.B.—If the milk is not quite boiling the wine will not curdle it.

4. We move the saucepan to the side of the fire, and let it stand for about *one minute*.

5. We then strain the *whey* into a glass.

N.B.—The curds are not digestible.

N.B.—Treacle posset is made in the same way, except that no sugar should be added to the milk, and the same quantity of treacle is used instead of wine.

Now it is finished.

SICK-ROOM COOKERY.

Lesson No. 12.

BRAN TEA.

Average cost of "*Bran Tea*" (*one quart*).

INGREDIENTS.

3 tablespoonsful of bran. } ½*d.*
Sugar or honey,
Time required, about twenty minutes.

Now we will show you how to make *Bran Tea*.

1. We put a kettle of *warm water* on the fire to boil.

2. We take *three tablespoonsful of bran* (not too coarse, for that is greasy) and put it into a large jug.

N.B.—Bran is the husk of the grain which is sifted from the flour after the wheat is ground by the miller.

3. When the *water* is quite boiling, we pour *one quart* into the jug.

4. We cover the jug and let it stand for a *quarter of an hour* to draw.

5. When it is drawn, we strain off the *tea* through a piece of muslin, and sweeten it according to taste with either *sugar* or *honey*.

N.B.—When wine is good for the patient it may be added to the tea, or lemon juice, but it is very good without.

N.B.—This is an invaluable drink for softening the throat.

Now it is finished.

SICK-ROOM COOKERY.

Lesson No. 13.
MUTTON BROTH.

Average cost of "*Mutton Broth*" (*two quarts*).

INGREDIENTS.

	s.	d.
4 lbs. of the scrag end of the neck of mutton	2	8
2 knuckles from the legs of mutton	1	0
A saltspoonful of salt }	0	0½
2 oz. of Patna rice }		
	3	8½

Time required for making,—the stock should be made the day before, and then the broth can be finished in about half an hour.

Now we will show you how to make *two quarts of Mutton Broth*.

1. We take *four pounds of the scrag end of the neck of mutton*, wash it well, put it on a board, cut away all the *fat*, and chop it up in large pieces.

2. We put these pieces into a stewpan, with *two knuckle-bones from the legs of mutton*.

3. We pour in *five pints of cold water* and add a *salt-spoonful of salt*.

4. We put the stewpan on the fire, just bring it to the boil, and then let it simmer for *four hours*.

5. We must watch it and skim it very often.

6. After that time we strain the *stock* into a basin, and put it aside until it is quite cold and in a stiff *jelly*.

7. We then take the *stock* and remove all the *fat* from the top with a spoon.

8. We take a clean cloth and dip it in hot water, and dab over the top of the *stock* so as to remove every particle of grease.

9. We must now take a clean dry cloth and wipe the top of the *stock* dry.

10. We take *two ounces of Patna rice*, and wash it well in two or three waters.

11. We put the *stock* into a stewpan.

12. We put the stewpan on the fire to boil.

13. When the *stock* is quite boiling we stir in the *rice*, and let it boil for *twenty-five minutes* to cook the *rice*.

N.B.—We should feel that the rice is quite tender.

14. We season it with *pepper* and *salt*, according to the patient's complaint.

15. For serving, we pour the *broth* into a basin.

N.B.—The *bones* should be put in the stock pot.

Now it is finished.

SICK-ROOM COOKERY,

Lesson No. 14.

MUTTON BROTH.

Average cost of this dish, *i.e.*, about *one quart of mutton broth* and a dish of *boiled mutton* with *parsley sauce*—

INGREDIENTS.

	s.	d.
2 lbs. of the scrag end of the neck of mutton	1	2
1 oz. of pearl barley or rice }	0	0¼
½ a saltspoonful of salt }		
½ oz. of butter	0	0¾
½ oz. of flour }	0	0½
2 sprigs of parsley }		
	1	3½

Time required, about two hours and forty minutes.

Now we will show you how to make *Mutton Broth.*

1. We take *two pounds of the scrag end of the neck of mutton*, and wash it well until it is quite clean.

2. We put the meat into a large saucepan with *three pints of cold water*, and put it on the fire to boil.

3. We take *one ounce of pearl barley or rice*, and wash it well in cold water.

4. When the water boils we put in the *pearl barley or rice* and *half a saltspoonful of salt* to help the scum to rise.

5. We now draw the saucepan to the side of the fire and let it simmer gently for *two hours and a half.*

6. We must watch it and skim it occasionally with a spoon.

7. If the meat is required for immediate use we should make *sauce* to pour over it.

8. We take a *sprig or two of parsley*, wash it and wring it in a cloth, put it on a board, and chop it up finely with a knife.

9. We put *half an ounce of butter* into a saucepan and put it on the fire.

10. When the *butter* is melted we stir in smoothly *half an ounce of flour* with a wooden spoon.

11. We take *one gill* (quarter pint) of *broth* from the *mutton*, pour it on to the *butter* and *flour*, and stir smoothly until it boils and thickens.

12. We now add the *chopped parsley* to the *sauce*, and move the saucepan to the side of the fire to keep warm till required for use.

13. When the *mutton* is sufficiently cooked, we take out the *meat* and put it on a hot dish.

14. We pour the *parsley sauce* all over the *mutton*.

15. We pour the *broth* into a basin to cool.

16. When it is cold we should remove all the *fat* before warming it up for use.

N.B.—If the *broth* is required for immediate use we can remove the *grease* with blotting paper or whitey-brown paper.

Now it is finished.

SICK-ROOM COOKERY.

Lesson No. 15.

BEEF TEA.

Average cost of "*Beef Tea*" (*one pint and a half*, 9*d.*).

INGREDIENTS.

1 lb. of gravy beef.......................... 9*d.*

Time required, about six hours.

Now we will show you how to make *Beef Tea*.

1. We take *one pound of gravy beef*, put it on a board, and cut it up very fine, removing all the *skin* and *fat*.

2. We put the *meat* into a saucepan with *one pint and a half of cold water, half a saltspoonful of salt*, and *two or three peppercorns* if allowed.

3. We put the saucepan on the fire, and just bring it to the boil.

4. We then move it to the side of the fire to simmer gently for *five or six hours*, but we must not let it reduce too much.

N.B.—The lid should be on the saucepan.

5. After that time we pour off the *beef tea*, or strain it through a coarse cloth into a basin, and let it get cold.

6. We should remove all *fat* from the *beef tea* before warming it up for use.

N.B.—*Fat* can be taken off *hot beef tea* with blotting paper or whitey-brown paper.

N.B.—It is better not to strain *beef tea*, as it removes all the little brown particles which are most nutritious.

Now it is finished.

SICK-ROOM COOKERY.

Lesson No. 16.

BEEF TEA.

(MADE WITH EQUAL QUANTITIES OF BEEF AND WATER.)

Average cost of "*Beef Tea*" (*half a pint*).

INGREDIENTS.

½ lb. of gravy beef .... 4½*d.*

Time required, about three hours and a quarter.

Now we will show you how to make *Beef Tea*.

1. We take *half a pound of gravy beef,* put it on a board, and cut it up very finely, removing all the *skin* and *fat*.

2. We put the *meat* into a stone jar, with *half a pint of water*.

N.B.—In making this *beef tea* the quantity of *meat* and *water* should be of equal weight, *i.e.*, one pint to one pound.

3. We put the lid on the jar, and tie a piece of paper over it.

4. We stand the jar in a saucepan of boiling water on the hob for *three hours*, or in the oven *for one hour and a half*.

N.B.—If the jar is put into the saucepan of boiling water, we should be careful that the water does not cover the jar, or it would get inside.

5. After that time we take out the jar, and pour off the *beef tea* into a cup.

N.B.—If allowed, we add *salt* according to taste.

Now it is finished.

SICK-ROOM COOKERY.

LESSON NO. 17.
LIEBIG'S QUICK BEEF TEA.

Average cost of "*Beef Tea*" (*half a pint*).

INGREDIENTS.

½ lb. gravy beef .... 4½*d*.

Time required, about a quarter of an hour.

Now we will show you how to make *Baron Liebig's quick Beef Tea.*

1. We take *half a pound of gravy beef*, put it on a board, and cut it up very fine, removing all the *skin* and *fat*.

2. We put it in a saucepan with its equal weight in water, *i.e.*, *half a pint*.

3. We put the saucepan on the fire and bring it quickly to the boil.

4. We let it boil for *five minutes,* and then pour it off into a cup.

Now it is finished.

SICK-ROOM COOKERY.

Lesson No 18

SAVOURY CUSTARD.

Average cost of "*Savoury Custard*" (*one gill*).

INGREDIENTS.

	d.
2 eggs............................. }	2
Salt................................ }	
1 gill of beef tea	2¼
	4¼

Time required, about twenty minutes.

Now we will show you how to make *Savoury Custard*.

1. We take the yolks of *two eggs* and the white of *one*, and put them in a small basin.

2. We add *one gill* of *beef tea*, and a *quarter of a salt-spoonful of salt*.

3. We whisk up the *eggs* and the *beef tea* well together.

4. We take a small gallipot and butter it inside.

5. We pour the mixture into the gallipot.

6. We take a piece of whitey-brown paper and butter it.

7. We put this buttered paper over the top of the gallipot, and tie it on with a piece of string.

8. We take a saucepan of hot water and put it on the fire.

9. When the water is quite boiling, we stand the little gallipot in it.

N.B.—The water must not quite reach the paper with which the gallipot is covered.

10. We draw this saucepan to the side of the fire, and let it simmer for a *quarter of an hour*.

N.B.—It must not boil, or the custard will be spoiled.

11. We take the gallipot out of the saucepan, take off the buttered paper, and the *custard* is ready for serving.

Now it is finished.

BUILDINGS REQUISITE FOR SCHOOLS FOR COOKERY.

A school where twelve students may be practised in the several necessary processes or branches of cookery requires as follows :—
1. A room about 20 ft. × 18 ft., and not less than 10 feet high, having a small suitable stove.
2. A scullery of somewhat less dimensions.
3. A larder, open to the north if possible.
4. A cellar for coal and wood.

This may be taken as the smallest amount of accommodation which is absolutely necessary for giving constant and systematic instruction. If it be desired to give lectures to numbers exceeding twelve, another room or rooms should be provided proportioned in size to the number of persons to be accommodated.

The premises for the NATIONAL TRAINING SCHOOL FOR COOKERY are temporary, and were constructed in a large iron shed. Such a shed is not to be recommended on account of the great variations of temperature in it; but the approximate dimensions of the Training School are given as affording some guide in providing the requisite accommodation for a *Training* school.
1. A lecture or demonstration room, accommodating, say 120 students, on seats rising above one another; size, 39 ft. × 36 ft.
2. Three practice kitchens, two for middle class cookery and one for artizan cookery, accommodating about twelve students in each room; size of each room, 18 ft. × 21 ft., not less than 10 feet high.
3. A scullery, or room used for practical lessons in cleaning utensils, &c., with sink draining out-of-doors; size, 20 ft. × 15 ft..
4. A larder; size, 15 ft. × 11 ft.
5. An office and meal room; size, 18 ft. × 21 ft.
6. A ladies' waiting-room and lavatory; size, 16 ft. × 14 ft.
7. A servants' waiting-room; size, 15 ft. × 11 ft.

To this list a store-room and coal-cellar should be added.

REGULATIONS AND FEES

OF THE

NATIONAL TRAINING SCHOOL FOR COOKERY, SOUTH KENSINGTON.

The National Training School for Cookery was established in the year 1874.

The chief object of the school was to train teachers who should become instructors of cookery in training schools, board schools, and similar institutions.

The courses of instruction in the school are :—

1. For educated persons who wish to qualify themselves to become teachers of cookery.

2. For students and cooks.

3. For those who wish to be able to practise cookery in their homes.

The course of instruction for a Teacher of cookery is as follows :—

She first goes as a pupil through the Scullery and Demonstrations; this takes, working every day except Saturday, one month, from 10 a.m. to 4 p.m., with an interval from 12 to 2 for rest and lunch. At the end of the month, the pupil goes up for a Theoretical Examination, and her note books are looked at. She then spends one month learning in the Artizan Practice Kitchen and a fortnight in teaching there what she has already learnt. She then goes into the Middle Class Practice Kitchen, and spends one month in learning, and a fortnight in teaching. The last month, is devoted to Practise in Demonstrating : first, a fortnight in private, and lastly, a fortnight in public, and for which the Lady Superintendent has drawn up careful and full rules, which are hung up close to where the student stands to give her Demonstration lesson.

The fee for this five months' course of training is £20. [May be paid by instalments in special cases.]

During her course of training at the School, the student can, if she likes, dine with the other pupils, for 1s., or if that is beyond her means, she is allowed to purchase any little dish that happens to be cooked as a lesson at a merely nominal charge. Students can get comfortable lodgings in the neighbourhood of the School, either with a Lady who has taken a house expressly for the purpose of accommodating the students of the various Art Schools at South Kensington, or at the house of the Head Cook, the charges for lodgings and partial board ranging from 16s. to 25s. a week. Saturday is a whole holiday at the School.

The staff teachers receive £2 a week all the year round, and their dinner at the School while employed in London, and when sent to reside out of London they receive a further sum of 30s. a week for board and lodging, and all their travelling expenses; three months' notice on either side terminates the engagement. When the staff teachers are all employed a few extra teachers are taken on "as improvers," at £1 a week, and thus they become competent to fill good appointments in the Provinces, when they offer. These engagements are terminable by a week's notice on either side.

The work of teachers on the staff varies somewhat according to the nature of their appointment, *i.e.*, if employed in the School itself, she would have to be in her kitchen by 9.30 a.m. to see that her kitchen-maid had everything in proper order for the pupils to begin work at 10 a.m., the lessons end at 4 p.m., the teacher would in most cases be able to leave the School at 5 p.m. and on Sunday she would be quite free.

If the staff teacher is sent to the Provinces the hours of work in that case depend greatly upon the Local Committee who for the time being employ her, but the number of hours of work are limited to 24 in the week, to be distributed by arrangement with the Local Committee and the teacher.

There is a shorter course for teachers wishing to train for Artizan teaching only, lasting ten weeks, the fee is £8 8s.

The fees for the courses of instruction for cooks and students are as follows:—

	£	s.	d.
Scullery cleaning, for five lessons .... 10 a.m. to 12 noon	0	10	6
Ten Middle Class Demonstrations and lectures .. 2 p.m. to 4 p.m.	2	2	0
Ten Artizan Demonstrations and lectures........ 10 a.m. to 12 noon	0	10	0
Ten Middle Class Practice lessons .... 10 a.m. to 4 p.m.	3	3	0
Ten Artizan Practice lessons .... 10 a.m. to 4 p.m.	2	2	0

The necessary Provisions are found in the "Practice Kitchens."

If the Scullery work be omitted by students in the Middle Class Practice Kitchen the fee would be £4 4s., and in the Artizan Kitchen £3 3s.

A limited number of daily pupils are now admitted in the Practice Kitchen at a fee of 10s. 6d. for each day's instruction to new pupils, and 6s. 6d. to old pupils.

R. O. C.

October, 1877.

INDEX.

	PAGE		PAGE
A-LA-MODE BEEF—Stews	94	Barley water (clear)—Sick-room cookery	389
Alexandra pudding—Puddings	281	— water (thick)—Sick-room cookery	390
Amber pudding—Puddings	275		
Anchovy sauce—Fish	199		
Apple charlotte—Puddings	264	Batter and fruit, baked—Puddings	303
— jelly—Jellies	327	— pudding, boiled—Puddings	284
Apples and tapioca—Puddings	298	— pudding, in a cup—Puddings	288
Apple turnovers and dumplings of short crust—Pastry	255		
— water—Sick-room cookery	391	Beans, haricot—Vegetables	234
Arrowroot, cup of—Sick-room cookery	386	Beef, à-la-mode—Stews	94
		— — —Soups	172
— pudding — Sick-room cookery	386	— braised fillets of—Entrées	68
		— essence—Sick-room cookery	384
Aspic jelly from calves' feet—Jellies	315	— olives—Entrées	81
		— steak pie	121
Australian meat—brown purée	42	— steak pudding	123
— caramel (browned sugar)	43	— — —Pastry	252
— curried rabbit	48	— stewed brisket of—Stews	100
— fricassée of mutton	52	— tea, Liebig's quick—Sick-room cookery	403
— Irish stew	44		
— mince	59	— — Sick-room cookery	401, 402
— mulligatawny	40	Biscuits, milk	372
— pie	50	— oatmeal	373
— rissoles	54	Blanc-mange—Puddings	283
— sausage rolls	46	Boiled batter—Puddings	284
— savoury hash	57	— cauliflower—Vegetables	229
		— cod—Fish	204
BACON, rolls of—Entrées	76	— fish	215
Baked batter and fruit—Puddings	303	— fowl	144
— fish in vinegar	212	— mutton and parsley sauce—Sick-room cookery	399
— mackerel or herring—Fish	208		
— potatoes—Vegetables	221	— new potatoes—Vegetables	218
— stuffed haddock—Fish	210	— pig's head, salted	128
Baking meat	22	— potatoes—Vegetables	217

Index.

	PAGE		PAGE
Boiled rice	92	Cakes—rock	366
— rice—Tripe	103	— seed cake	359
— sheep's head	137	— Shrewsbury	365
— tripe, with milk and onions—Tripe	104	— sultana cake	353
— turbot—Fish	187	Caramel (browned sugar)—Australian meat	43
Boiling meat	20	Carrots and turnips—Vegetables	227
Bonne femme—Soups	158	Carrot pudding—Puddings	279
Braised fillet of veal	109	Carrots—Vegetables	237
— fillet of beef—Entrées	68	Cauliflower au gratin—Vegetables	230
Bran tea—Sick-room cookery	396	— boiled—Vegetables	229
Brawn—boiled pig's head	129	Charlotte russe—Creams	333
Brazilian stew—Stews	96	Chaudfroid of chicken—Entrées	72
Bread	379	Cheese with maccaroni	346
— pudding—Puddings	292	— soufflé—Soufflés	338
— sauce—Roast fowl	151	— straws	349
— unfermented	381	Chicken broth—Sick-room cookery	383
Brisket of beef (cold) stewed—Stews	100	— chaudfroid of—Entrées	72
Broth—Dr. Kitchener's—Soups	173	— fricassée of—Entrées	77
— mutton—Sick-room cookery	399	— croquettes or rissoles of—Entrées	87
— mutton—Sick-room cookery	397	— panada—Sick-room cookery	382
— from sheep's head—Sheep's head	137	Clarifying butter—Frying	25
Brown bread pudding—Puddings	277	— dripping—Frying	25
— purée of Australian meat	42	— fat—Frying	25
— sauce—Sauces	239	Cleaning a close kitchen range	13
— stock	183	— a copper stewpan	15
Browned sheep's head	139	— a gas stove	14
Brussels sprouts—Vegetables	226	— an enamelled stewpan	15
Buns	368	— an iron saucepan	15
— rice	370	— an open kitchen range	12
Bullock's heart, stuffed and roasted	111	Clear soup—Soups	152
Butter, clarifying—Frying	25	Cod, boiled—Fish	204
		Cold cabinet pudding—Puddings	305
Cabbage, pickled	351	— chicken, fricassée of—Entrées	79
— soup—Soups	177	— meat—curry	33
Cabinet pudding—Puddings	260	— — fried rissoles	37
— — (cold)—Puddings	305	— — goblet pie	31
Cakes—Corn-flour cake	363	— — hashed meat	26
— dough cake	364	— — meat fritters	29
— German pound cake	355	— — minced meat	39
— plain cake	357	— — shepherd's pie	35
— plum cake	361	Cooked meat—curry	33

Index.

	PAGE
Cooked meat—fried rissoles	37
— — goblet pie	31
— — hashed meat	26
— — meat fritters	29
— — minced meat	39
— — shepherd's pie	35
Corn-flour cake—Cakes	363
— pudding—Puddings	289
— — in a cup—Puddings	284
Cornish pasties	115
Cow-heel jelly—Jellies	321
— stewed, with onion sauce—Jellies	322
Cream of barley — Sick-room cookery	385
Creams—charlotte russe	333
— strawberry cream	331
— vanilla cream	329
Croquettes of potato—Vegetables	224
— or rissoles of chicken—Entrées	87
Crowdie—Soups	174
Cup of arrowroot — Sick-room cookery	386
Curate's pudding—Puddings	291
Curried rabbit — Australian meat	48
— rabbit or veal—Entrées	90
Curry, of cold meat	33
— of tripe—Tripe	102
— (Indian)—Entrées	61
Custard pudding—Puddings	269
— sauce—Soufflés	336
Cutlets, lobster—Fish	200
— mutton—Entrées	70
— veal—Entrées	74
DOUGH cake—Cakes	364
Drinks—apple water—Sick-room cookery	391
— barley water (clear)—Sick-room cookery	389
— barley water (thick)—Sick-room cookery	390
— bran tea—Sick-room cookery	396

	PAGE
Drinks— lemonade— Sick - room cookery	392
— rice water — Sick - room cookery	388
— toast and water—Sick-room cookery	393
— treacle posset—Sick-room cookery	395
— white wine whey—Sick-room cookery	395
Dripping, clarifying—Frying	25
Dr. Kitchener's broth—Soups	173
Dumplings—hard dumplings	309
— Norfolk dumplings	310
Dutch sauce—Sauces	242
EGG sauce—Boiled fowl	146
— — Fish	192
Entrées—beef olives	81
— braised fillets of beef	68
— chaud-froid of chicken	72
— croquettes or rissoles of chicken	87
— curried rabbit or veal	90
— curry (Indian)	61
— fricassée of chicken	77
— fricassée of cold chicken	79
— haricot mutton	85
— Irish stew	83
— mutton cutlets	70
— quenelles of veal	65
— veal cutlets	74
Essence of beef— Sick-room cookery	384
FAT, clarifying—Frying	25
Fillet of veal, braised	109
Fillets of beef, braised—Entrées	68
— of sole à la maître d'hôtel—Fish	196
— of sole, fried—Fish	198
Fire, to lay a	13
Fish baked in vinegar	212
— baked mackerel or herring	208
— baked stuffed haddock	210
— boiled	215

Index.

	PAGE
Fish, boiled cod	204
— boiled turbot	187
— fillets of sole à la maître d'hôtel	196
— fish pudding	190
— fried fillets of sole	198
— fried plaice	213
— grilled salmon	206
— lobster cutlets	200
— pudding—Fish	190
— sole au gratin	194
— whitebait	193
Flaky crust (for pies and tarts)—Pastry	258
Fowl, boiled	144
— for boiling, trussing a	144
— for roasting, trussing a	148
— roasted	148
Fricassée of chicken—Entrées	77
— of cold chicken—Entrées	79
— of mutton — Australian meat	52
Fried fillets of sole—Fish	198
Fried plaice—Fish	213
— potato-chips — Vegetables	222
— rissoles of cold meat	37
— slices of potato — Vegetables	223
Fruit tart of short crust—Pastry	247
Frying	24
GENOESE pastry—Pastry	248
German pea-soup—Soups	180
— pound-cake—Cakes	355
— sauce—Puddings	278
Giblet soup—Soups	165
Ginger-bread nuts	371
Goblet pie—Cooked meat	31
Grilled salmon—Fish	206
— steak	117
Gruel—Sick-room cookery	394
HADDOCK baked and stuffed—Fish	210
Hard dumplings—Dumplings	309
Haricot beans—Vegetables	234
— mutton—Entrées	85

	PAGE
Hash, savoury, of Australian meat	57
Hashed meat- -Cooked meat	26
Herring or mackerel, baked—Fish	208
ICELAND moss jelly—Jellies	319
Invalid pudding—Puddings	300
Irish stew—Entrées	83
— — of Australian meat	44
— —Stews	98
JAM tart—Pastry	259
Jellies—apple jelly	327
— aspic jelly from calves' feet	315
— cow-heel jelly	321
— Iceland moss jelly	319
— milk jelly from cow-heel	321
— ox-foot jelly	323
— porter jelly	325
— stewed cow-heel, with onion sauce	322
— stewed ox-foot	326
— wine jelly from calves' feet	311
LEMON pudding—Puddings	262
Lemonade—Sick-room cookery	392
Liebig's quick beef-tea—Sick-room cookery	303
List of cleaning materials and utensils required in a kitchen	11
— utensils required in a first class school kitchen	7
— utensils required in a second class school kitchen	9
Liver and bacon	119
Lobster cutlets—Fish	200
— sauce—Fish	188
MACCARONI in milk—Maccaroni	346
— with cheese —	346
— soup—Soups	181
— stewed in stock	348
Mackerel or herring, baked—Fish	208
Mashed potatoes—Vegetables	220
— turnips—Vegetables	235
Mayonnaise—Sauces	240

Index

	PAGE
Meat, Australian—brown purée	42
— — caramel(browned sugar)	43
— — curried rabbit	48
— — fricassée of mutton	52
— — Irish stew	44
— — mince	59
— — mulligatawny	40
— — pie	50
— — rissoles	54
— — sausage rolls	46
— — savoury hash	57
— baking	22
— boiling	20
— fritters—Cooked meat	29
— hashed—Cooked meat	26
— minced—Cooked meat	39
— pie, of Australian meat	50
— pie, beef-steak	121
— pudding, beef-steak	123
— re-cooked—Curry	33
— re-cooked—Fried rissoles	37
— re-cooked—Goblet pie	31
— re-cooked—Hashed meat	26
— re-cooked—Meat fritters	29
— re-cooked—Minced meat	39
— re-cooked—Shepherd's pie	35
— roasting	17
Milk biscuits	372
— jelly from cow-heel—Jellies	321
— rolls	376
— soup—Soups	175
Mince, of Australian meat	59
Minced meat—Cooked meat	39
Mock-turtle—Soups	167
Mutton, boiled, with parsley sauce—Sick-room cookery	399
— broth—Sick-room cookery	397
— — Sick-room cookery	399
— cutlets—Entrées	70
— fricassée, of Australian meat	52
— haricot—Entrées	85
Mulligatawny, of Australian meat	

	PAGE
New potatoes boiled—Vegetables	218
Norfolk dumplings—Dumplings	310
Oatmeal biscuits	373
Omelet, savoury	344
— soufflé	342
Onion sauce—Boiled pig's head	128
Ox-foot jelly—Jellies	323
Oyster sauce—Fish	205
Pancakes—Puddings	266
Pastry—beef-steak pie	121
— beef-steak pudding	252
— cornish pasties	115
— flaky crust, for pies and tarts	258
— fruit tart of short crust	247
— Genoese pastry	248
— patty cases of puff paste	245
— pie—Australian meat	50
— pork pie	131
— puff paste	243
— rissoles of Australian meat	54
— rissoles of chicken—Entrées	88
— rough puff paste, for pies, tarts, and tartlets	250
— sausage rolls	133
— sausage rolls of Australian meat	46
— short crust	246
— short crust for apple turnovers and dumplings	255
— suet crust	252
— tartlets of puff paste	244
Patty cases of puff paste—Pastry	245
Pea soup (German)—Soups	180
— —Soups	178
Peas—Vegetables	233
Pickle for meat	352
Pickled cabbage	351
Pie of Australian meat	50
— beef-steak	121
Pie, shepherd's, of cold meat	35
Pie, pork	131
Pig's fry—Poor man's goose	125

Index.

	PAGE
Pig's head, salted and boiled	128
Piquante sauce—Sauces	241
Plaice, fried—Fish	213
Plain cake—Cakes	357
Plum cake—Cakes	361
— pudding—Puddings	270, 296
Poor man's goose—Pig's fry	126
Pork pie	131
Porter jelly—Jellies	325
Potato chips, fried—Vegetables	222
— croquettes—Vegetables	224
— fried slices of—Vegetables	223
— soufflé—Soufflés	340
Potatoes, baked—Vegetables	221
— boiled—Vegetables	217
— mashed—Vegetables	220
— new, boiled—Vegetables	218
— purée of—Soups	160
— sauté—Vegetables	221
— steamed—Vegetables	218
Pot-au-feu, or soup—Soups	170
Puddings—Alexandra pudding	281
— amber pudding	275
— apple charlotte	264
— arrowroot — Sick - room cookery	386
— baked batter and fruit	303
— batter pudding in a cup	288
— beef-steak	123
— beef steak—Pastry	252
— blanc-mange	283
— boiled batter	284
— bread-pudding	292
— brown bread pudding	277
— cabinet pudding	260
— carrot pudding	279
— cold cabinet pudding	305
— corn-flour pudding	289
— corn-flour pudding in a cup	286
— curate's pudding	291
— custard pudding	269
— fish—Fish	190
— invalid pudding	300
— lemon pudding	262
— pancakes	266

	PAGE
Puddings—plum pudding	270
— plum puddings	296
— rice pudding	268
— rice pudding (with egg)	290
— semolina pudding	302
— suet pudding	307
— tapioca and apples	298
— treacle pudding	294
— Viennoise or Vennoise pudding	273
— Yorkshire puddings	308
Puff paste—Pastry	243
— rough, for pies, tarts, and tartlets—Pastry	250
Purée, brown—Australian meat	42
— of potatoes—Soups	160
Quenelles of veal—Entrées	65
Rabbit curried—Australian meat	48
— curry of—Entrées	90
Rice, boiled	92
— — Tripe	103
— buns	370
— water—Sick-room cookery	388
— pudding (with egg)—Puddings	290
— pudding	268
Rissoles, fried—Cooked meat	37
— of Australian meat	54
— or croquettes of chicken—Entrées	87
Roast bullock's heart, stuffed	111
— fowl	148
Roasting meat	17
Rock cakes	366
Rolls of bacon—Entrées	76
Rough puff paste, for pies, tarts, and tartlets—Pastry	250
Salmon, grilled—Fish	206
Sauce, anchovy—Fish	199
— bread	151
— brown—Sauces	239
— custard—Soufflés	336
— Dutch—Sauces	242
— egg	146

	PAGE
Sauce—egg—Fish	192
— for boiled fish—Fish	215
— German—Puddings	278
— lobster—Fish	188
— mayonnaise—Sauces	240
— oyster—Fish	205
— piquante—Sauces	241
— Tartare—Fish	207
— white—Sauces	238
— wine—Soufflés	336
— wine or brandy—Puddings	272
Sausage rolls	133
— of Australian meat	46
Sauté potatoes—Vegetables	221
Savoury custard—Clear soup	154
— — Sick-room cookery	404
— hash of Australian meat	57
— omelet	344
Scones	374
Sea pie	135
Seed cake—Cakes	359
Semolina pudding—Puddings	302
Sheep's head, boiled	137
— — broth	137
— — browned	139
Shepherd's pie—Cooked meat	35
Shrewsbury cakes	365
Short-bread	375
Short crust—Pastry	246
— for apple dumplings and turnovers—Pastry	255
Sick-room cookery—apple water	391
— — arrowroot pudding	386
— — barley water (clear)	389
— — barley water (thick)	390
— — beef tea	401, 402
— — boiled mutton, with parsley sauce	399
— — bran tea	396
— — chicken panada	382
— — cream of barley	385
— — cup of arrowroot	386
— — gruel	394
— — lemonade	392
— — Liebig's quick beef tea	403

	PAGE
Sick-room cookery—mutton broth	397, 399
— — rice water	388
— — savoury custard	404
— — toast and water	393
— — treacle posset	395
— — white wine whey	395
Sole à la maître d'hôtel, fillets of —Fish	196
— au gratin—Fish	194
— fried fillets of—Fish	198
Soufflé—cheese—Soufflés	338
— omelet	342
— potato—Soufflés	340
— vanilla—Soufflés	334
Soups—bonne femme soup	158
— cabbage soup	177
— clear soup	152
— crowdie	174
— Dr. Kitchener's broth	173
— German pea soup	180
— giblet soup	165
— maccaroni soup	181
— milk soup	175
— mock turtle soup	167
— mulligatawny soup—Australian meat	40
— pea soup	178
— pot-au-feu	170
— purée of potatoes	160
— spring vegetable soup	162
— tapioca cream	156
Spinach—Vegetables	231
Spring vegetable soup—Soups	162
Steak, grilled	117
— stewed	141
Steamed potatoes—Vegetables	218
Stewed beef or ox-cheek, with vegetables—Pot-au-feu	170
— cow-heel, with onion sauce —Jellies	322
— ox-foot—Jellies	326
— steak	141
Stew, Irish, of Australian meat	44
— — Entrées	83
Stews—à-la-mode beef	94

	PAGE		PAGE
Stews—Brazilian stew	96	Veal—curry of—Entrées	90
— Irish stew	98	— cutlets—Entrées	74
— stewed brisket of beef (cold)	100	— quenelles of—Entrées	65
Stock, brown	183	Viennoise, or Vennoise pudding—Puddings	273
— made with vegetables	185	Vegetables, baked potatoes	221
— white	183	— boiled cauliflower	229
Strawberry cream—Creams	331	— boiled new potatoes	218
Suet crust—Pastry	252	— boiled potatoes	217
— pudding—Puddings	307	— brussels sprouts	226
Sultana cake—Cakes	353	— carrots	237
		— carrots and turnips	227
TAPIOCA and apples—Puddings	298	— cauliflower au gratin	230
— cream—Soups	156	— fried potato chips	222
Tart filled with jam—Pastry	259	— fried slices of potato	223
Tartare sauce—Fish	207	— haricot beans	234
Tartlets of puff paste—Pastry	244	— mashed potatoes	220
Toad-in-the-hole	143	— mashed turnips	235
Toast and water — Sick-room cookery	393	— peas	233
		— potato croquettes	224
Treacle posset—Sick-room cookery	395	— sauté potatoes	221
		— spinach	231
— pudding—Puddings	294	— steamed potatoes	218
Tripe à la Coutance—Tripe	106	Vegetable stock	185
— boiled, with milk and onions	104		
— curried tripe	102	WHITEBAIT—Fish	193
Trussing, a fowl for boiling	144	White sauce—Sauces	238
— a fowl for roasting	148	— stock	183
Turbot, boiled—Fish	187	— wine whey — Sick-room cookery	395
Turnips and carrots—Vegetables	227		
— mashed—Vegetables	235	Wine jelly from calves' feet—Jellies	311
UNFERMENTED bread	381	— or brandy sauce—Puddings	272
		— sauce—Soufflés	336
VANILLA cream—Creams	329		
— soufflé—Soufflés	334	YORKSHIRE pudding—Puddings	308
Veal, fillet of, braised	109	Yorkshire tea cakes	377

THE END.

www.ingramcontent.com/pod-product-compliance
Lightning Source LLC
Chambersburg PA
CBHW030602300426
44111CB00009B/1073